THE THIRD BOOK OF BOTANICAL TANG

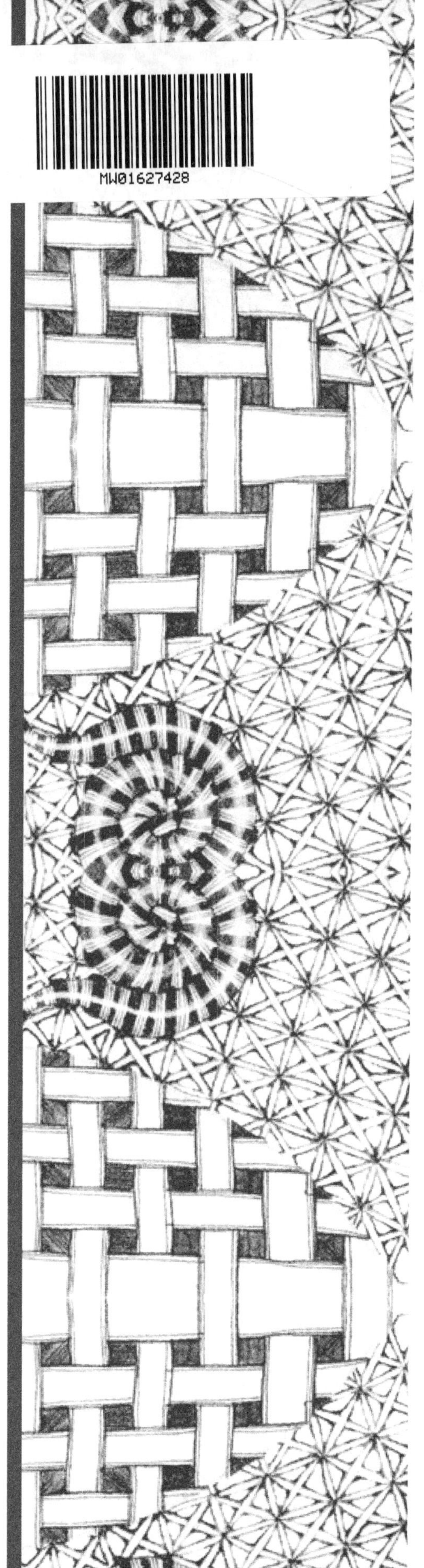

WELCOME!

I really hope you enjoy this book as much as I have enjoyed putting it together for you. This is the 3rd book in my botanical tangles series and as always it brings together many new tangles and inspiration from CZTs® (Certified Zentangle® Teachers) and tanglers from all over the world. I hope you find the book inspiring and helpful as you embark on a creative journey.

With much love,
MZ

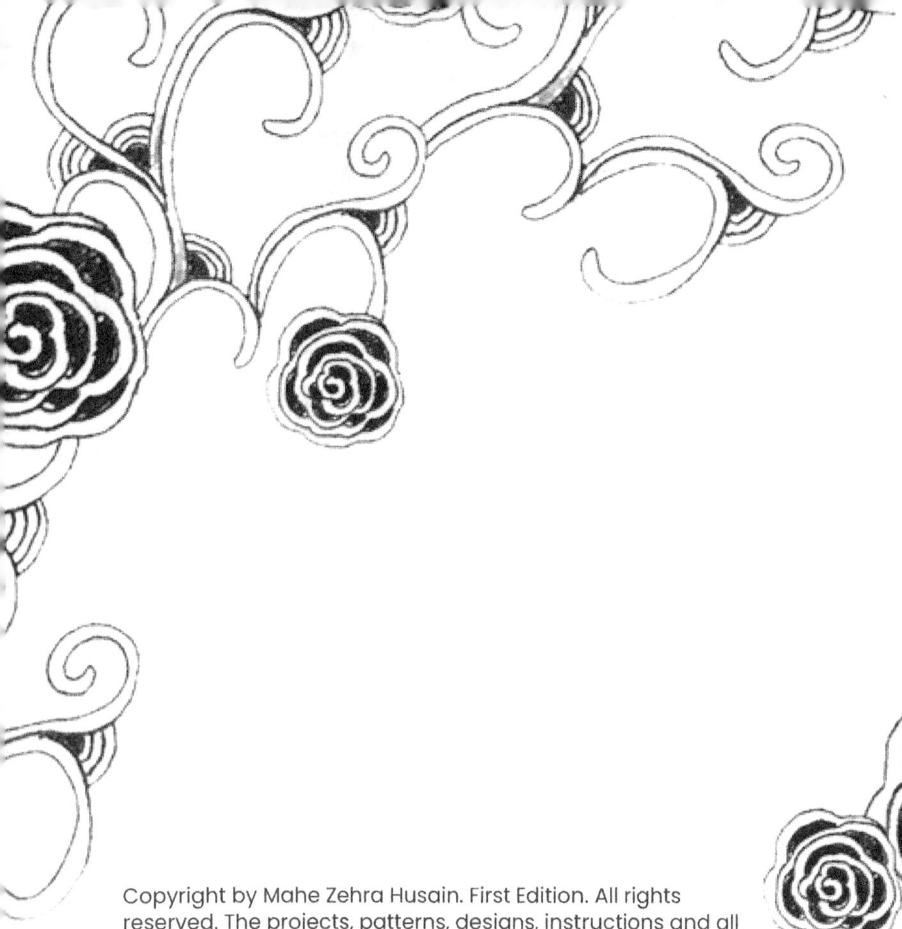

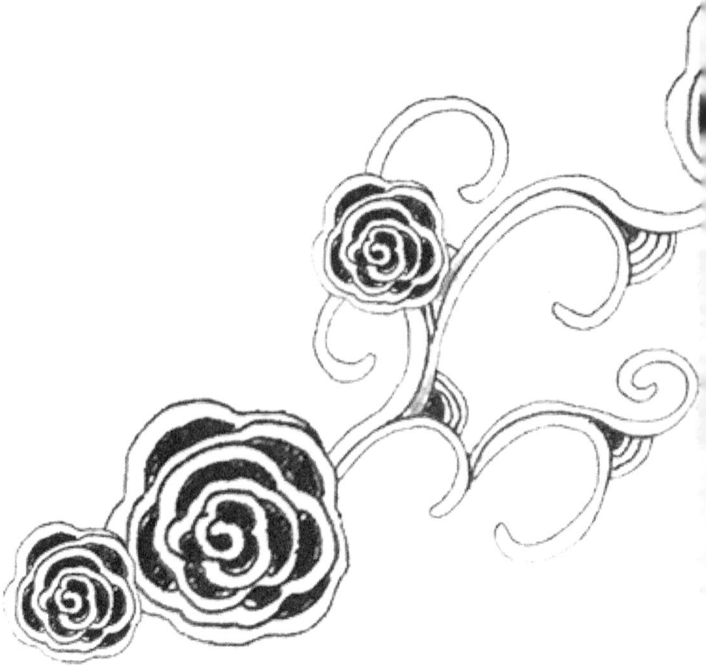

MAHE ZEHRA HUSAIN

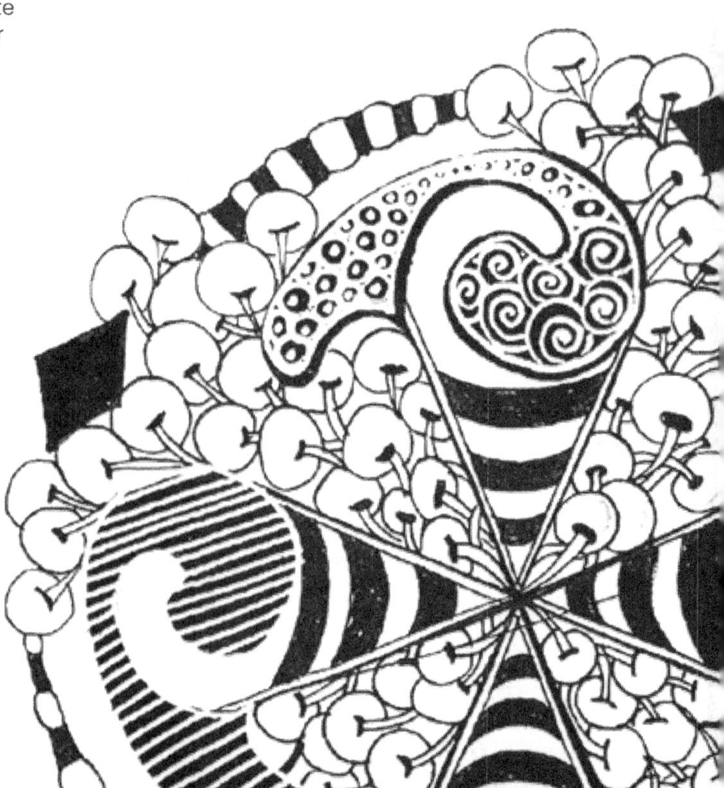

Check out our Free Zentangle Art Class on

www.mzcreates.com | Youtube: MZCreates

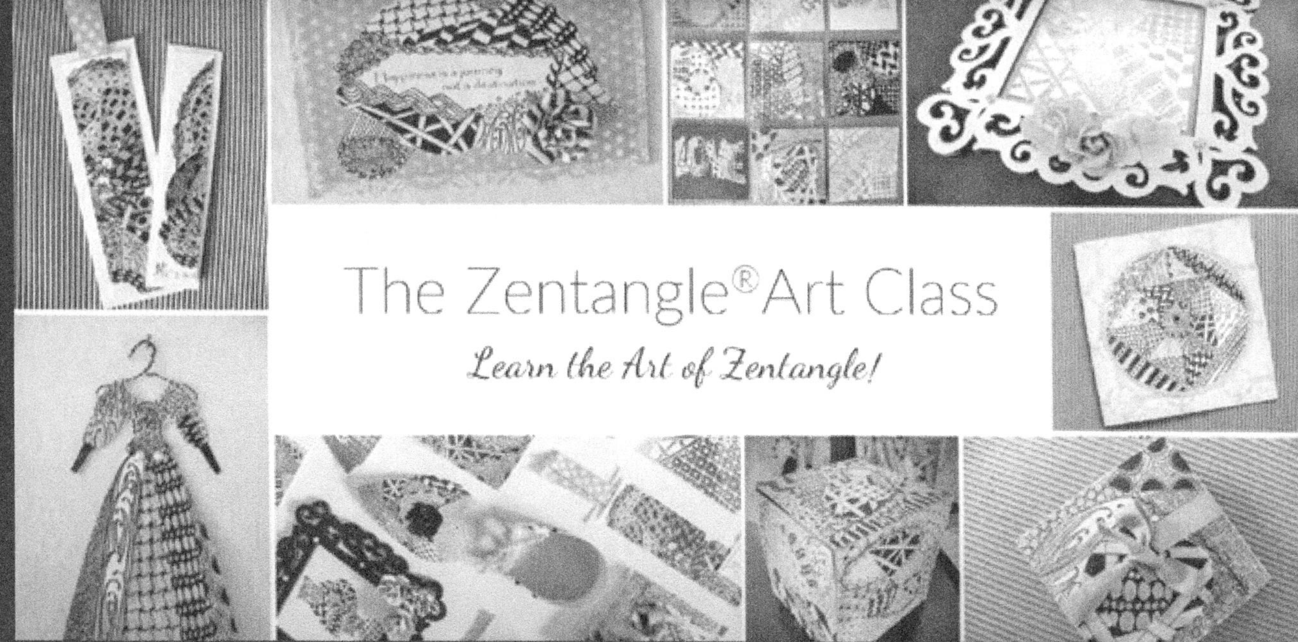

Leave a Review

If you like this book please take out some time to review it on Amazon. It helps us to spread the word about our budget friendly arts and crafts guides. If you have any questions or concerns, please reach out to us through our website.

www.mzcreates.com

Free Zentangle Course!

Check out our YouTube channel - MZ Creates - for a free class called The Zentangle Art Class!

www.mzcreates.com

YouTube Channel

Check out our YouTube channel for fun arts, crafts and lifestyle videos. From journaling to tangling, from collage to lettering, our videos are great fun!

https://www.youtube.com/mzcreates

Facebook and Instagram Community

Join our community of crafters on Facebook and Instagram for daily inspiration and free giveaways!

@MZCreates

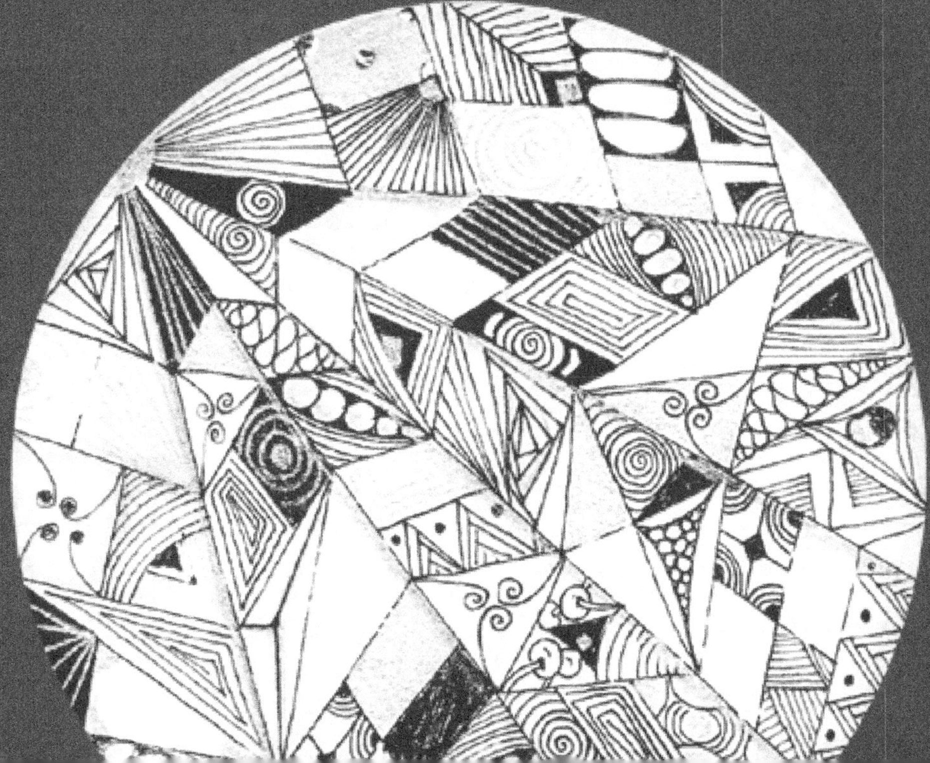

TABLE OF CONTENTS

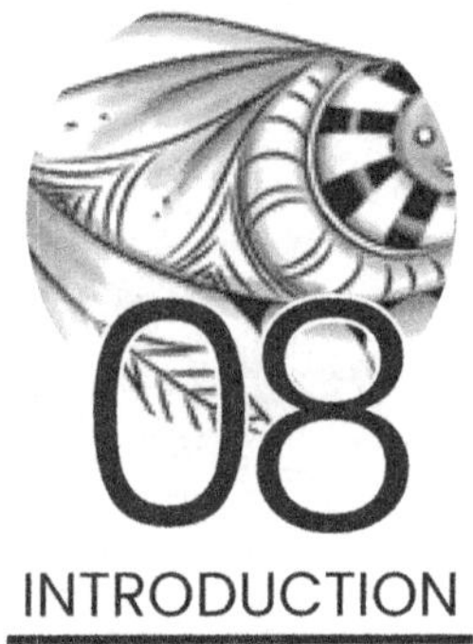
08 INTRODUCTION

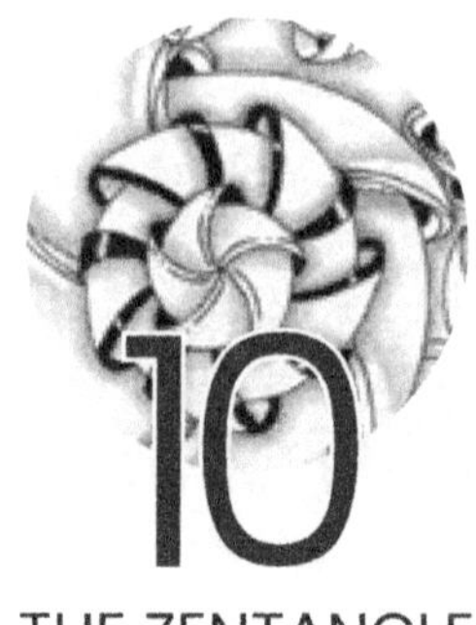
10 THE ZENTANGLE METHOD

12 TOOLS AND SUPPLIES

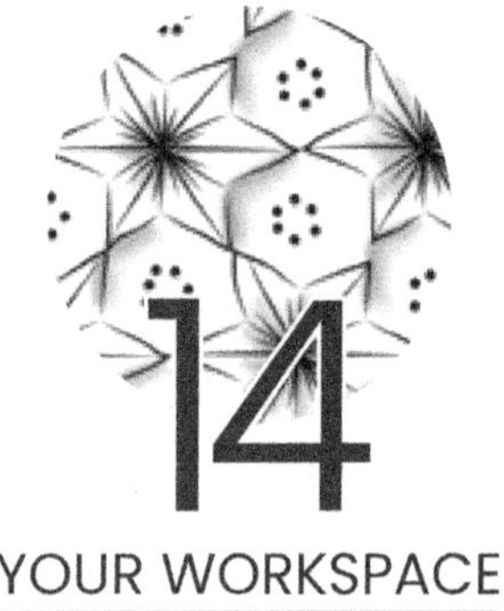
14 YOUR WORKSPACE

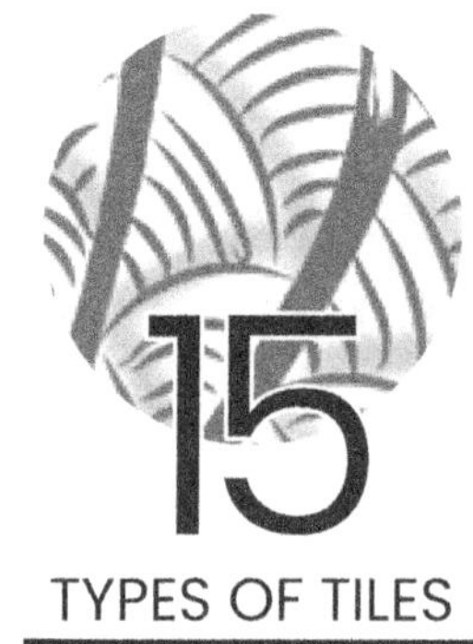
15 TYPES OF TILES

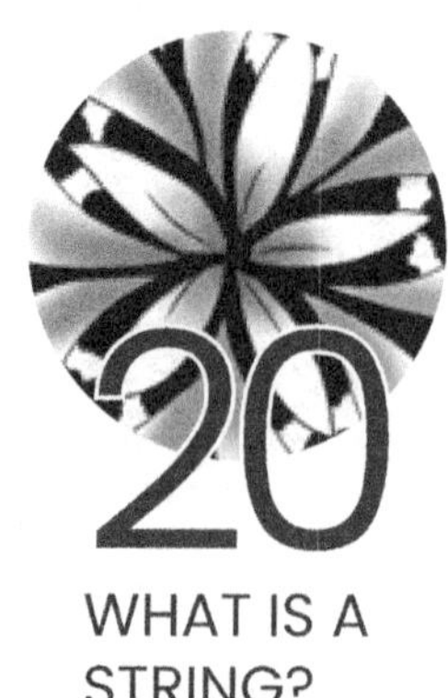
20 WHAT IS A STRING?

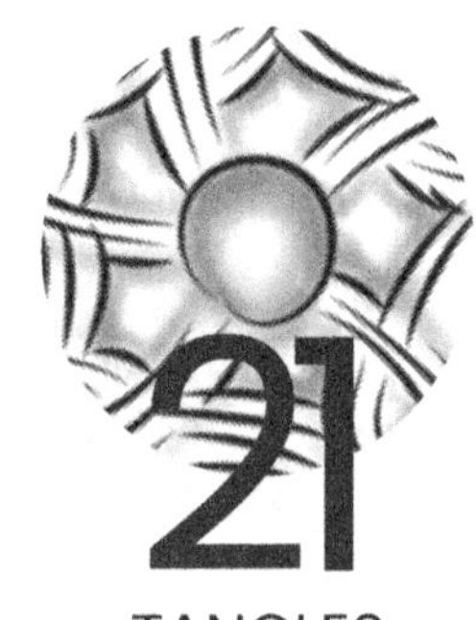
21 TANGLES

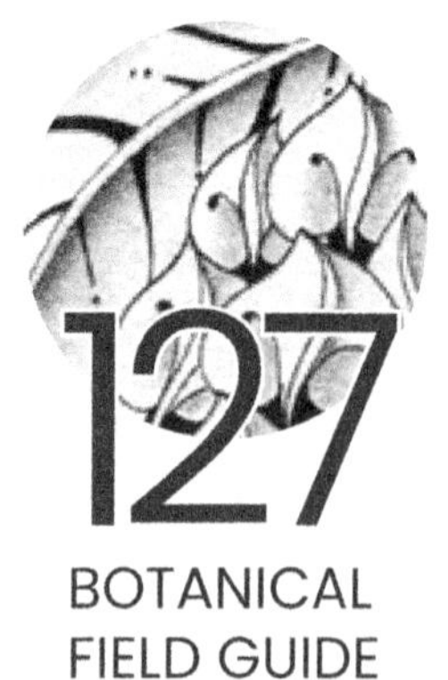
127 BOTANICAL FIELD GUIDE

133 ARTIST GALLERY

Introduction

What started as a small project and book idea has grown into a full-blown series! I had no idea so many people would like the book as much as they did. It makes me feel immensely grateful to know that so many beautiful souls all over the world hold a book I created with a lot of love and hard work.

When I started compiling some botanical tangles, for the first Book of Botanical Tangles, I knew that there were quite a few tanglers who, like me, loved organic tangles and wanted to find them in an easy reference book or guide.

Sometimes the world of tangles can be a little overwhelming and I wanted to take away a little of that by creating a resource with a set number of tangles. This just makes it a little easier when you want to set aside some creative time. Instead of going down the YouTube-Google rabbit hole, you pick up a book, choose a few tangles, look at a couple of project ideas and start.

That was my goal-to make it easy to enjoy some creative tangling time and to make it easy for anyone to just pick up the book and start creating something. I believe that when we give ourselves some time to create, we are giving ourselves what our soul needs.

I am a data scientist/statistician, and all my life I have used creative pursuits to balance my numbersdriven, life. It has been my refuge, my lifesaver. It didn't matter whether what I created was 'good' or not. The important thing was that I was taking the time out to let my brain balance itself. We all have a left and right side. I do not believe that one is more dominant than the other. It is up to us to choose to fuel both sides.

We are all born creative and logical. The challenge is to keep a balance between the two. Often, we get caught up in our careers and jobs and stop feeding our soul with the creative time it needs.

Zentangle® is the perfect artform to add to your life – whether you are a beginner or an experienced creative – there is something for everyone to learn. Most of all, the lesson I take away from this artform is the slogan from Zentangle® HQ.

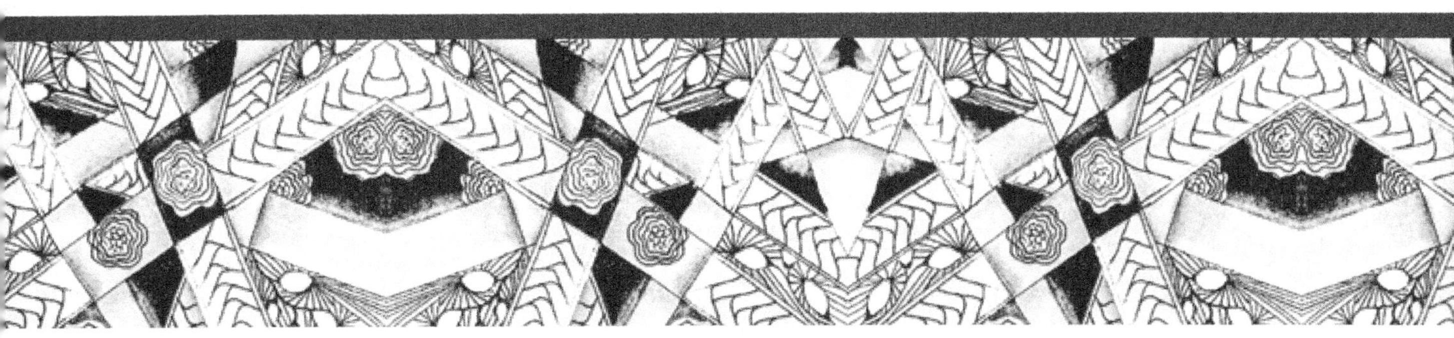

"Anything is possible, One stroke at a time.™"

As I see the tile build up with each little stroke and I see it evolve into something I didn't think I could create, it helps me to remember that all challenges are like that. We must take one step at a time. This philosophy has really helped me over the years.

The tangling community that you will find yourself a part of is one of the most generous and loving groups of people I have ever had the pleasure to be with! I am a CZT (Certified Zentangle Teacher) and cannot express in words hw generous my fellow CZTs are. You will see a lot of their work and tangles in my books. They have so generously shared their creativity with all of us. Without them, my work would not be possible.

The joy and the strength that comes with tangling is something I wish the whole world knew, and so this is my attempt to bring a little creativity to you. No matter where you are or what you do or whether you 'think' you are creative or not. Give tangling a try! You will be hooked for life and your life will feel a little more balanced.

Every time I read a review for my books, I am grateful for the love. I am also grateful for the critique. I learn from mistakes made and feel that is the only true way to move forward. A lot of the feedback I got for book one will make this book much better. (I will also make updates to volume one. Cant have the book that has made this one possible, suffer) So please know that I read what you have to say about my books and all feedback is appreciated!

I truly hope you will enjoy this journey with me. I have so many ideas for what I want to do in the future, and I can't wait to share them with you.

Love,
MZ

The Zentangle® Method

The Zentangle® method was developed by Rick Roberts and Maria Thomas. If you decide to train to be a CZT you will actually meet them at the seminars they conduct!

They are a lovely couple. Maria is an artist and Rick who has worn many professional hats throughout the years, is now a tangler. They both bring their unique experiences and skillsets to the Art of Zentangle®.

When Maria was working on some art - Rick noticed the meditation aspect of her work. That's when Zentangle® was born. You can read their entire story and more on their website - www.zentangle.com. I can't at all do it justice in a few lines!

They built the Zentangle® method so that anyone could take up drawing and create beautiful works of art. They wanted the entire process to be mindful and slow and almost like an act of meditation.

Too often now we are rushing from one place to the next and from one chore to the next. Our mind is racing with thoughts of our to-do lists and everything else we have yet to do or have left undone.

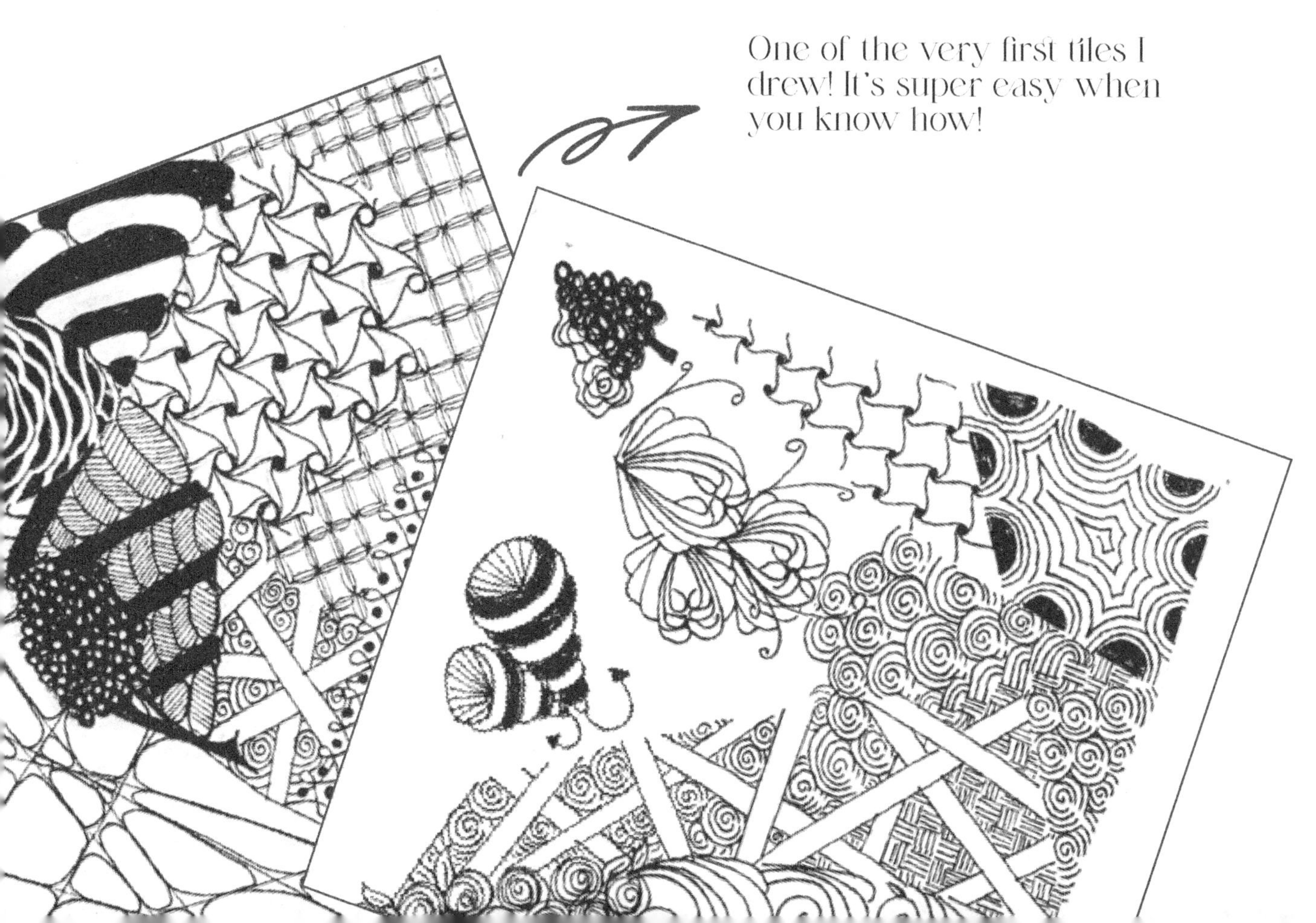

One of the very first tiles I drew! It's super easy when you know how!

Zentangle® came at a perfect time. Exactly when the world needed it most.

The Zentangle® method has been created to be quite simple and easy to follow.

1. You start with a tile - this can be a 3.5 inch square or a Zendala or other variations that have now been introduced. These can be white, black and beige with new ones coming in. That's the best thing about Zentangle® - it is constantly evolving.

2. Then you make 4 dots on the 4 corners of your tile a little bit in from the edge.

3. Then you join these with a penciled line. This line can be wonky as long as it stretches from dot to dot.

4. Add a string inside the tile. This is a penciled line that can curve and bend and loop around and go all over your tiles within the confines of the lines connecting the dots.

5. Now you can fill in the sections created by your string with tangles!

To introduce you to the basic concepts of Zentangle® I've created some videos on YouTube that you can watch.

My YouTube channel is MZ Creates and you have to look for The Zentangle® Art Class videos. If you're a beginner tangler and don't know any basics of the Zentangle® method, I highly reccommend you watch those videos and then continue with this book. This will allow you to see how tangling is done in a way that I can never explain in a book. When you come back to the book you will be ready to take on botanical tangling.

If you know the basics of tangling, read on!

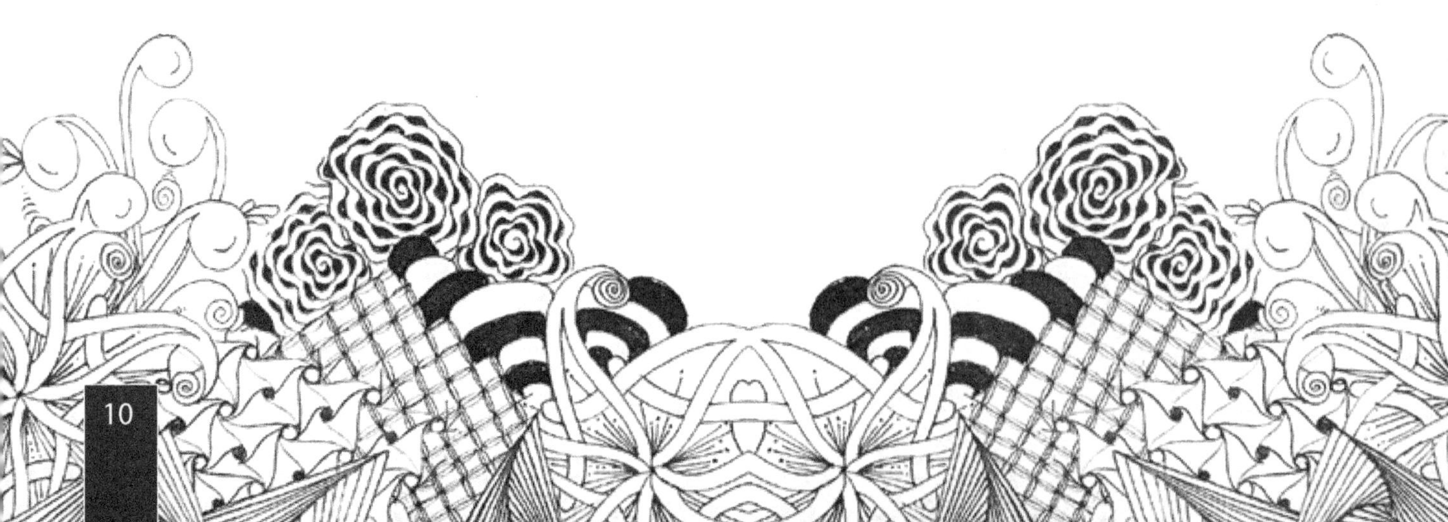

Tools and Supplies

The best thing about Zentangle® is that you need very few materials to start. If you want to get going right now all you need is a pen and paper to start practicing the tangles.

Emphasis in this art form is on the quality of the supplies that you use. The thinking behind that is that better supplies lead to better art and also that you are worth the good stuff! Very often we hold off on using good quality things saving them for another time or thinking our art is not good enough. That stops with Zentangle®. Your art is amazing so use good materials.

You will need:
1. Surfaces or tiles - You can buy them from Zentangle® HQ through their website or cut your own using good quality watercolor paper and the templates I've provided at the back of the book.
2. Micron pens in 01 black - these are what I use mostly for white tiles. You can also get 005 to add line width variation in your work.
3. Sakura white gelly roll pen for black tiles.
4. A pencil.
5. A Tortillon or a cotton earbud for shading.

I have found that next to the paper, the pens I use are super important. They really impact the quality of the finished artwork.

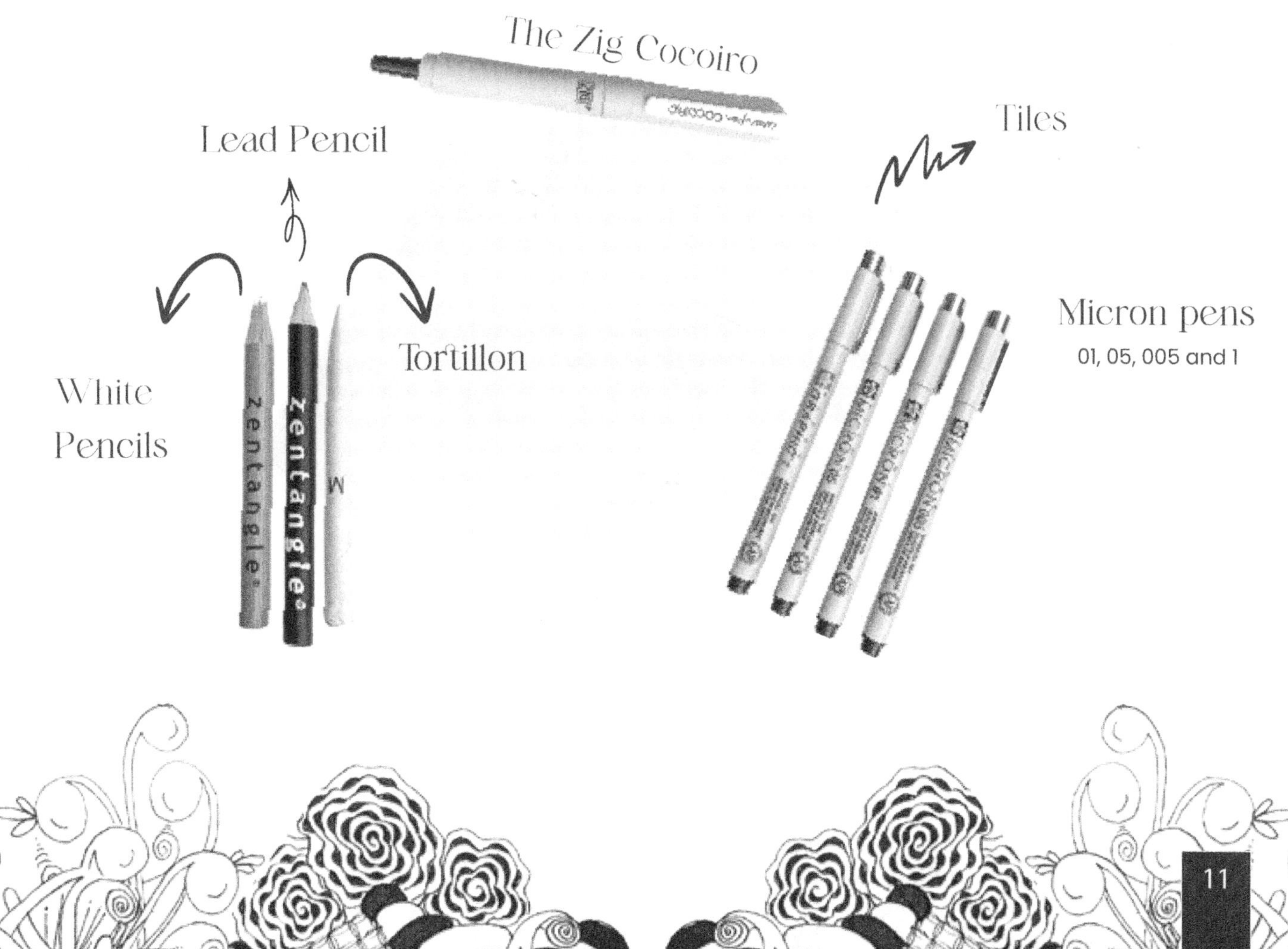

Whenever you can, use Micron 01 pens. They are recommended by Zentangle Headquarters for a reason. They are incredible! The line width is perfect and makes the finished work look very intricate. It's also the perfect line width to work with on a small surface. The Micron pens are also waterproof. Another very important factor.

Other than these basic micron 01 pens, you will come across brown pens and white pens and the world of color as well.

I don't go into too much color theory and examples in this series of botanical books. The color tangling projects are part of my upcoming series of short zine format books on Zentangle. But one little Google search will open a world of color for you!

If you're just starting out, I recommend playing with limited supplies. Just work with good quality tiles and black pens. When you want to add something extra to your tiles you can venture into the world of black tiles. What a wonderful world that is!

The only challenge is you need a white pen that will work for you. I have tried the Signo and Sakura white pens. Most people swear by them and really love them. I have found white pens to be a matter of luck as far as I am concerned. Sometimes they flow well and other times they don't. After trying quite a few pens in quite a few countries I have concluded that currently the Gelly Roll 08 by Sakura is my favorite white pen. I am saying currently because in my Amazon cart I have several new white pens I want to try and so the quest continues! But for now this one is my favorite.

If you want to experiment with other pens you most definitely should. Half the fun is experimenting and finding what works best for you. Maybe you like the line weight to be a bit more - in which case go for a Micron 05, or maybe you want to tangle in color. The choice is yours. I am only making suggestions based on what I have learned.

At heart I am a bit of an upcycler. I love to save bits and pieces and turn them into something new. I hate wastage of any kind. So, when I started my Zentangle journey I was a bit reluctant to go for the best tiles I could find. Surely, I could make art with anything? Any surface I could find? Yes, that is true, but I found the experience of using quality paper just incredible. The ink flows better, the final look is better, the shading is better and the most important thing of all, I am spending so much time on this practice, I deserve the best I can afford.

There is no need to go out and buy the entire art store. Like I said before, we need very few supplies for tangling. I would recommend getting the best you can afford.

Your Workspace

You don't need a lot of space to tangle. Any work surface will do. What I do recommend is that you make sure you're comfortable.

1. Your back should be supported and the chair should be comfortable.

2. The desk height should be right for you.

3. The lighting should be good so as not to strain your eyes. Tangling can get pretty intricate and involved so you need to make sure of that.

4. I like burning some incense or a candle when I tangle - it just adds to the meditation effect of the ritual for me.

5. Instrumental soft music is also amazing!

6. At all times take care of your posture. You want to keep standing up and stretching after 15 minutes and make sure your body is refreshed.

7. Optional: Your favorite beverage!

Now let's get tangling!!!

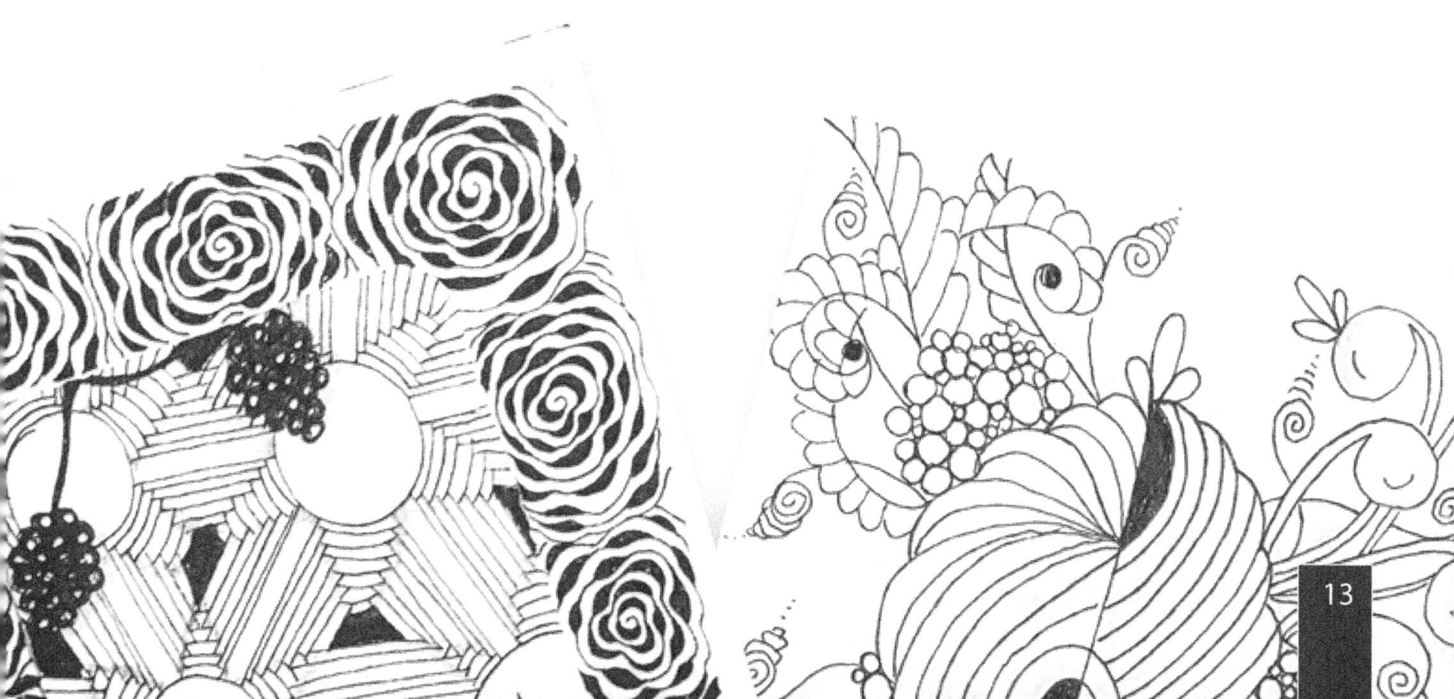

Types of Tiles

The world of tangling surfaces has grown since I trained to become a CZT. I love that this art form is constantly evolving, with more surfaces, more techniques and more tangles becoming a part of our toolkit.

This table is supposed to be a simple at a glance look at the current list of 'official' tangling surfaces .

Name	Shape	Color	Size
Square Tile		White, Black, Tan or Grey	3.5 inches by 3.5 inches
Zendala		White, Black, Tan or Grey	4-5/8 inches diameter
Bijou Square Tile		White, Black, Tan or Grey	2 inches by 2 inches

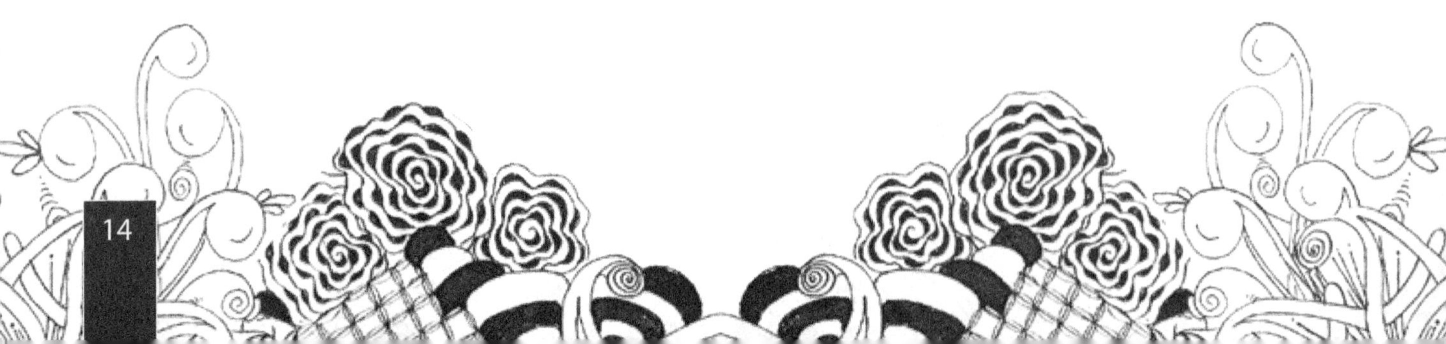

Name	Shape	Color	Size
Opus Tile	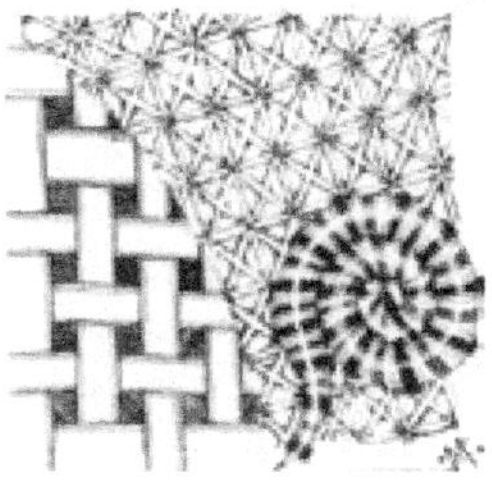	White, Black, Tan or Grey	10.5 inches by 10.5 inches
3Z Tile	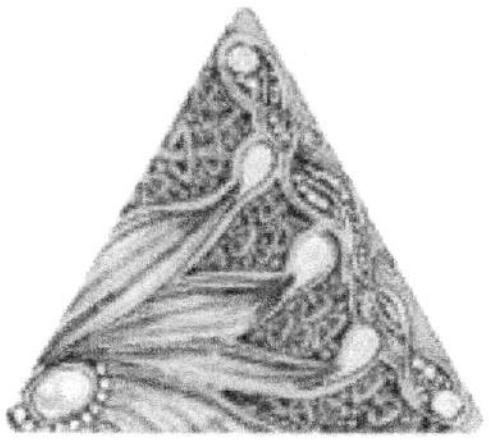	White, Black, Tan or Grey	A 3.5 inches equilateral triangle
Phi Tile	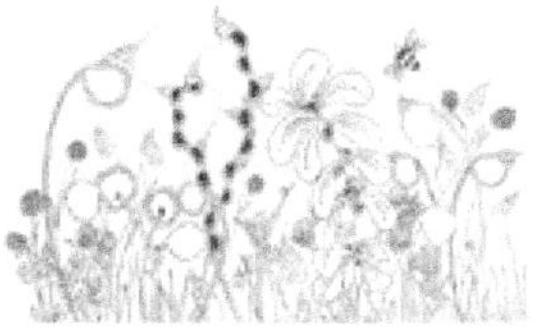	White, Black, Tan or Grey	5 inches by 3.1 inches

These are the current official options, which means these are the tiles you will find on the Zentangle website. They offer all these options in assorted color packs in case you want to buy from the official website.

You can also take good quality watercolor paper and cut your own. I have included templates for all these sizes at the back of the book. You can tear out those pages and glue them onto good card-stock and then cut them out and keep them as templates to use whenever you want.

The fun with having so many different sizes is that you can try putting them together in different ways. The figures on the next page are just a few examples of what you can do with your tiles to create larger art pieces or collaborative art!

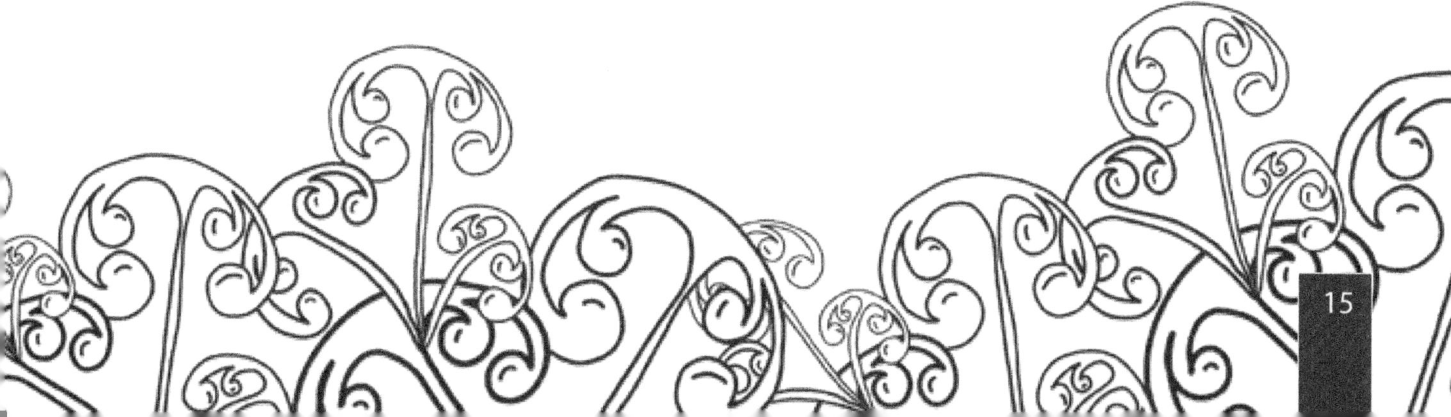

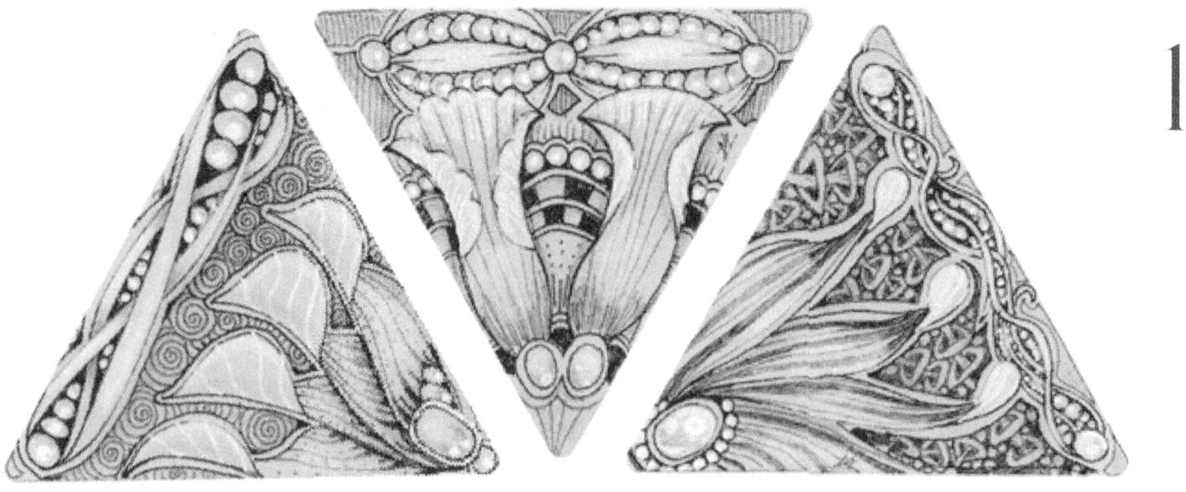

1

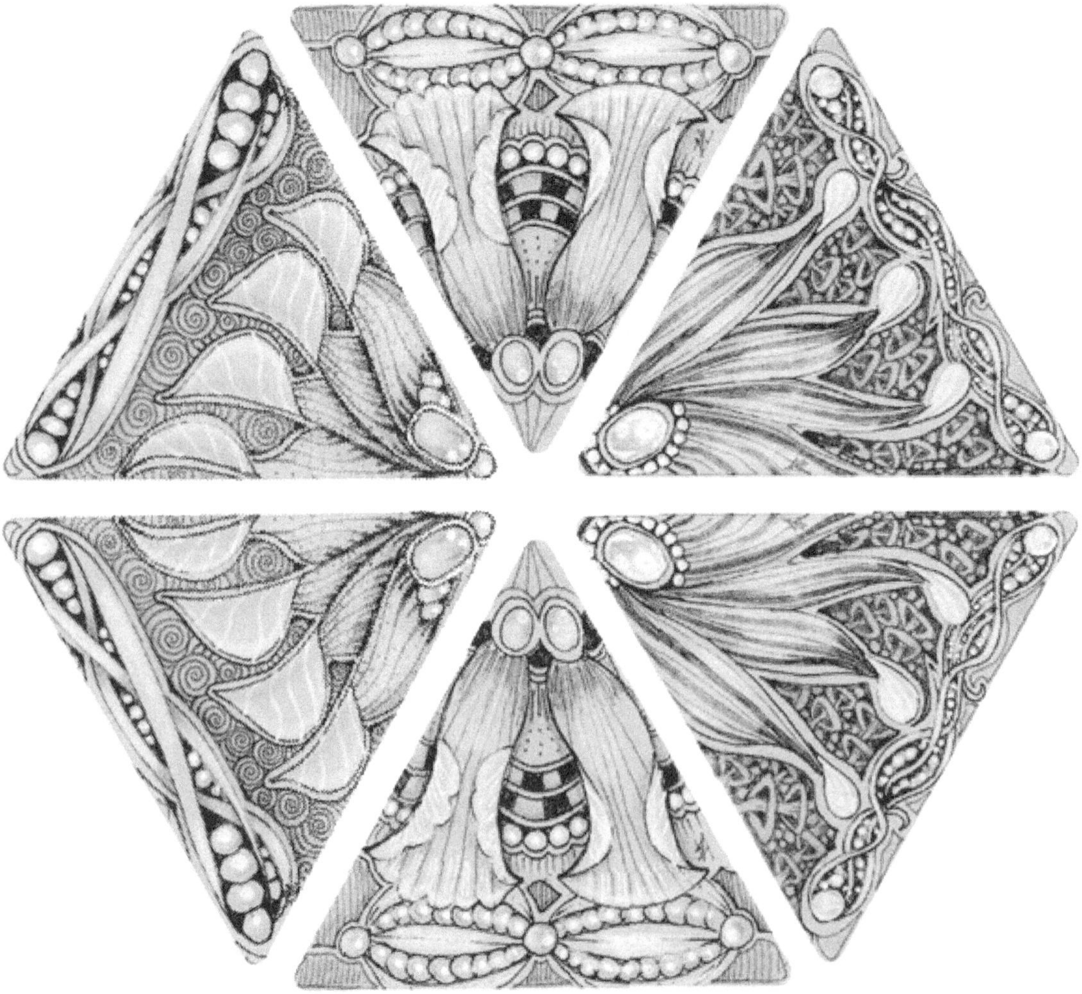

2

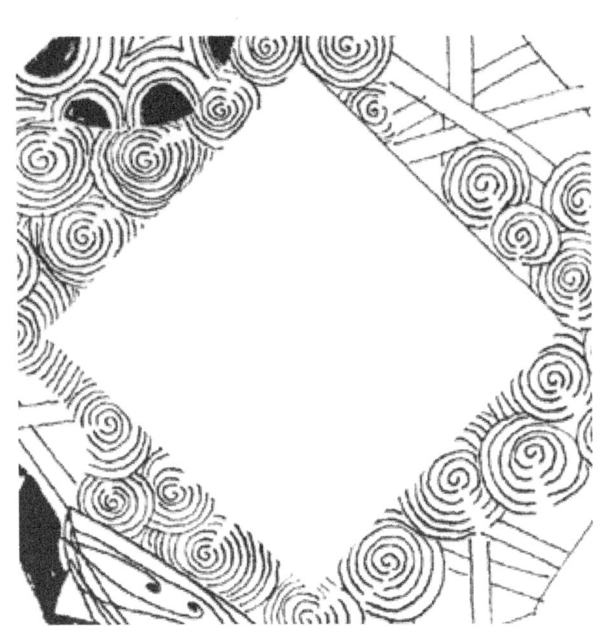

Layer a smaller Bijou tile on a regular tile.

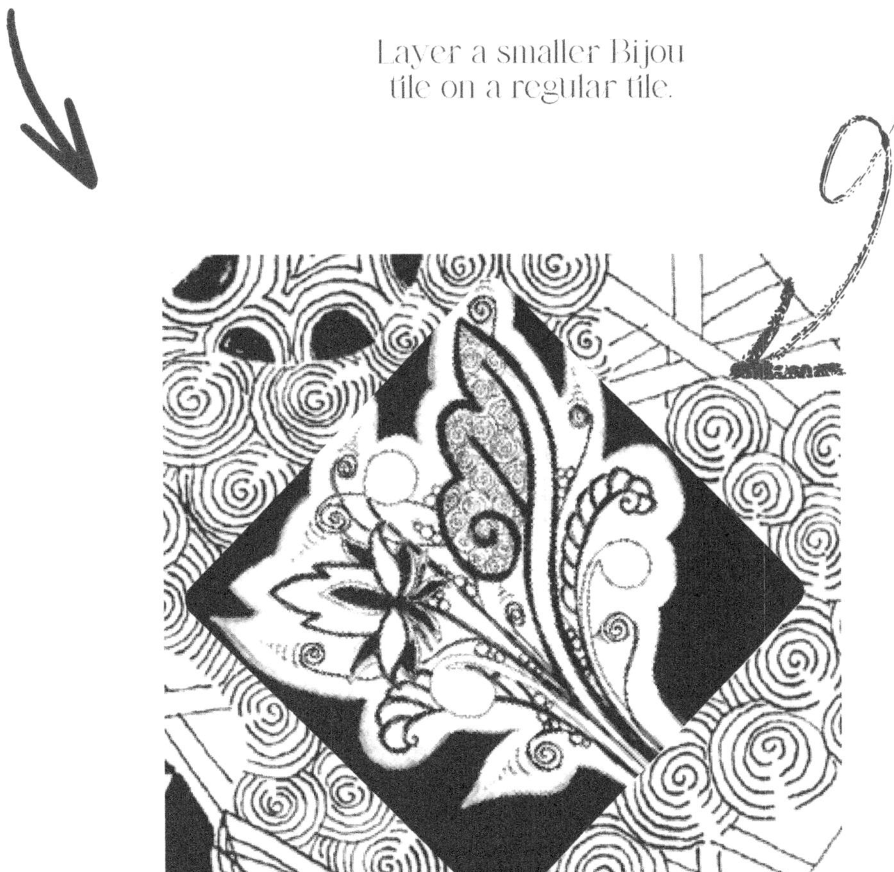

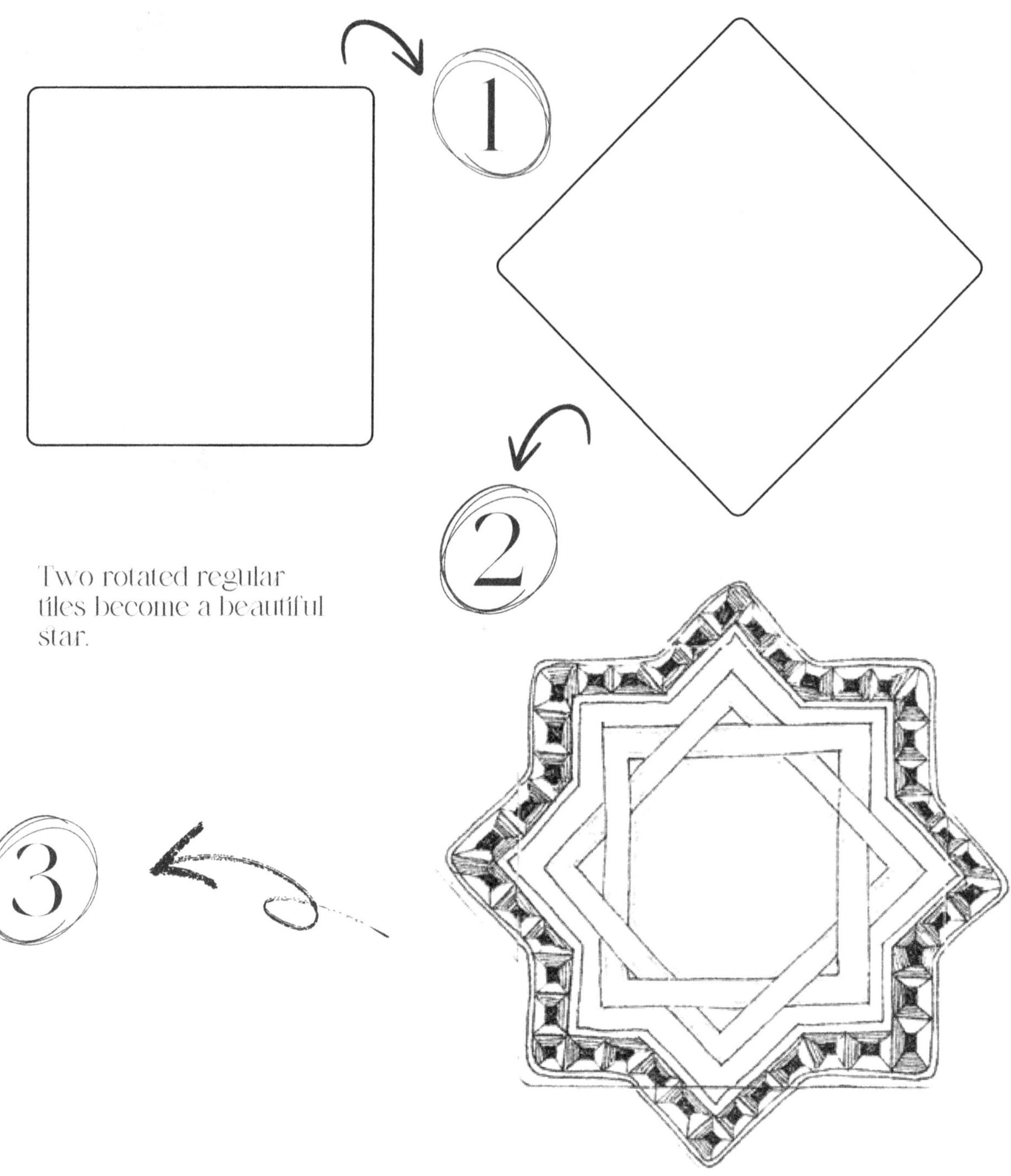

Two rotated regular tiles become a beautiful star.

What is a String?

There are so many ways to start your tile. And there is just one simple way to do it too. Totally depends on what you want.

According to the official Zentangle method you start your tile by:

1. Making four very light dots using your pencil on the 4 corners of your tile.

2. Join these dots with very loose and light lines. These can be straight, wavy, looped anything you want.

3. Now inside this space, that is bound by the four lines you have drawn, start at any edge and create a 'string' ending at any edge. The string is a line you make within this boundary. Again, it can take any form you want and is drawn as a light pencil line.

The idea behind the light pencil lines is that they disappear as you add the tangles and so there is no need of an eraser while tangling.

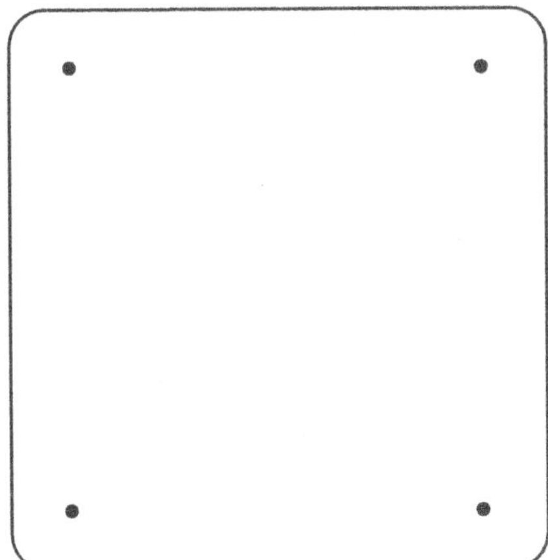

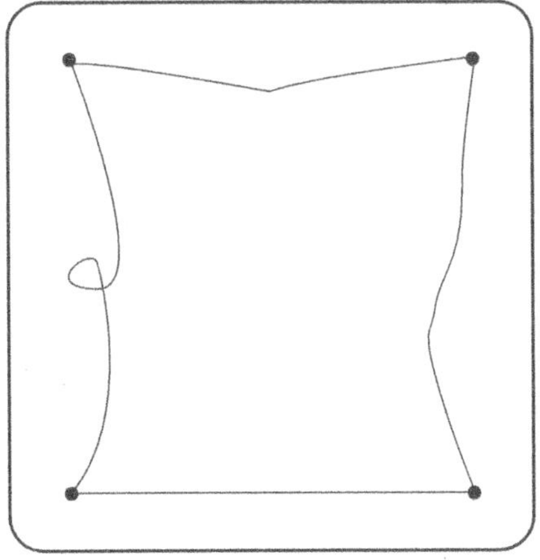

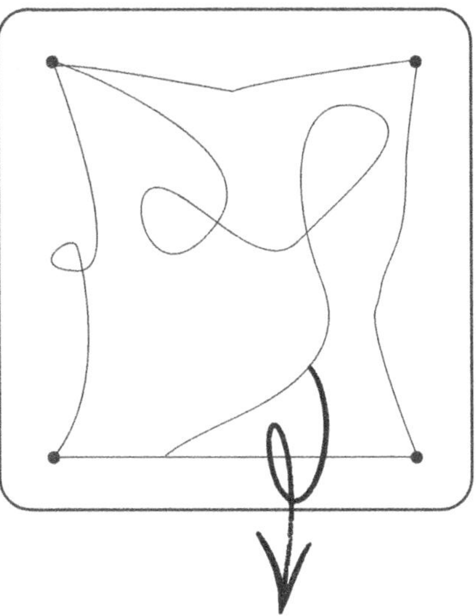

This is a string. It breaks your tile into portions that you can fill with different tangles.

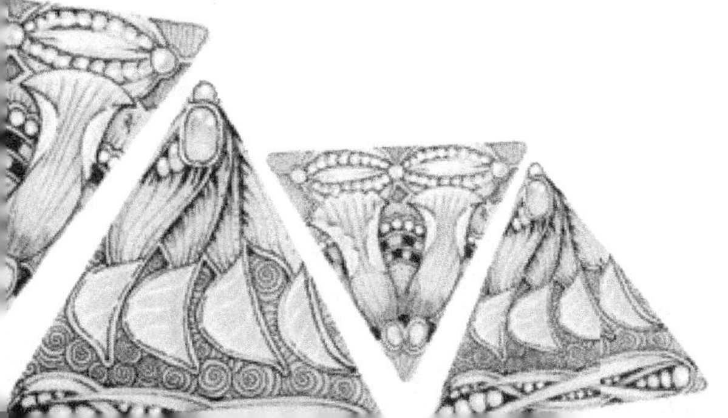

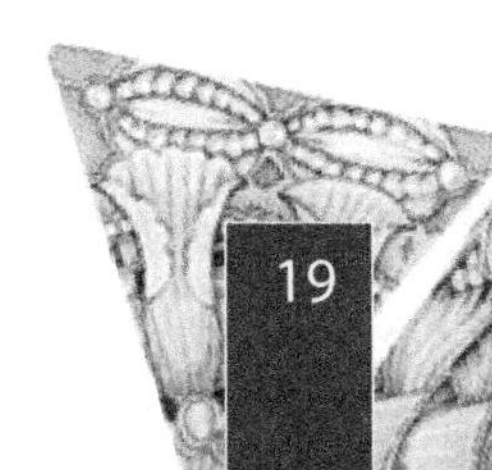

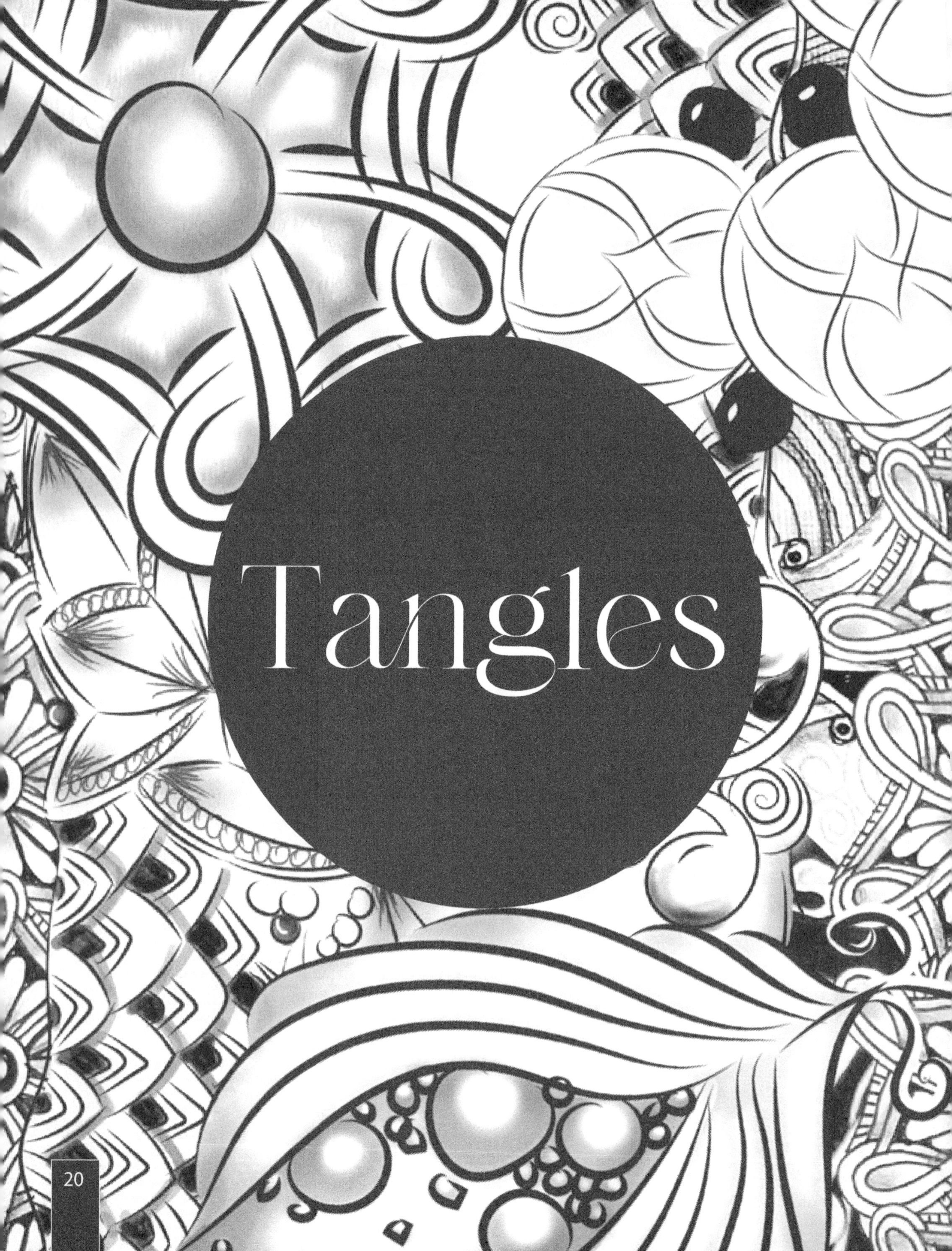

Tangles

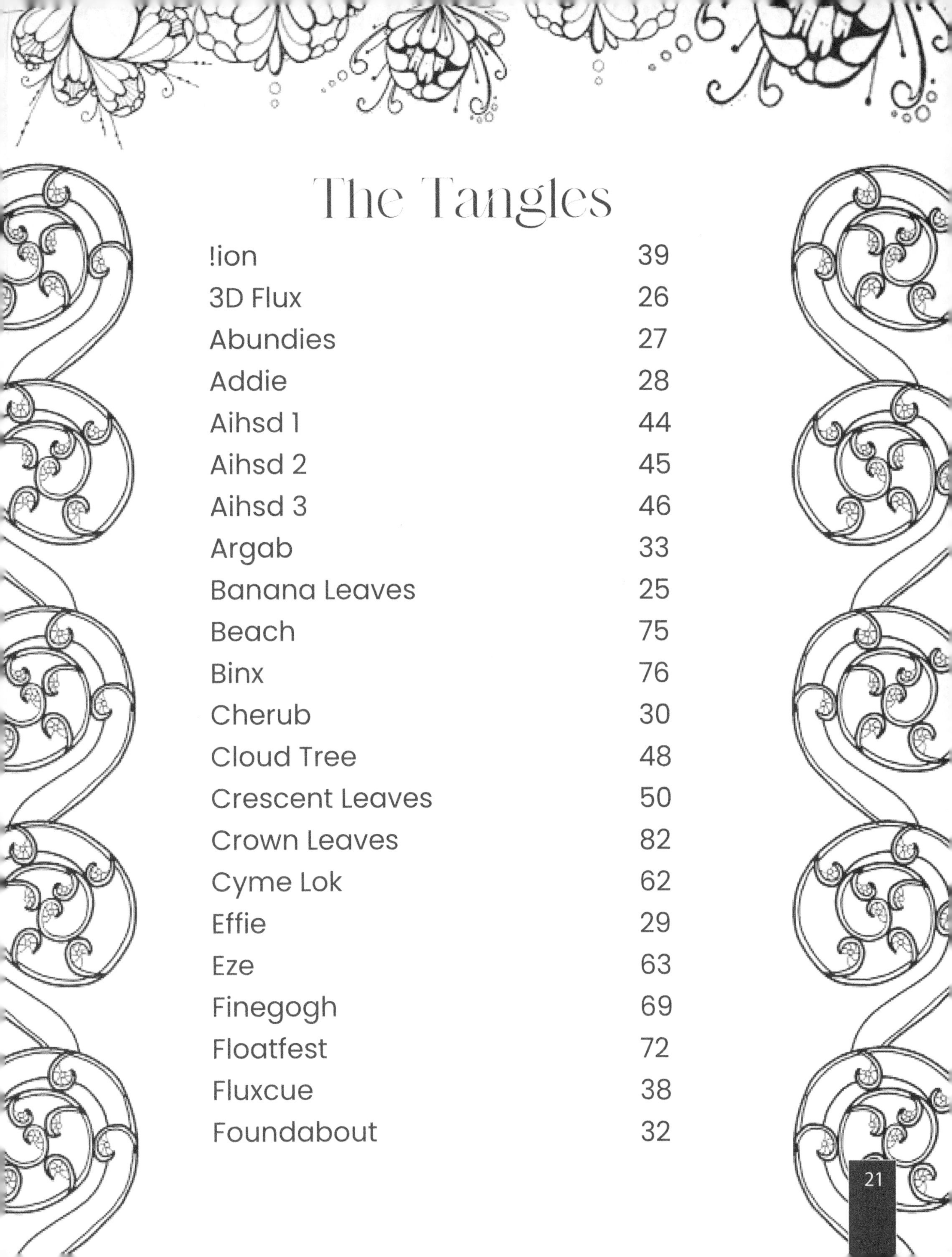

The Tangles

!ion	39
3D Flux	26
Abundies	27
Addie	28
Aihsd 1	44
Aihsd 2	45
Aihsd 3	46
Argab	33
Banana Leaves	25
Beach	75
Binx	76
Cherub	30
Cloud Tree	48
Crescent Leaves	50
Crown Leaves	82
Cyme Lok	62
Effie	29
Eze	63
Finegogh	69
Floatfest	72
Fluxcue	38
Foundabout	32

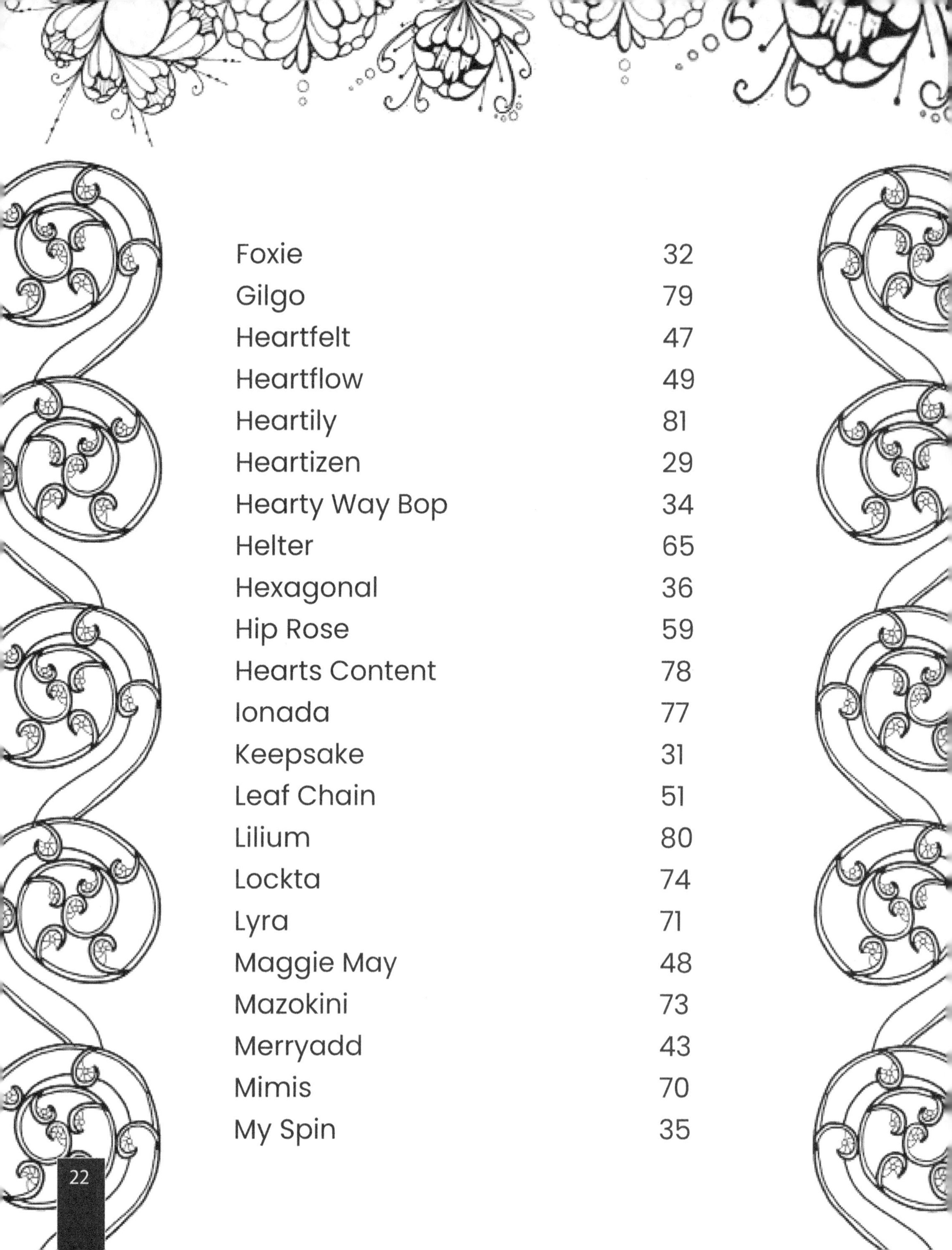

Foxie	32
Gilgo	79
Heartfelt	47
Heartflow	49
Heartily	81
Heartizen	29
Hearty Way Bop	34
Helter	65
Hexagonal	36
Hip Rose	59
Hearts Content	78
Ionada	77
Keepsake	31
Leaf Chain	51
Lilium	80
Lockta	74
Lyra	71
Maggie May	48
Mazokini	73
Merryadd	43
Mimis	70
My Spin	35

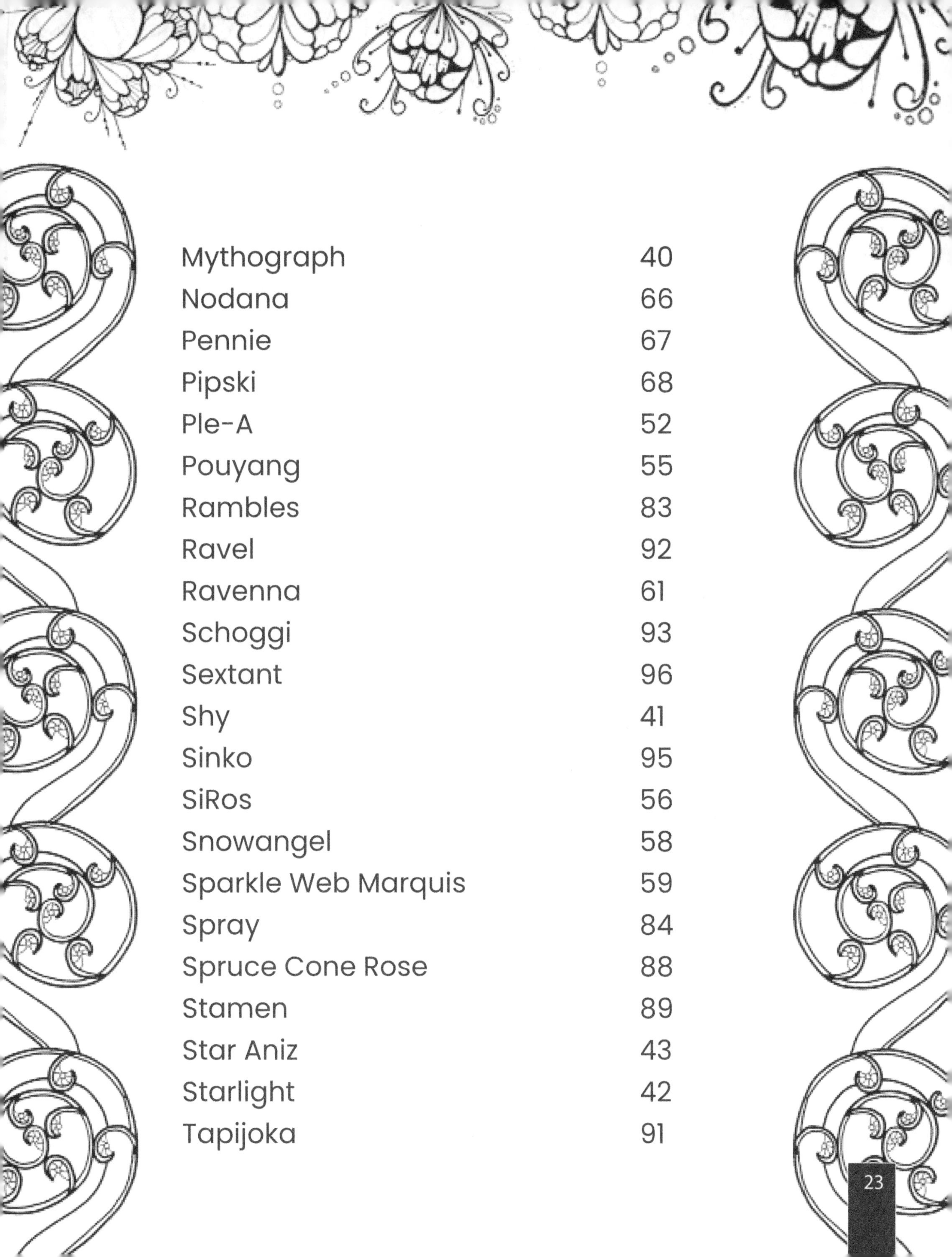

Mythograph	40
Nodana	66
Pennie	67
Pipski	68
Ple-A	52
Pouyang	55
Rambles	83
Ravel	92
Ravenna	61
Schoggi	93
Sextant	96
Shy	41
Sinko	95
SiRos	56
Snowangel	58
Sparkle Web Marquis	59
Spray	84
Spruce Cone Rose	88
Stamen	89
Star Aniz	43
Starlight	42
Tapijoka	91

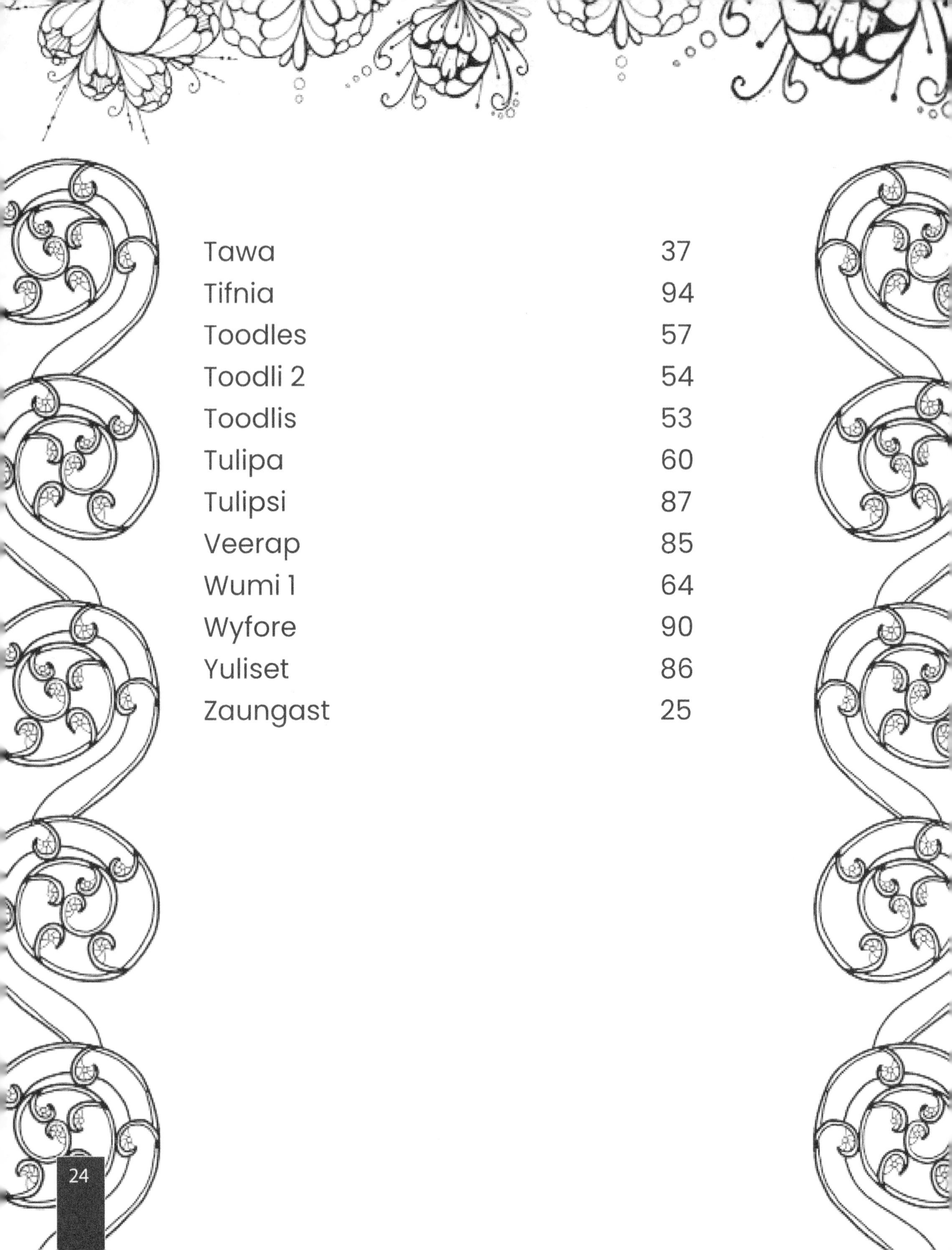

Tawa	37
Tifnia	94
Toodles	57
Toodli 2	54
Toodlis	53
Tulipa	60
Tulipsi	87
Veerap	85
Wumi 1	64
Wyfore	90
Yuliset	86
Zaungast	25

Banana Leaves

Dolly Bolen CZT

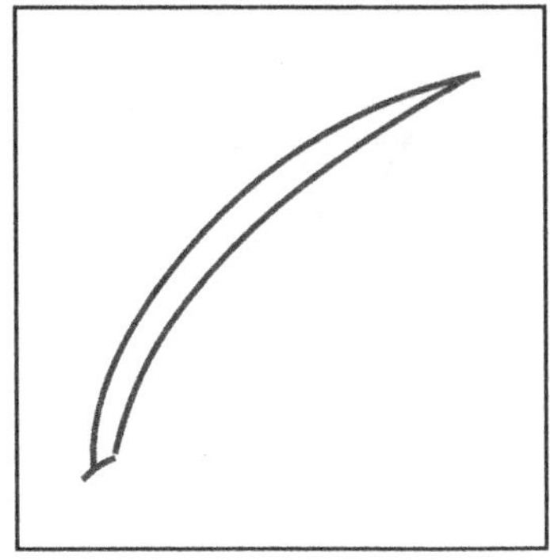

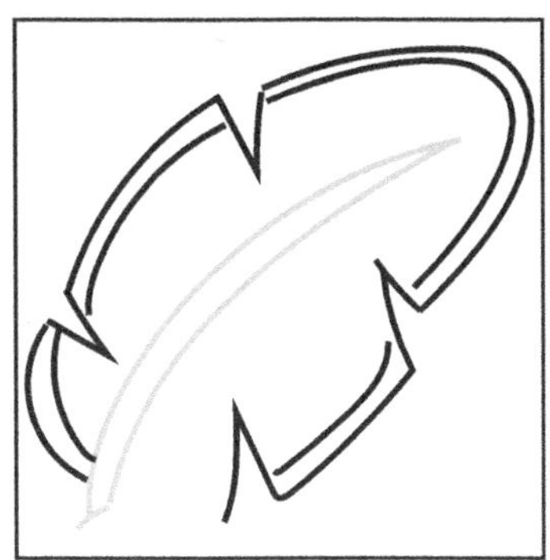

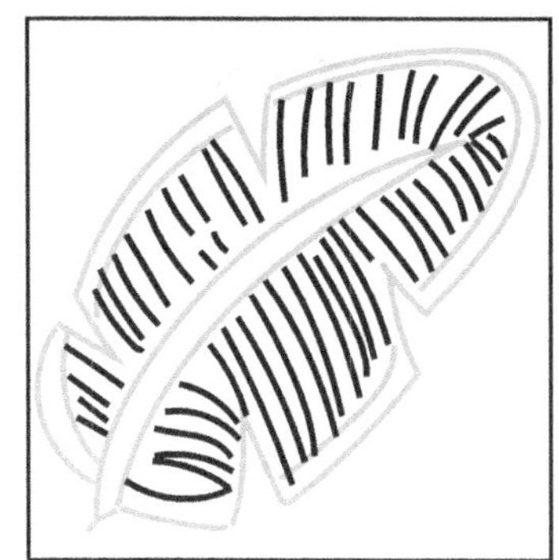

Zaungast

Annett Rumpler CZT

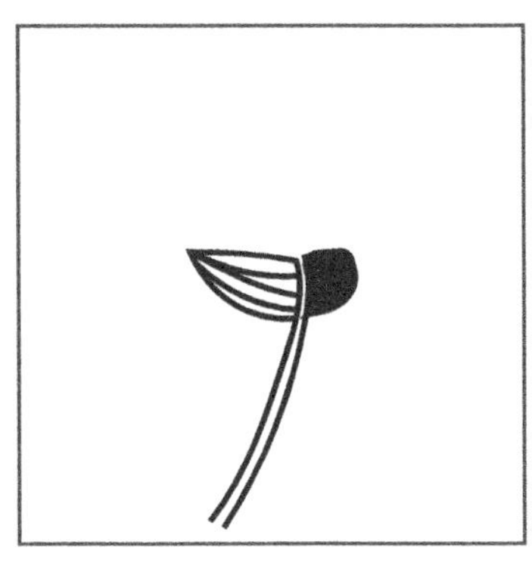

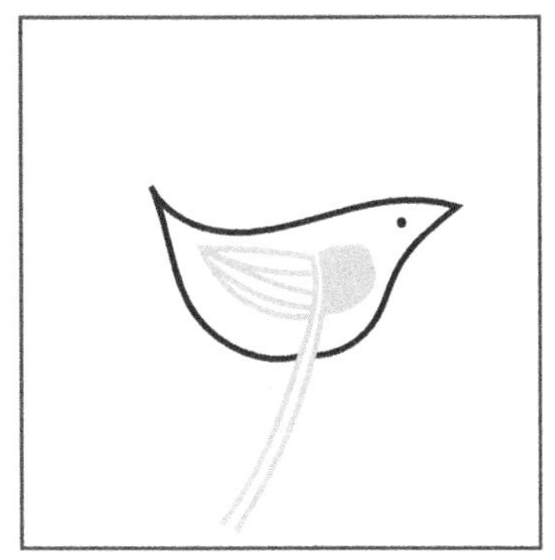

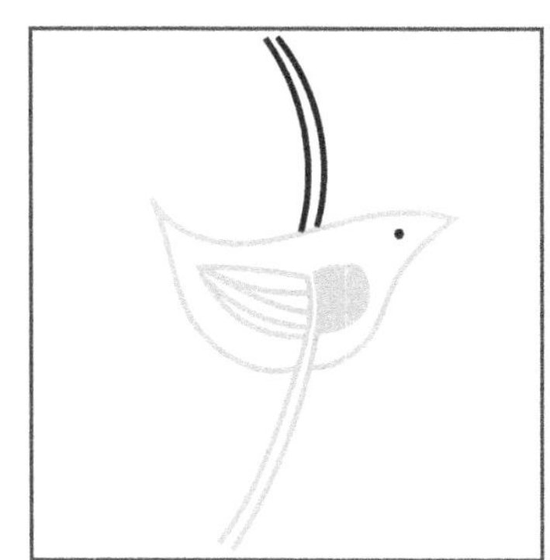

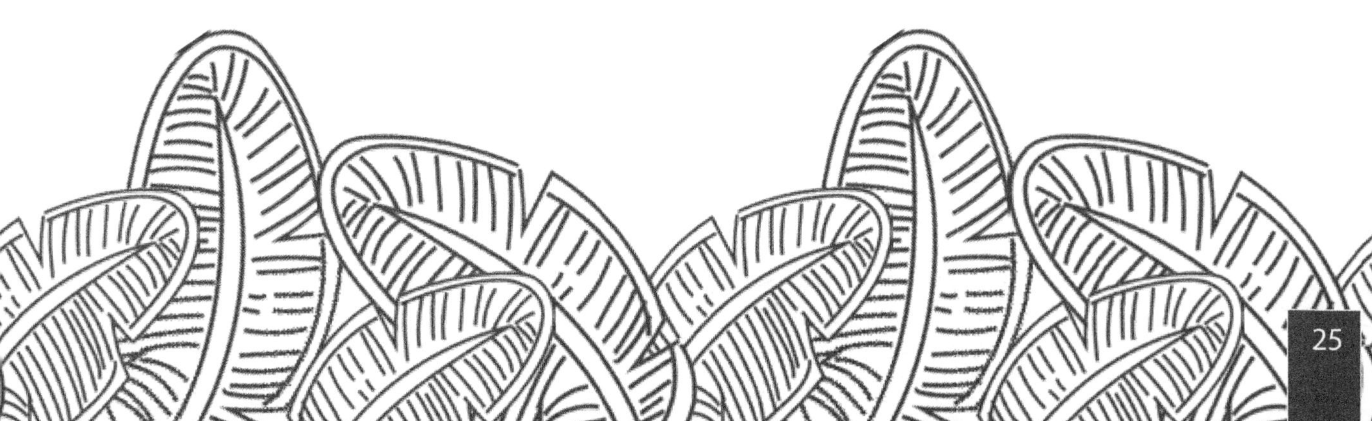

3D Flux

Barbara Duel Johnson CZT

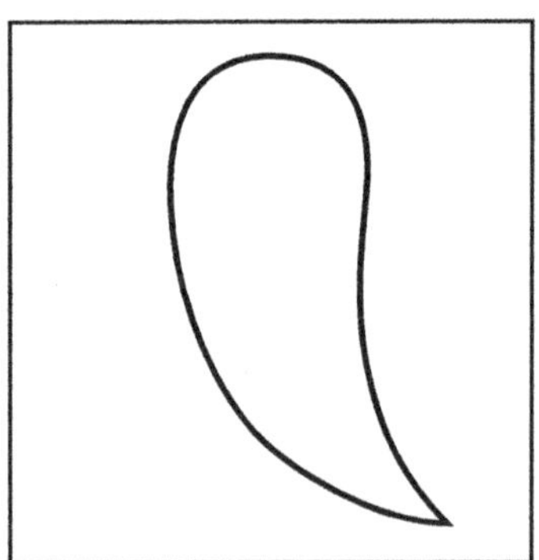
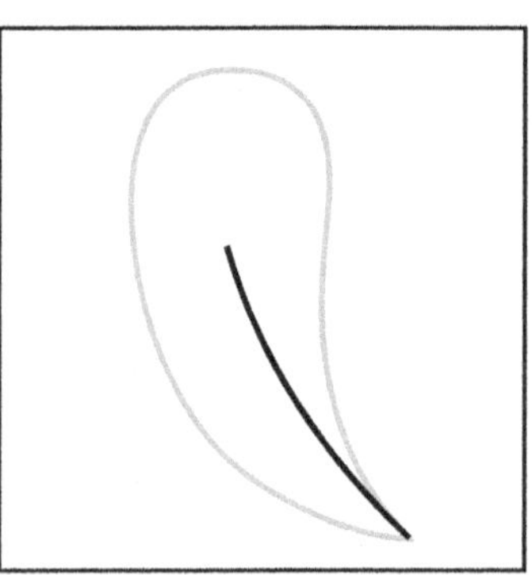
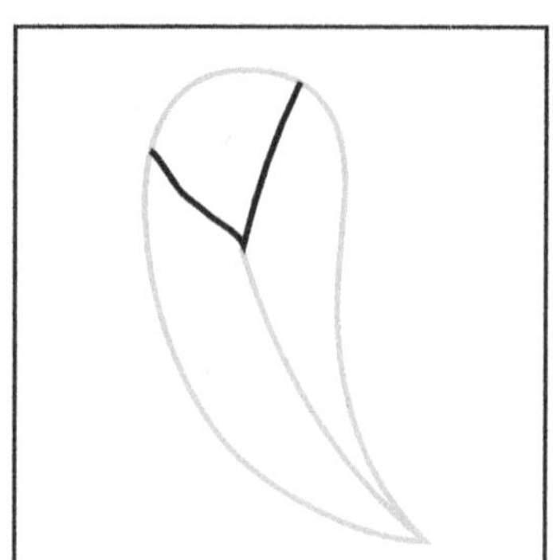
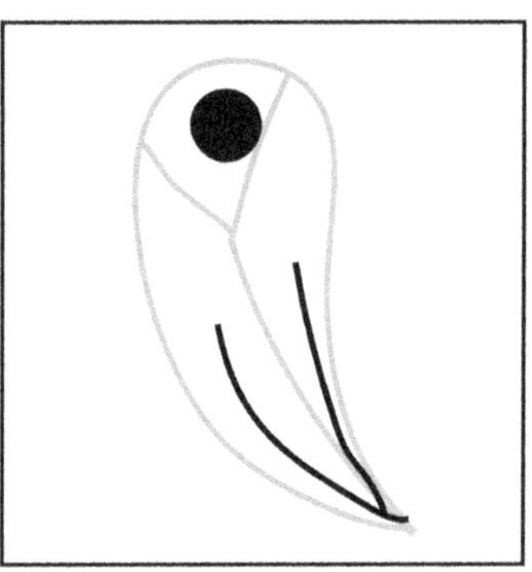
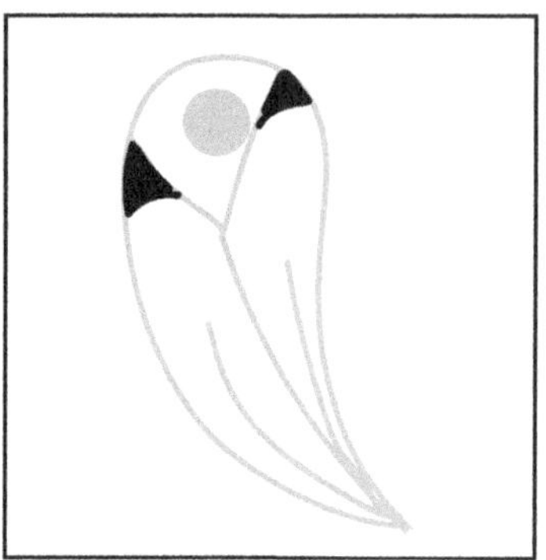

Abundies

Hanny Waldburger CZT

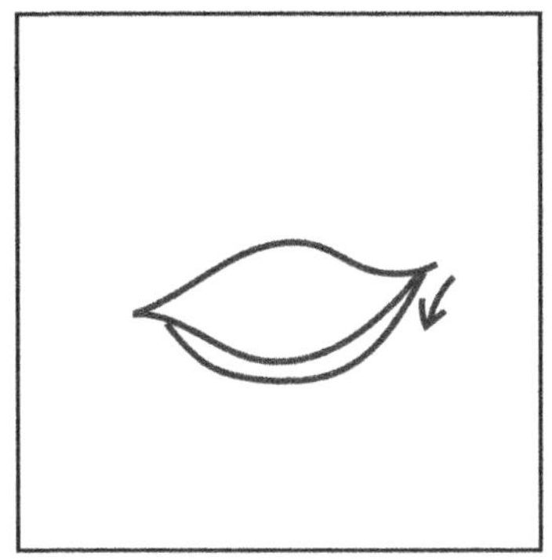
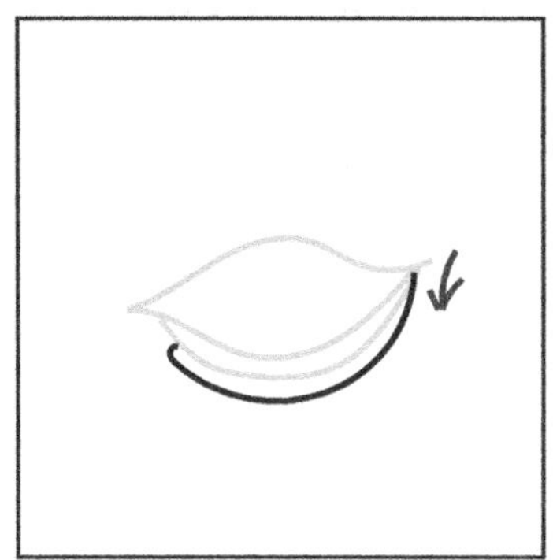
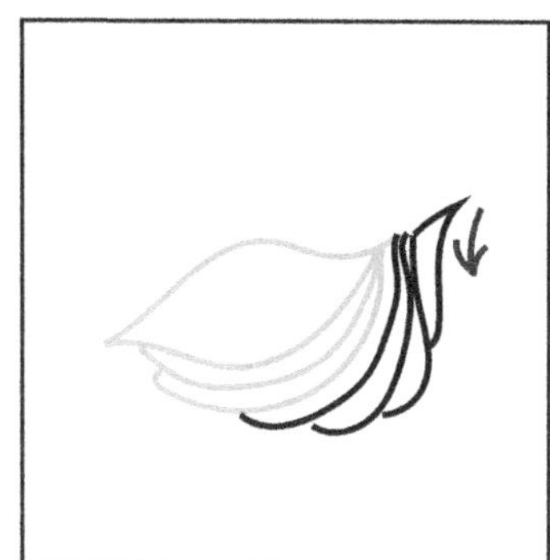
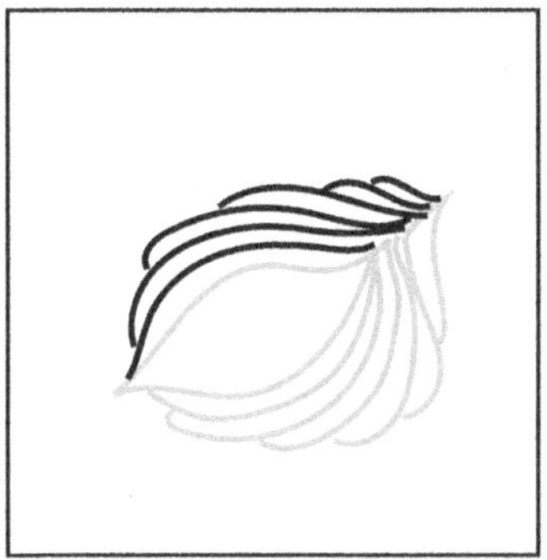
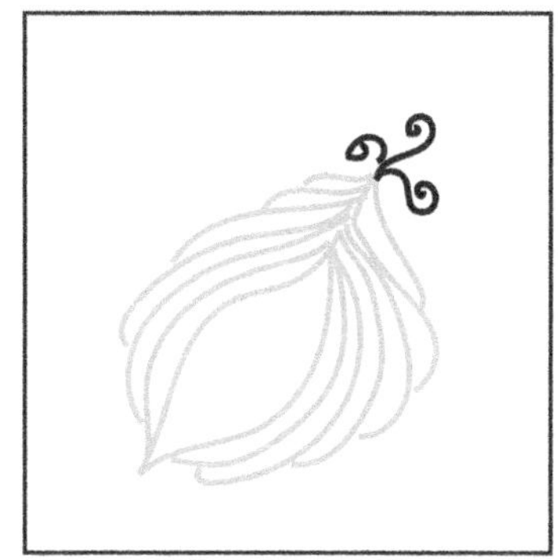
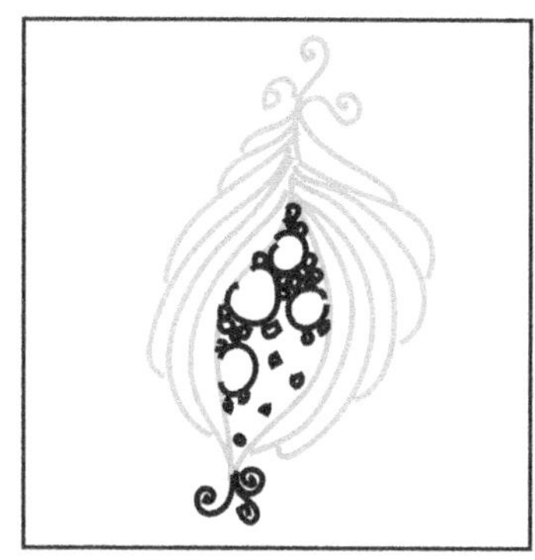

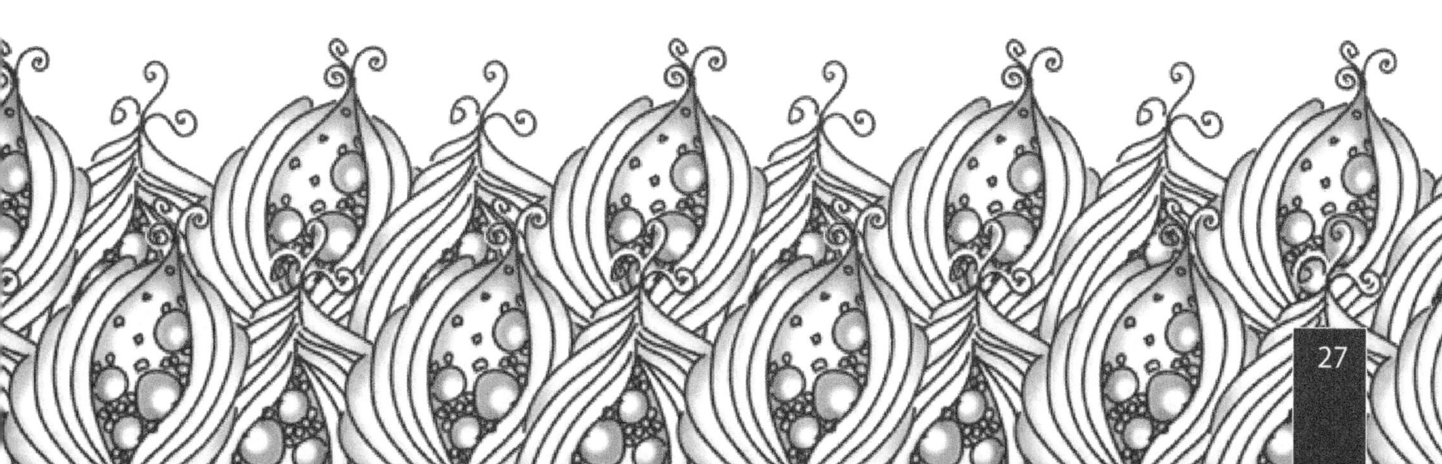

Addie

Barbara Duel Johnson CZT

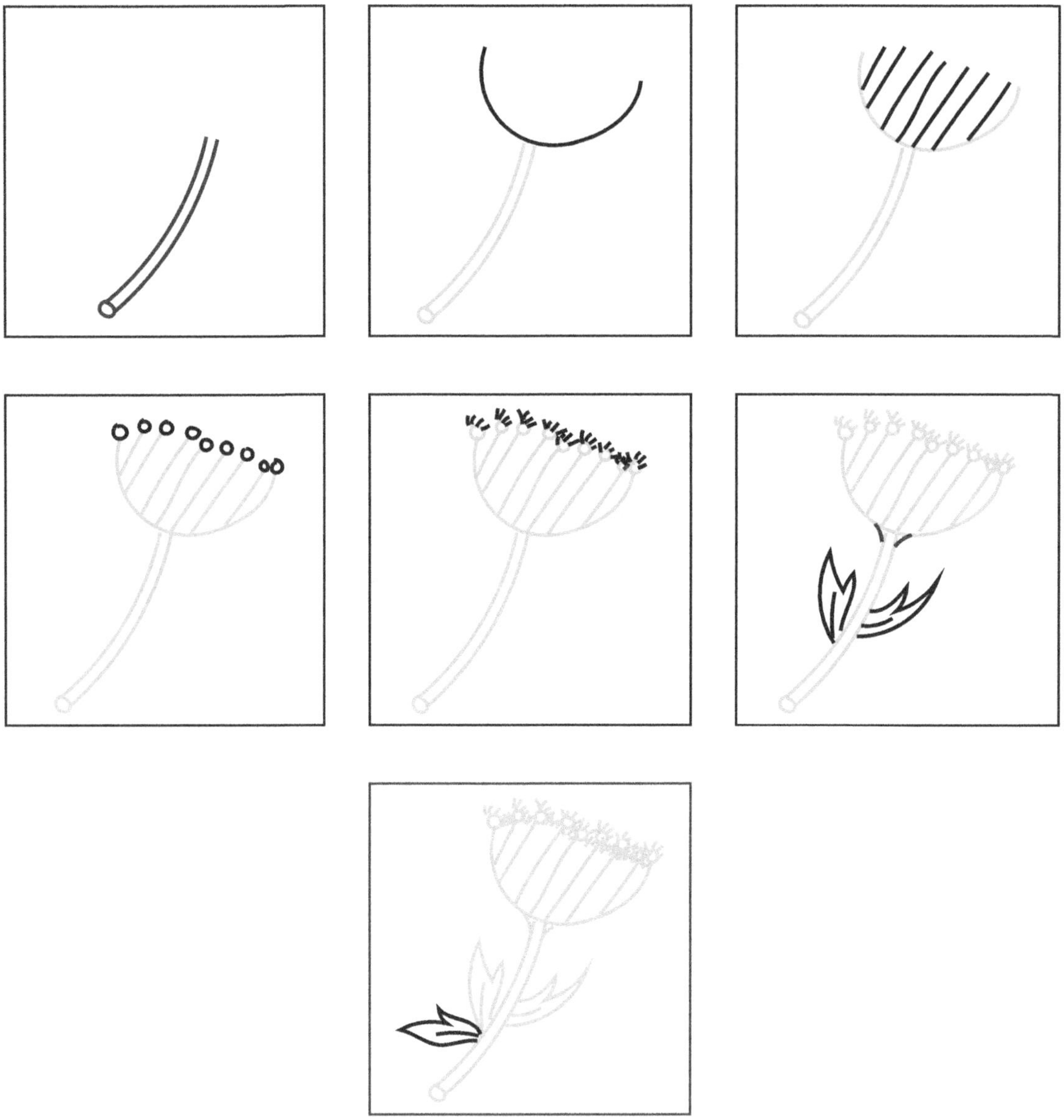

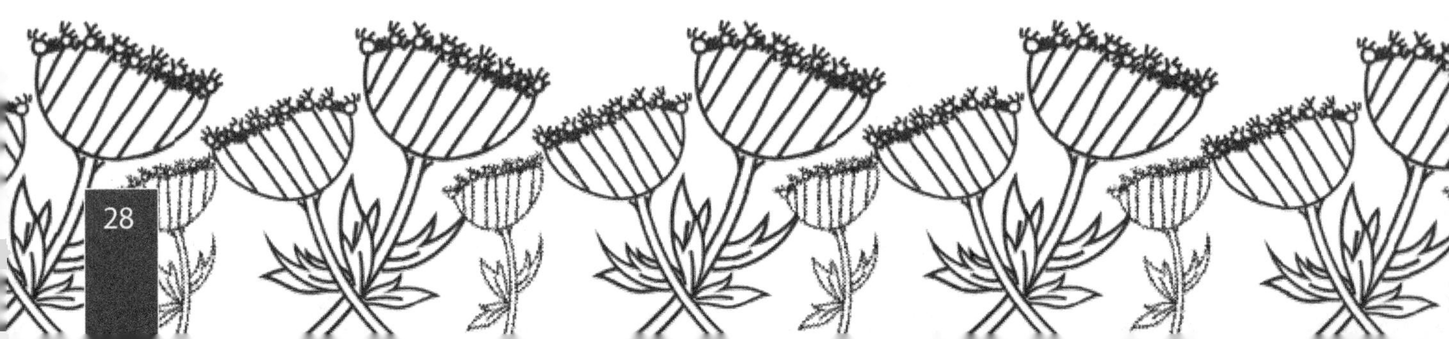

Heartizen

Aishwarya Dharba CZT

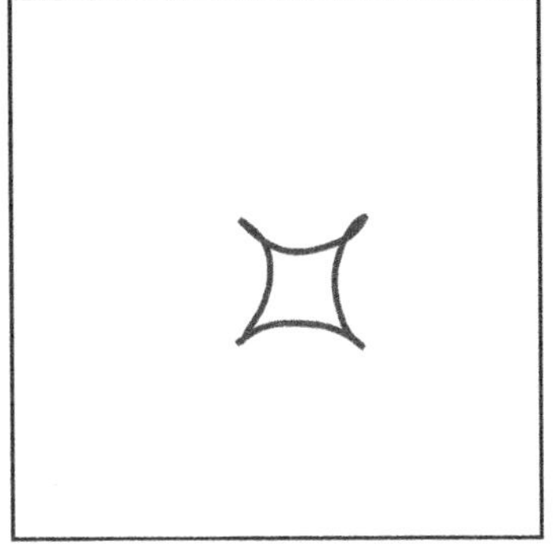
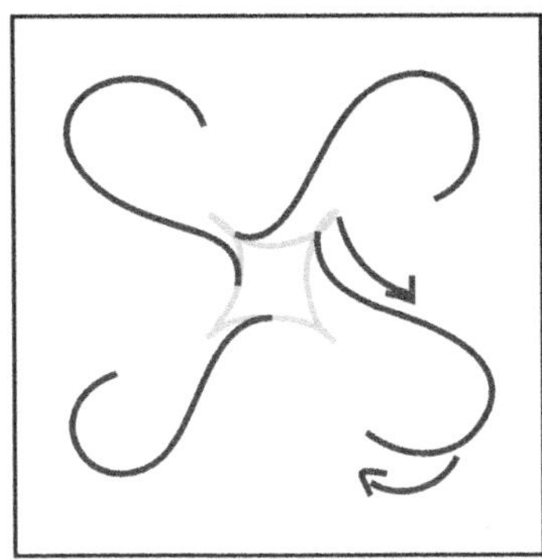
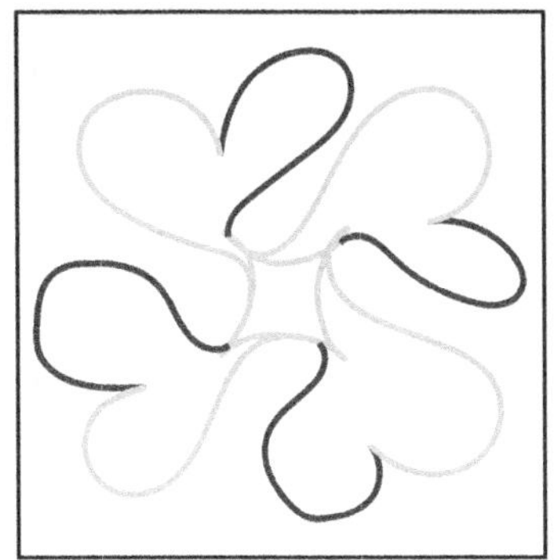

Effie

Annett Rumpler CZT

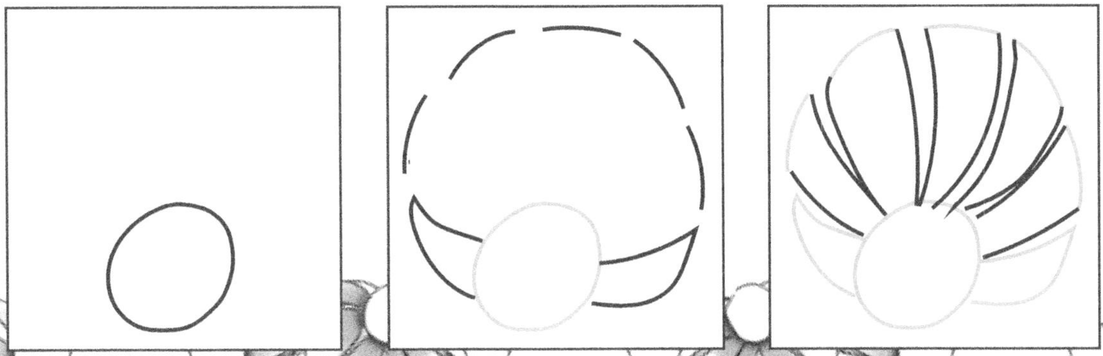

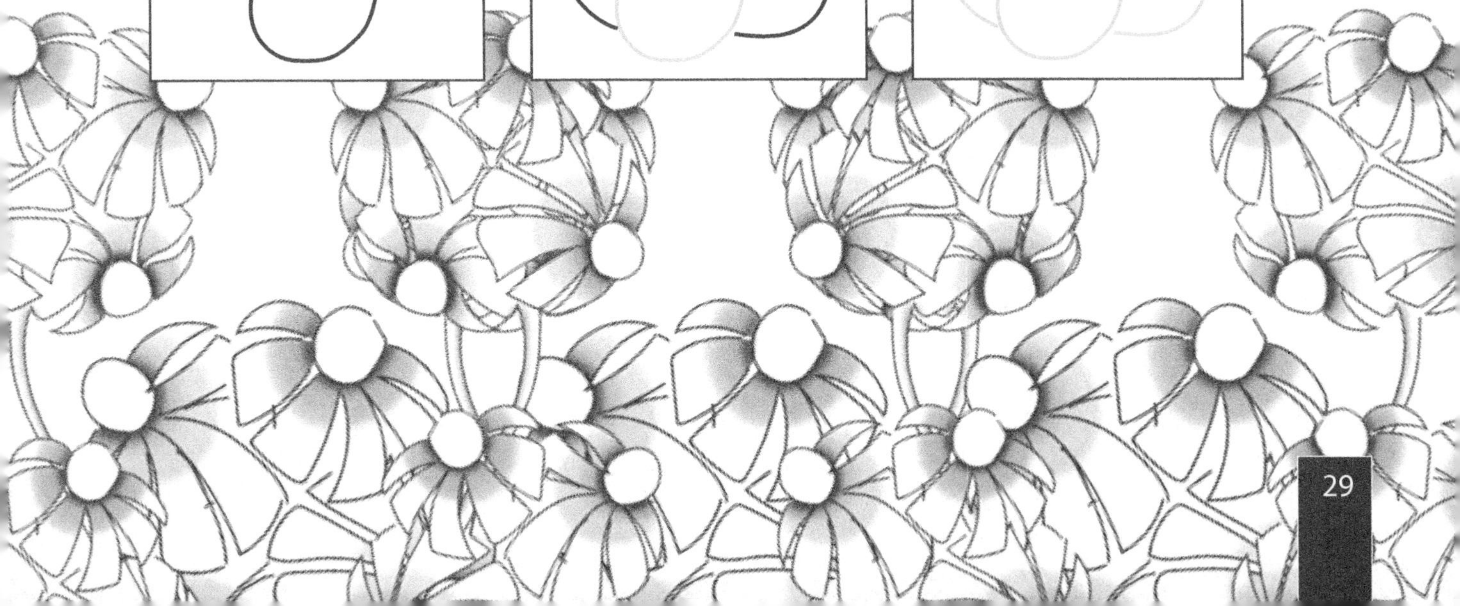

Cherub

Debbie Raaen CZT

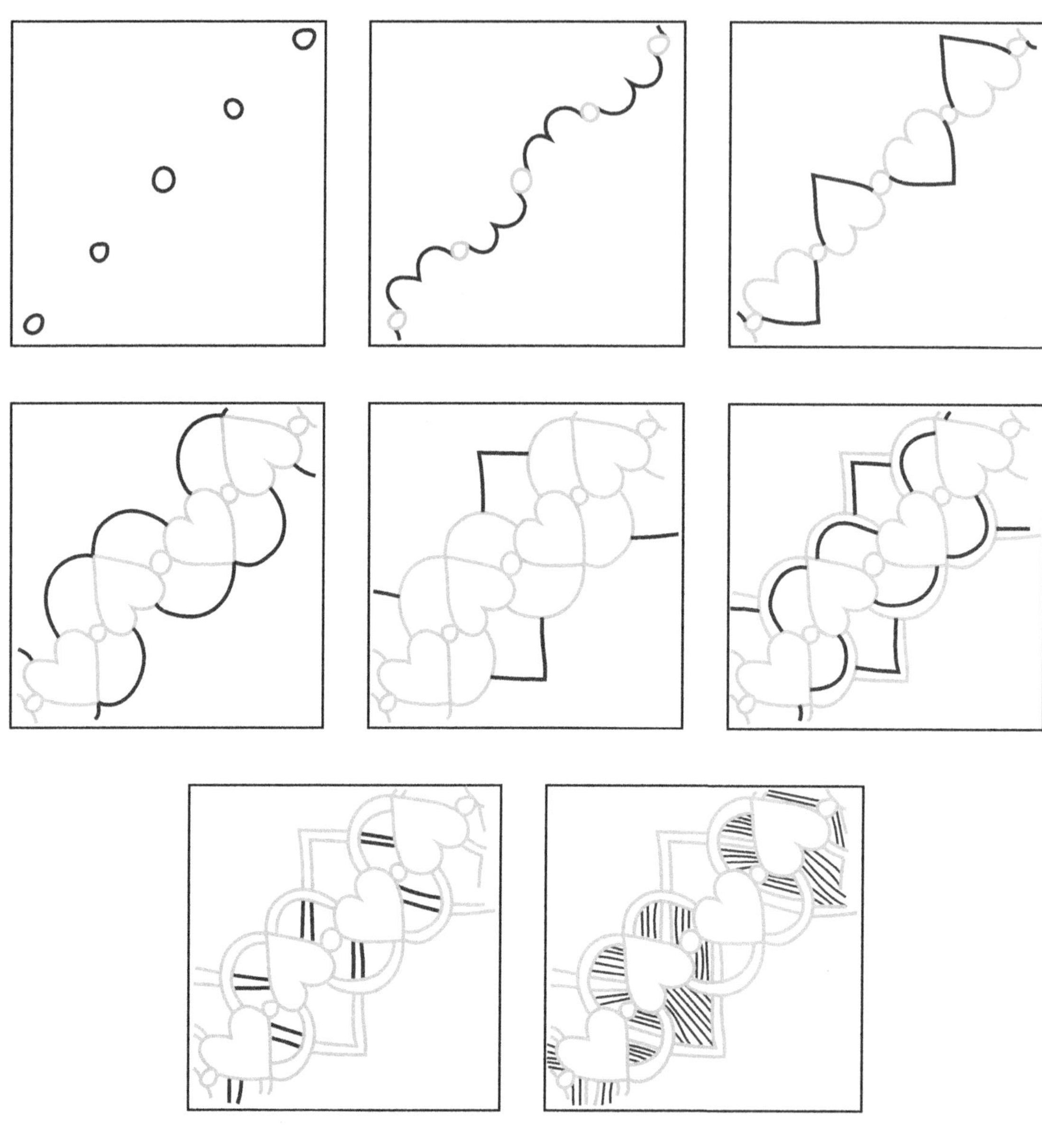

Keepsake

Simone Menzel CZT

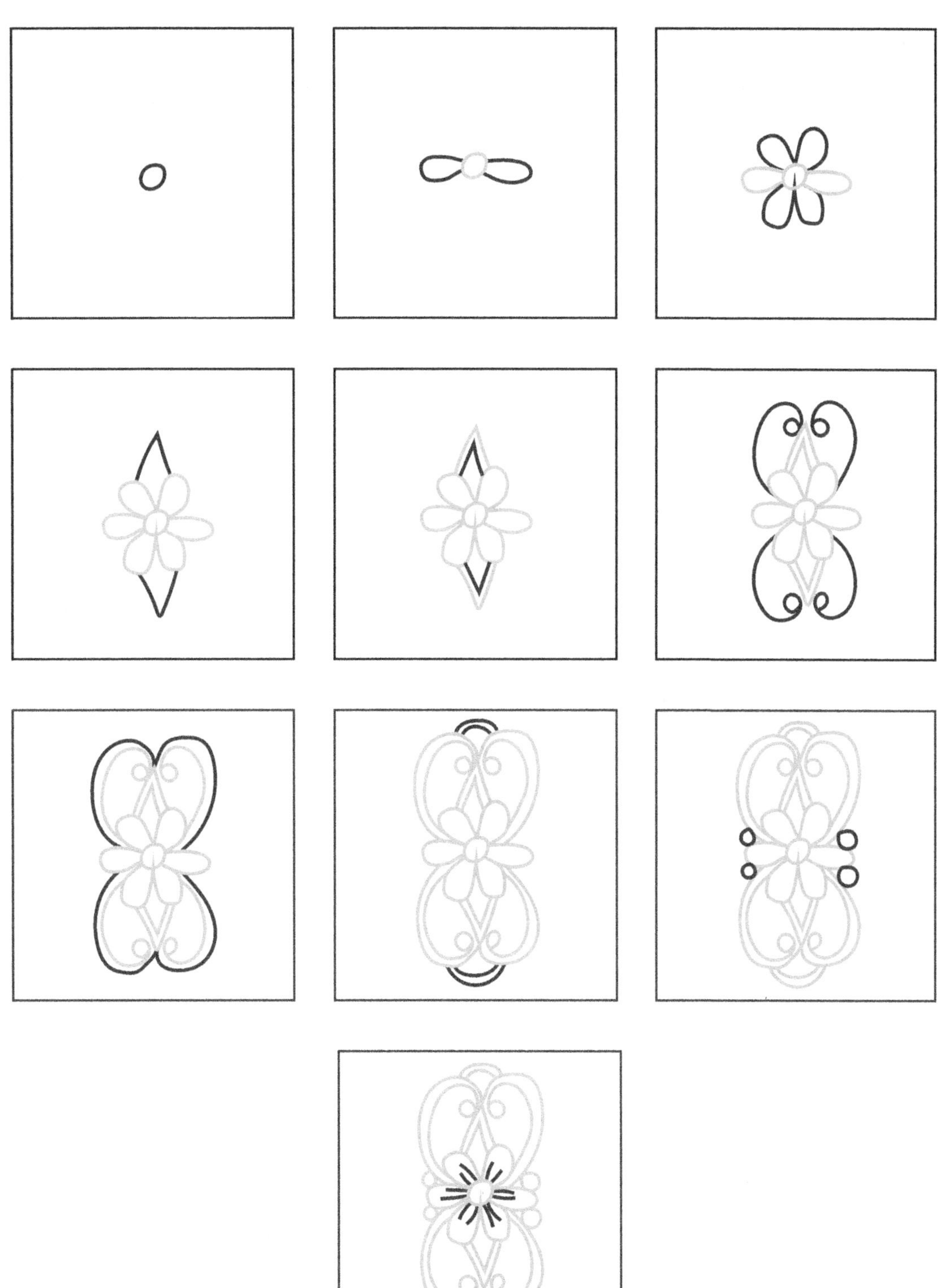

Foundabout

Official Zentangle Pattern

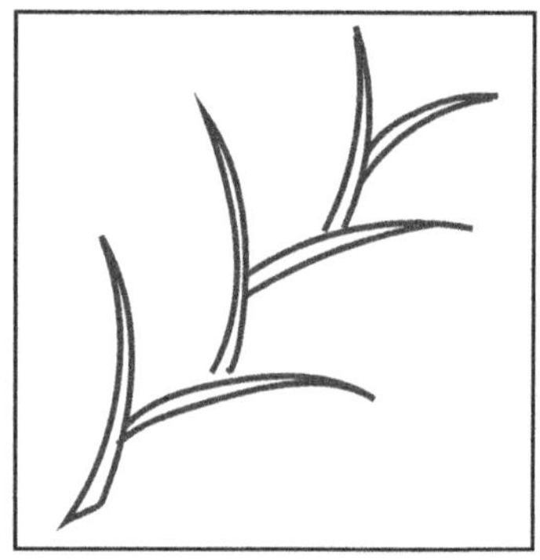
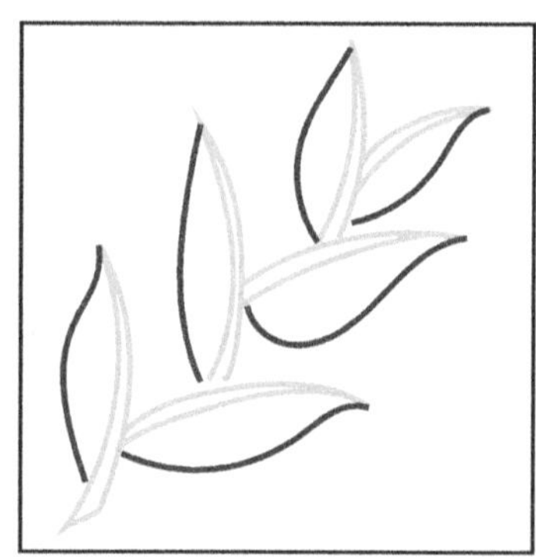
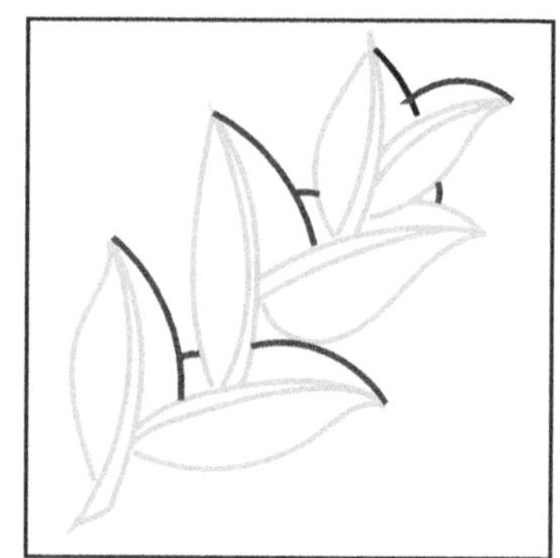

Foxie

Barbara Duel Johnson CZT

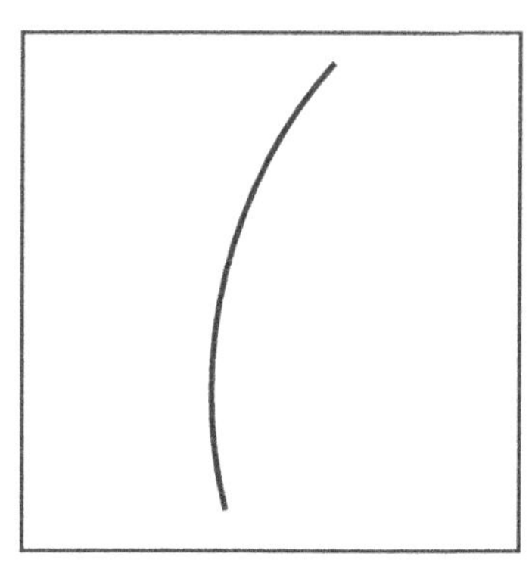
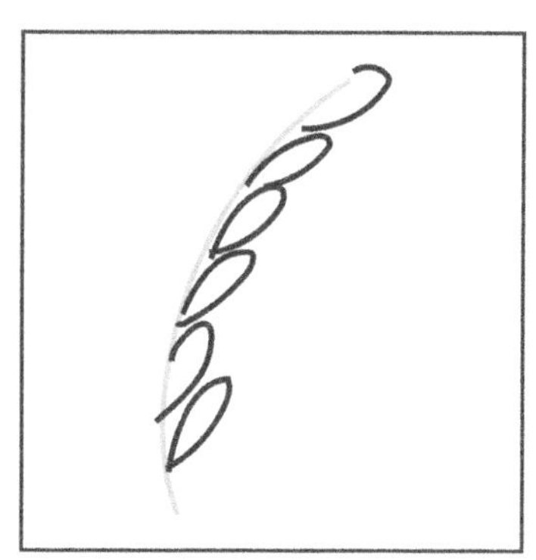
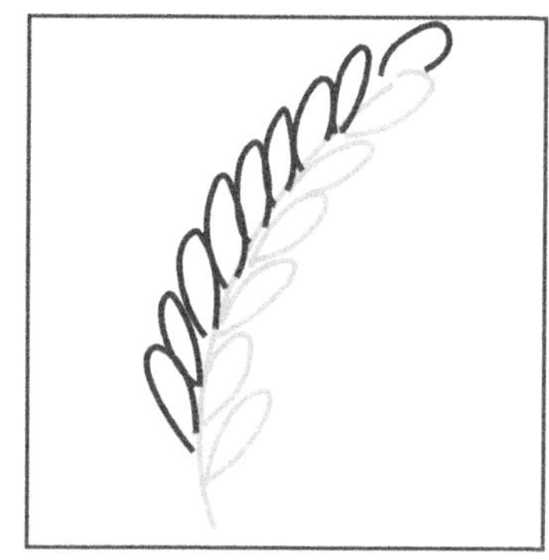

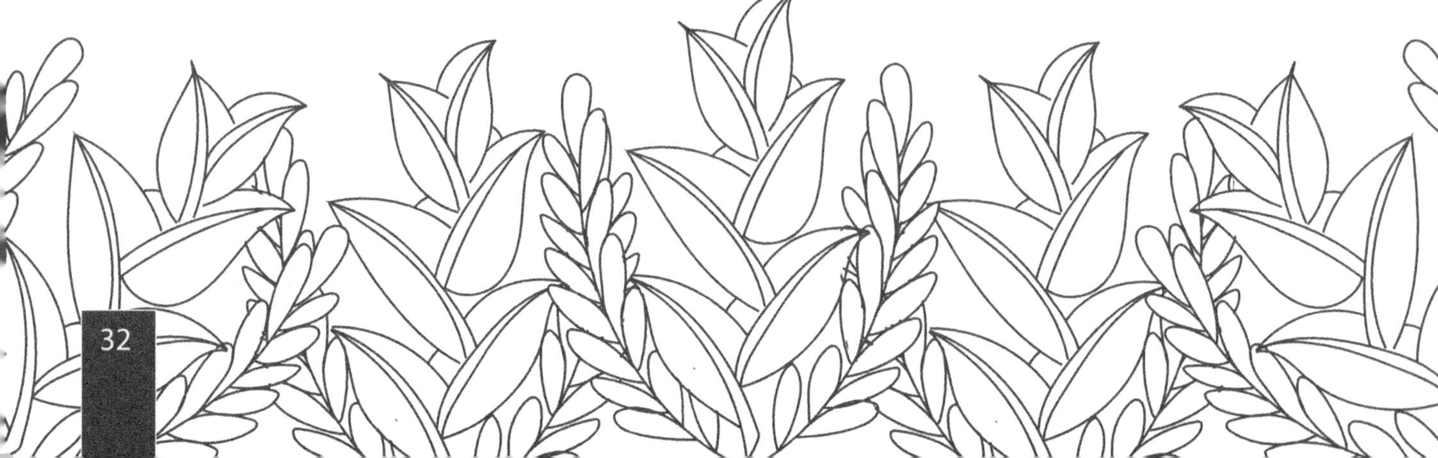

Argab

Simone Menzel CZT

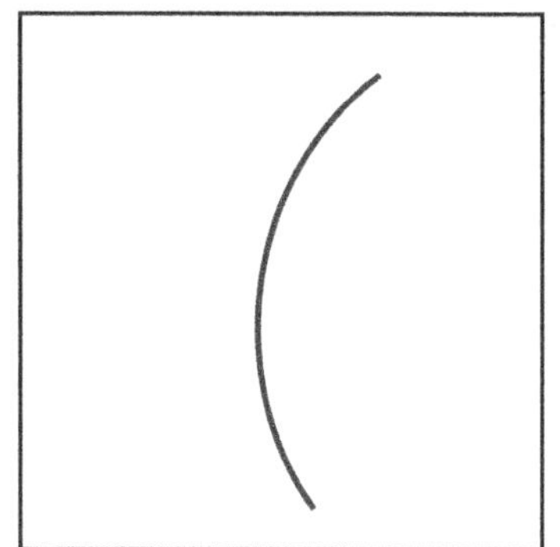
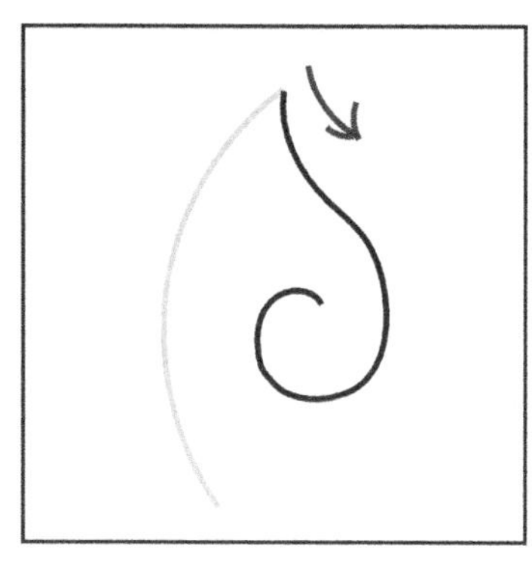
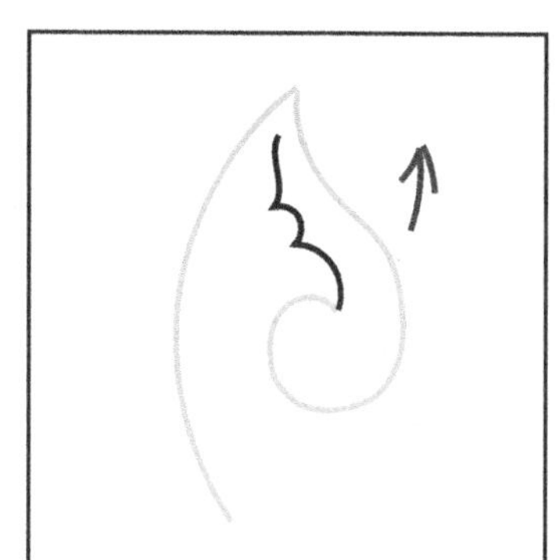
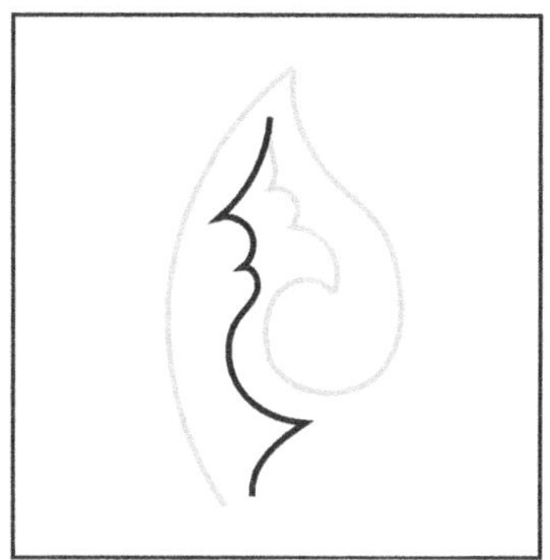
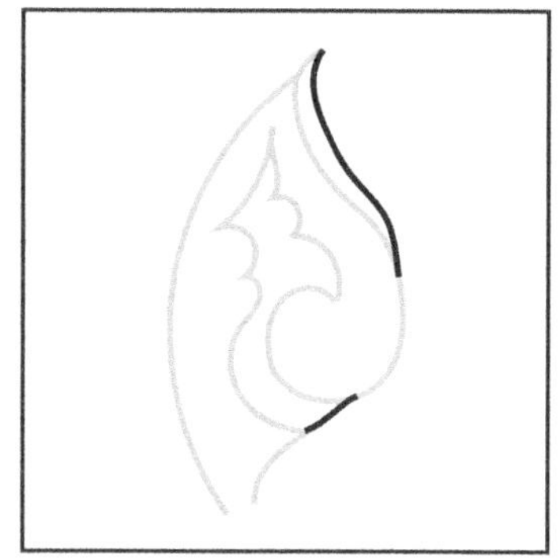
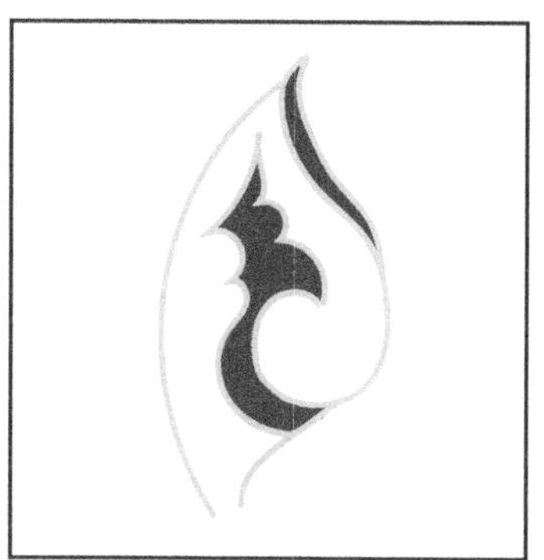

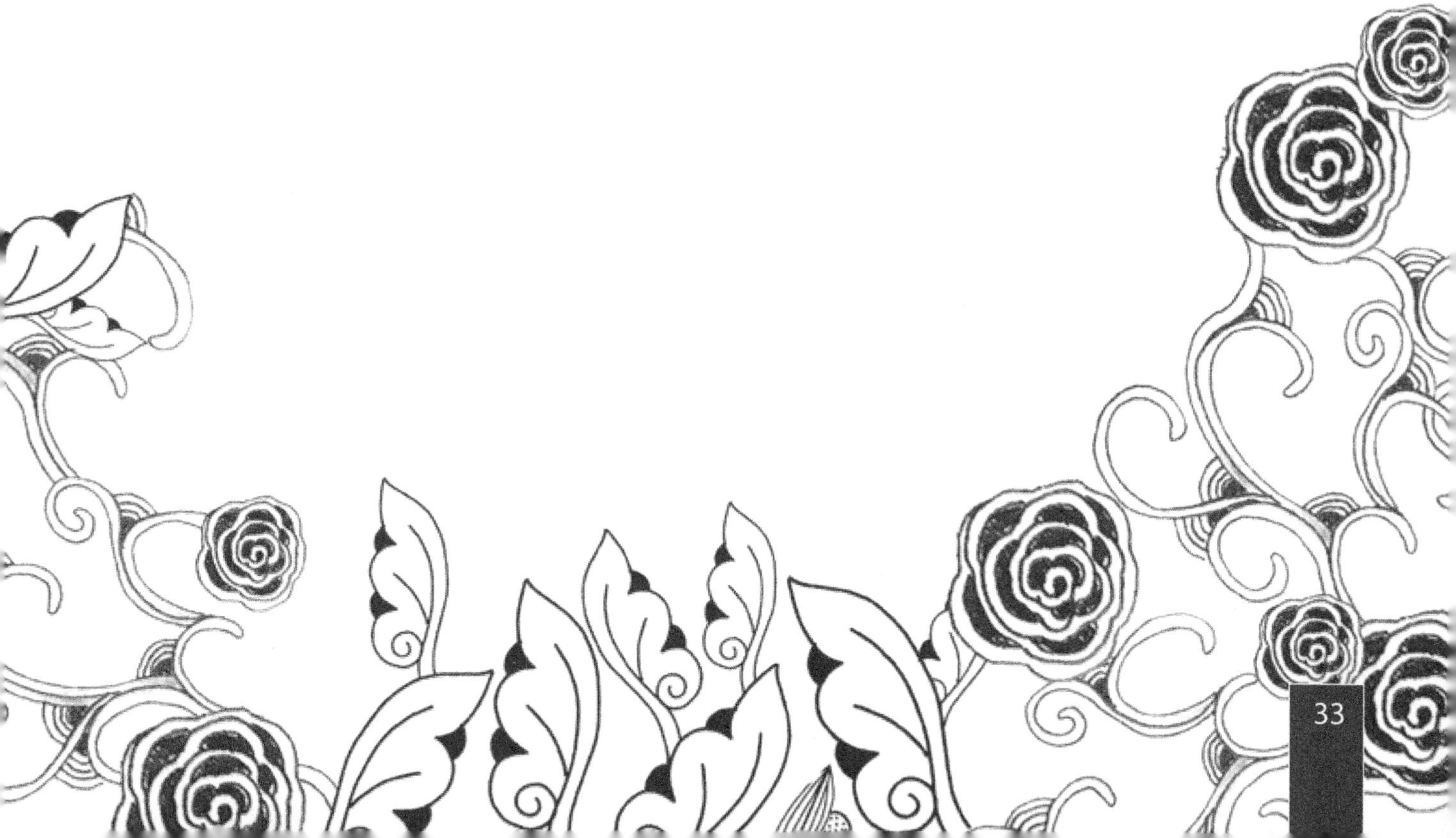

Hearty Way Bop

Official Zentangle Pattern

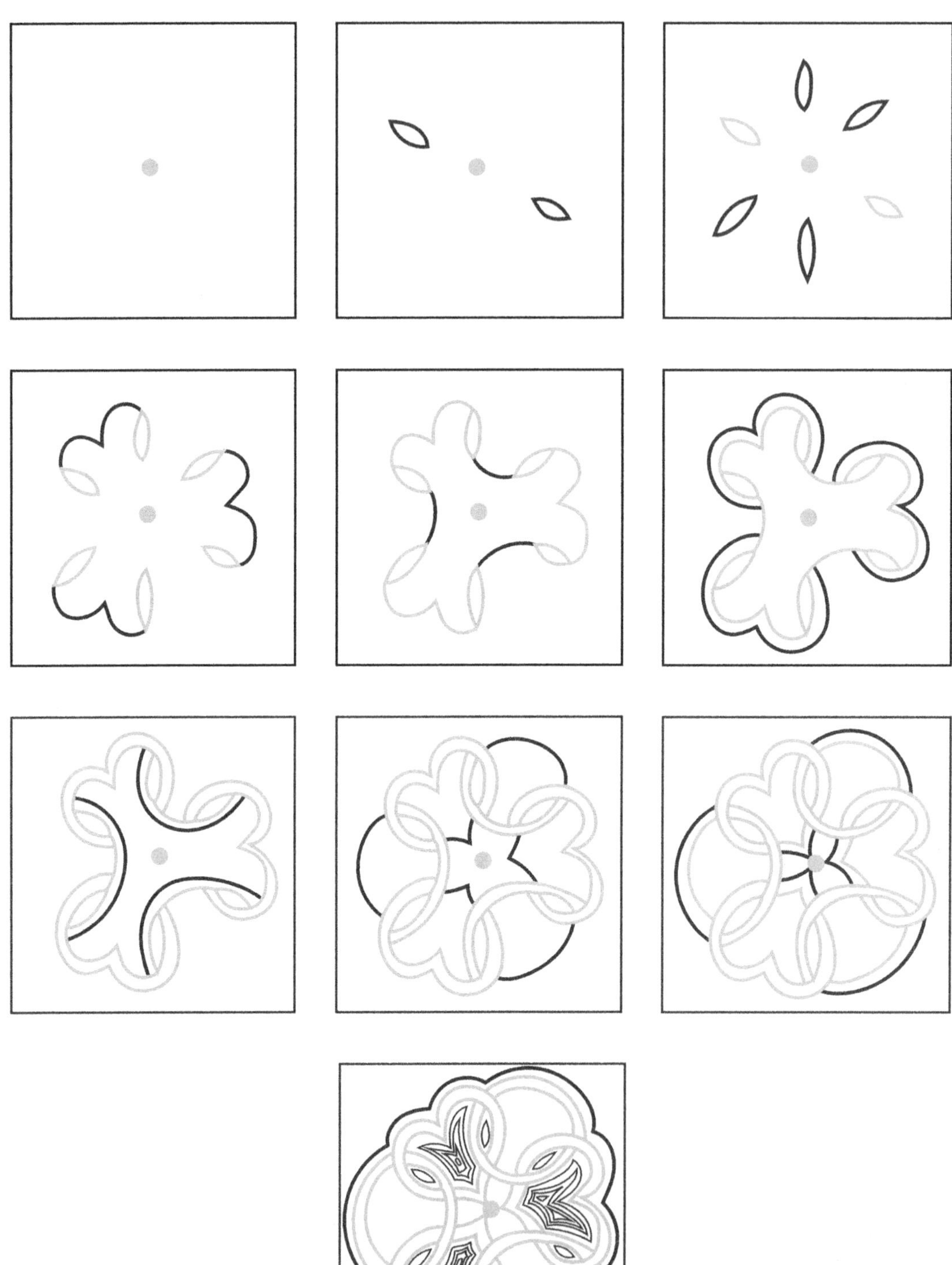

My Spin

Simone Menzel CZT

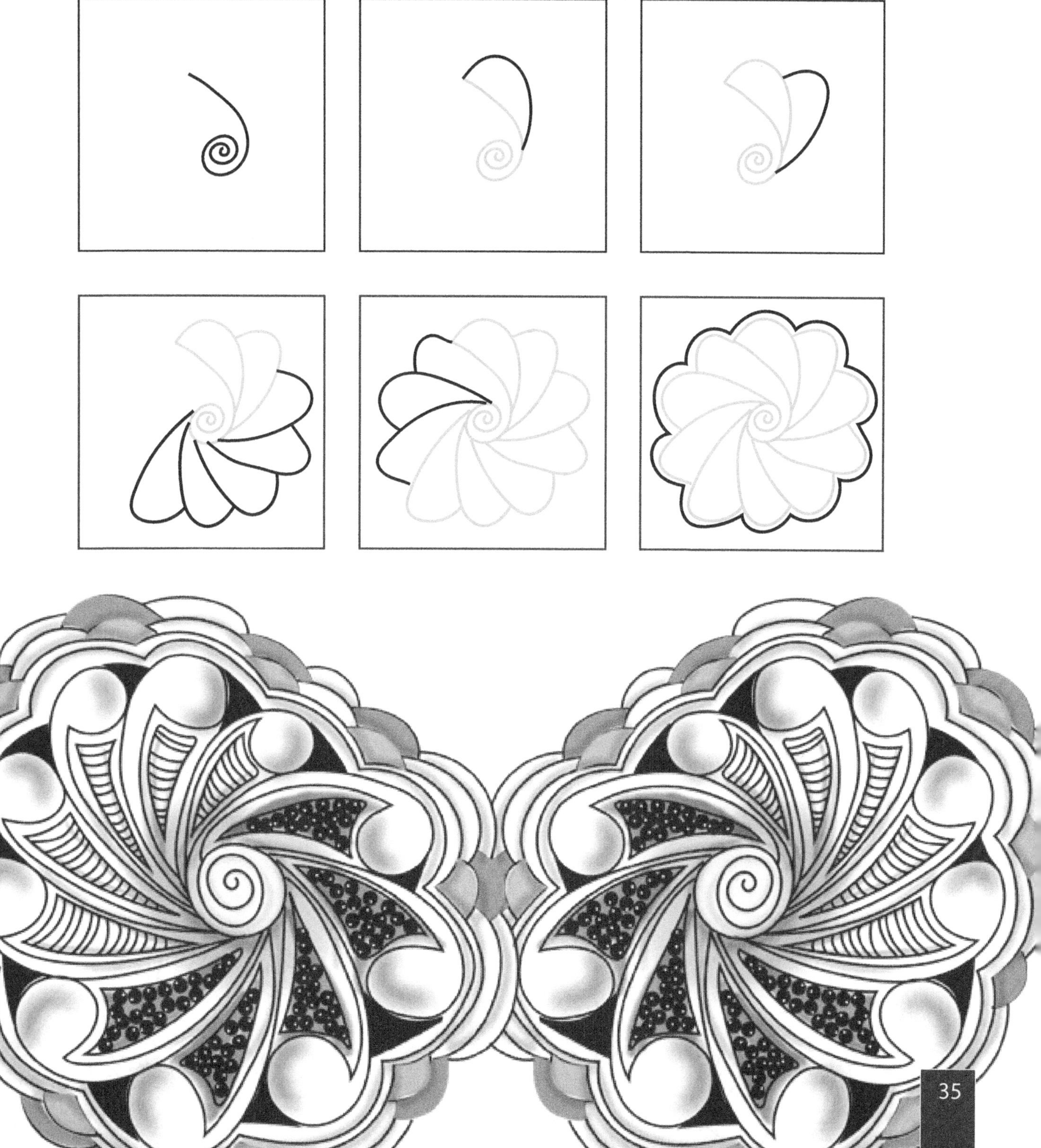

Hexagonal

Aishwarya Dharba CZT

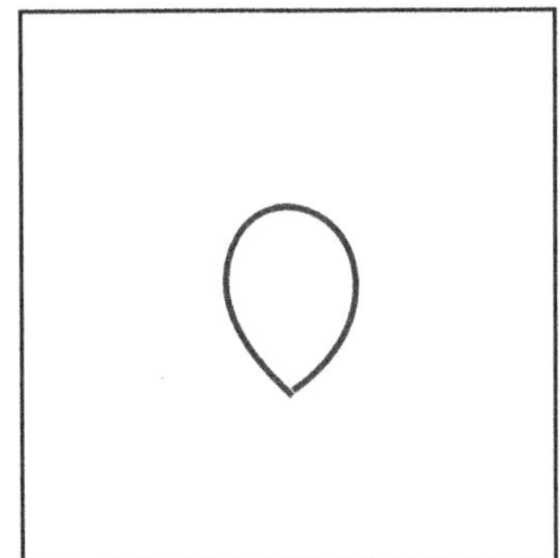
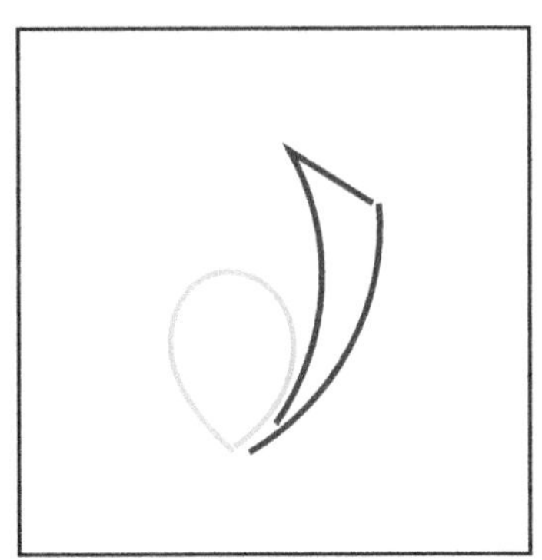

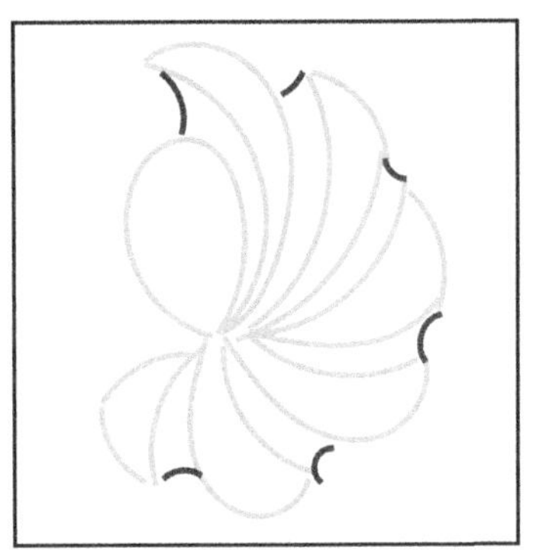
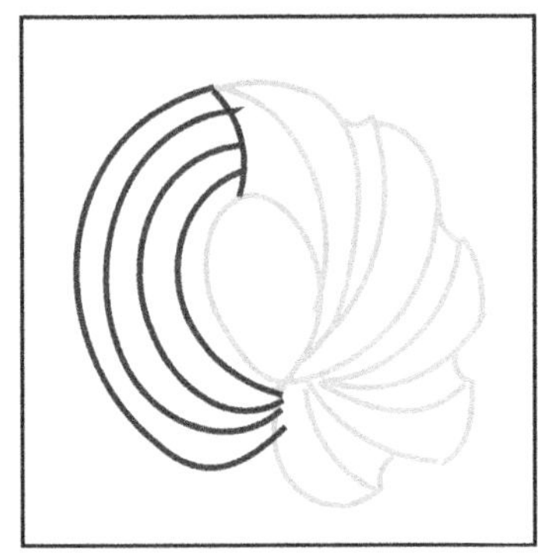
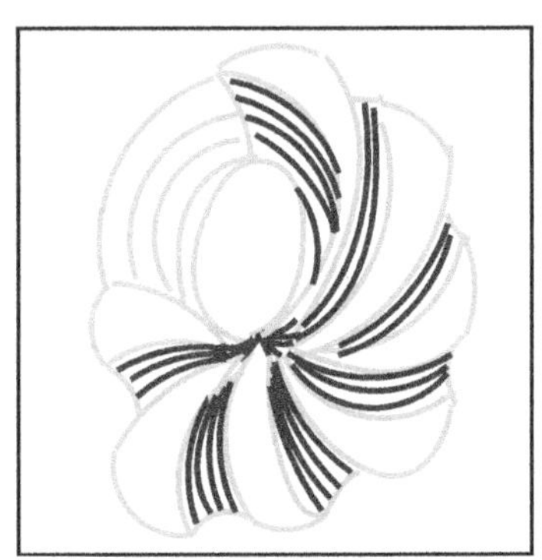

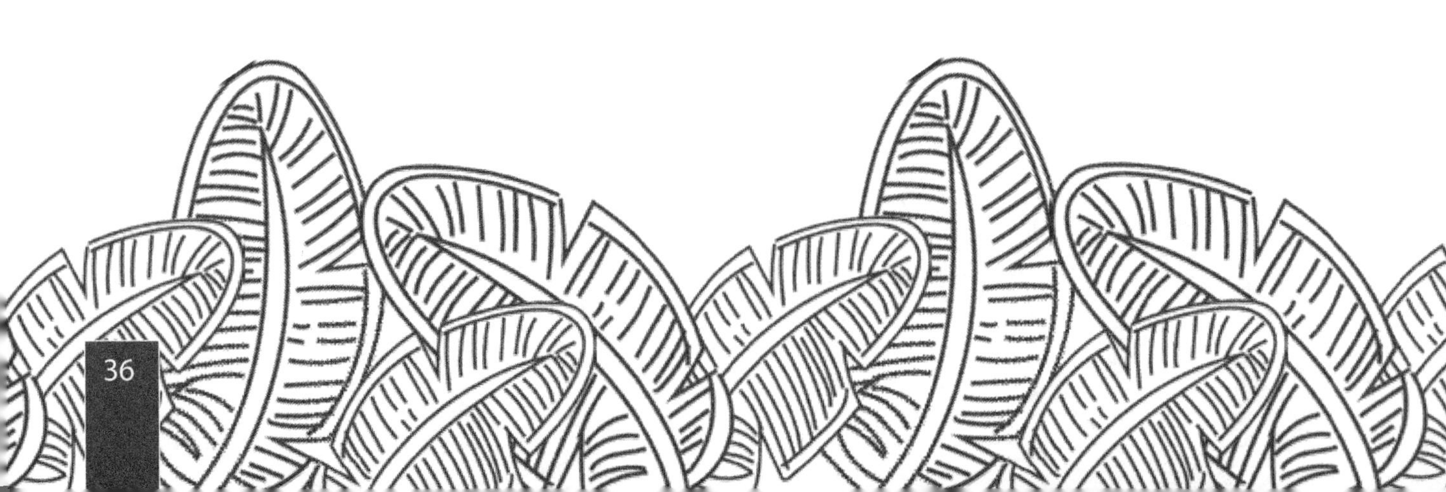

Tawa

Miranda Gerber CZT

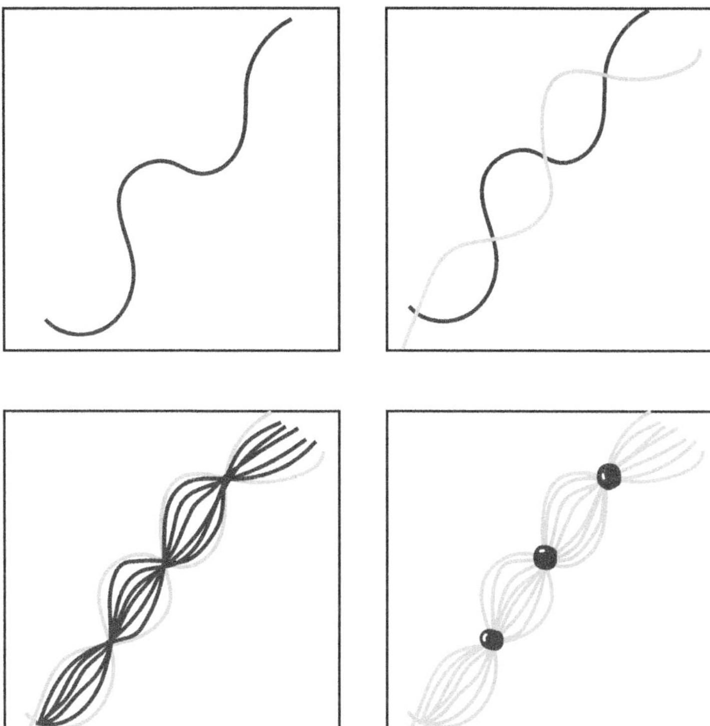

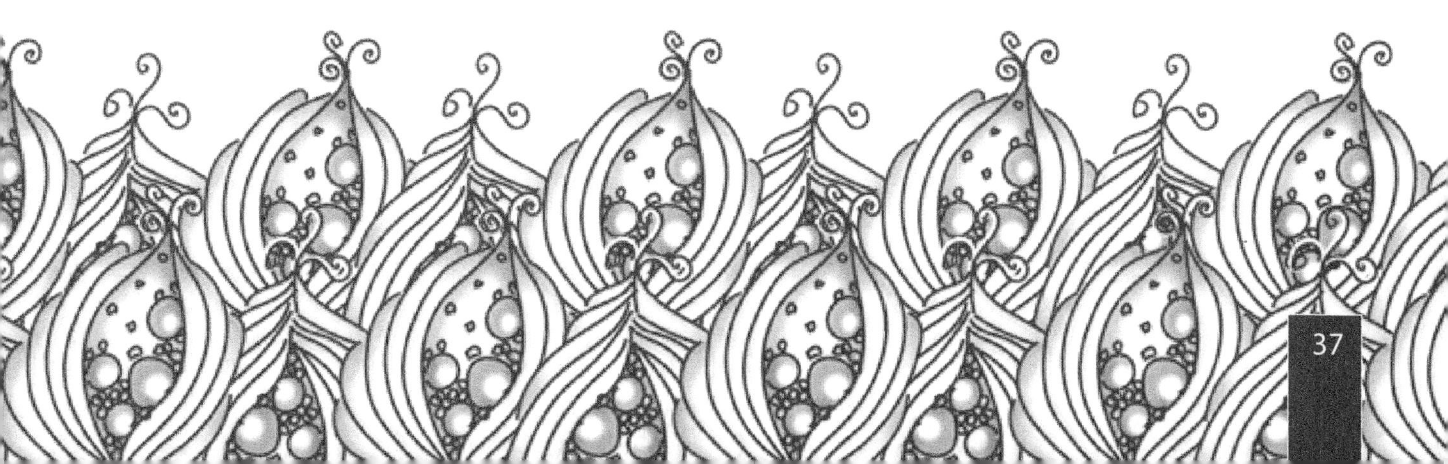

Fluxcue

Sunali Shah CZT

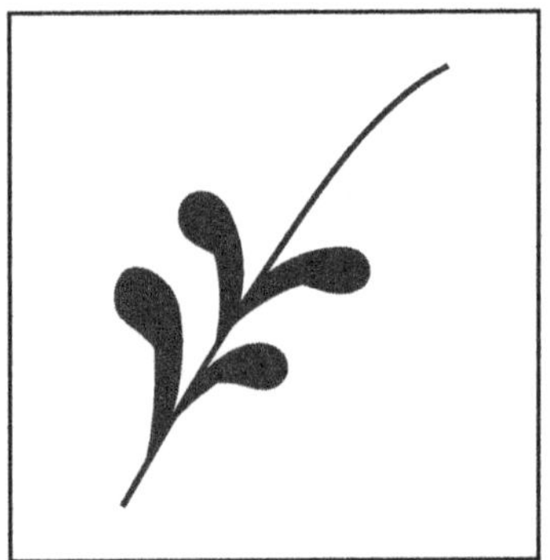
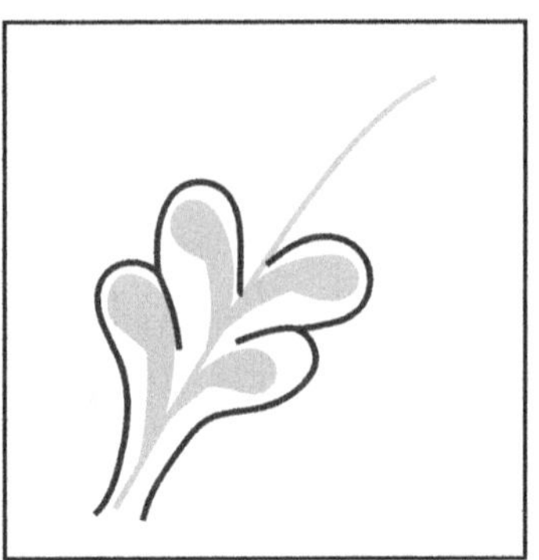
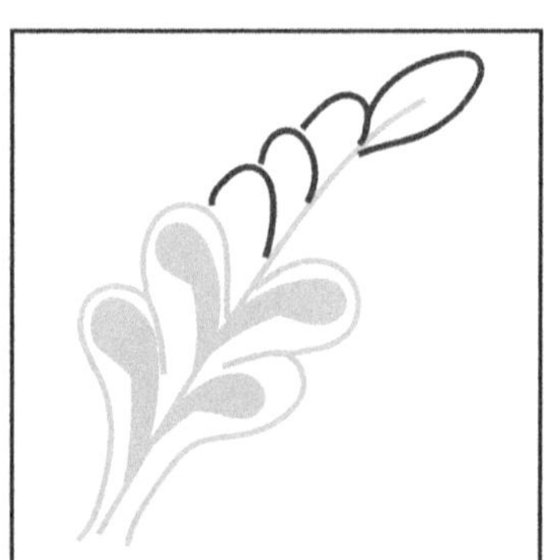
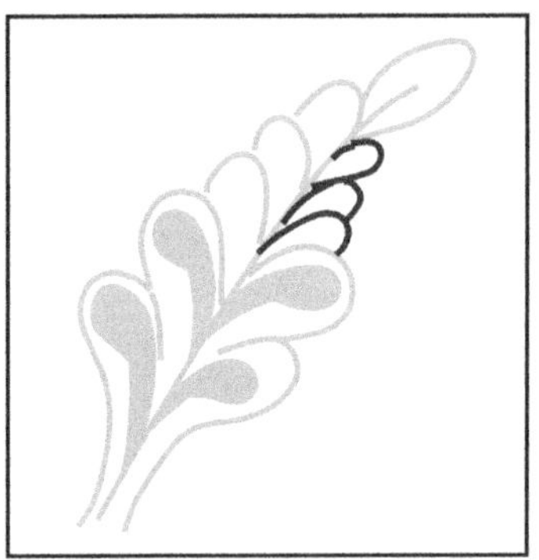
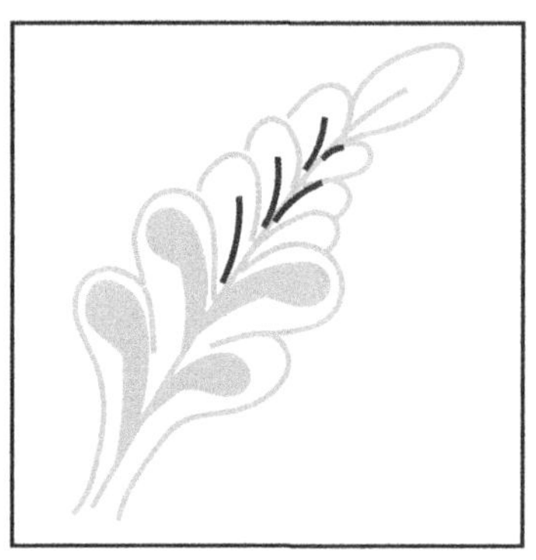

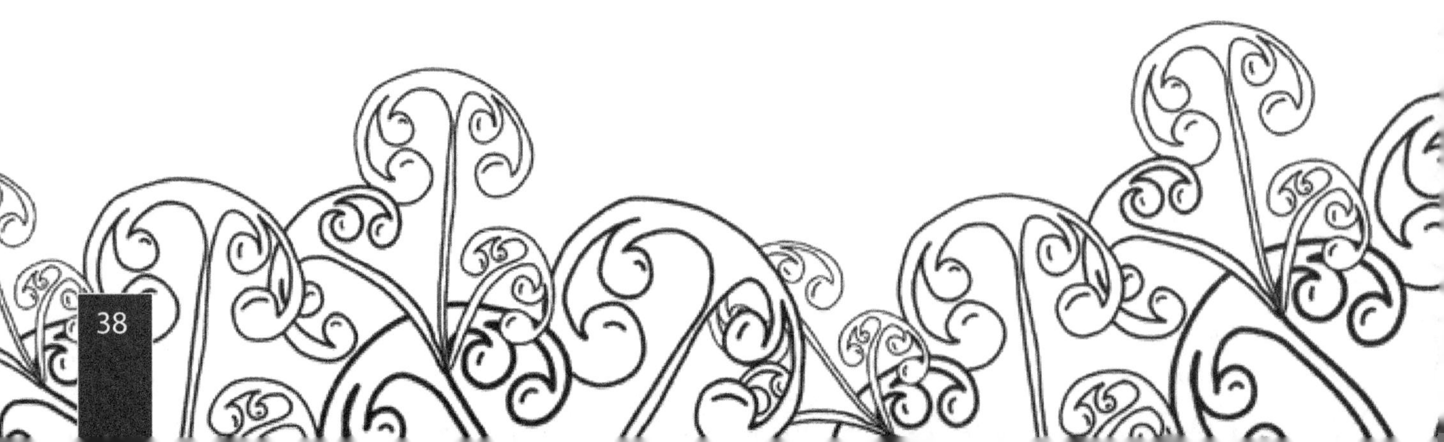

!ion

Theresa Fessler CZT

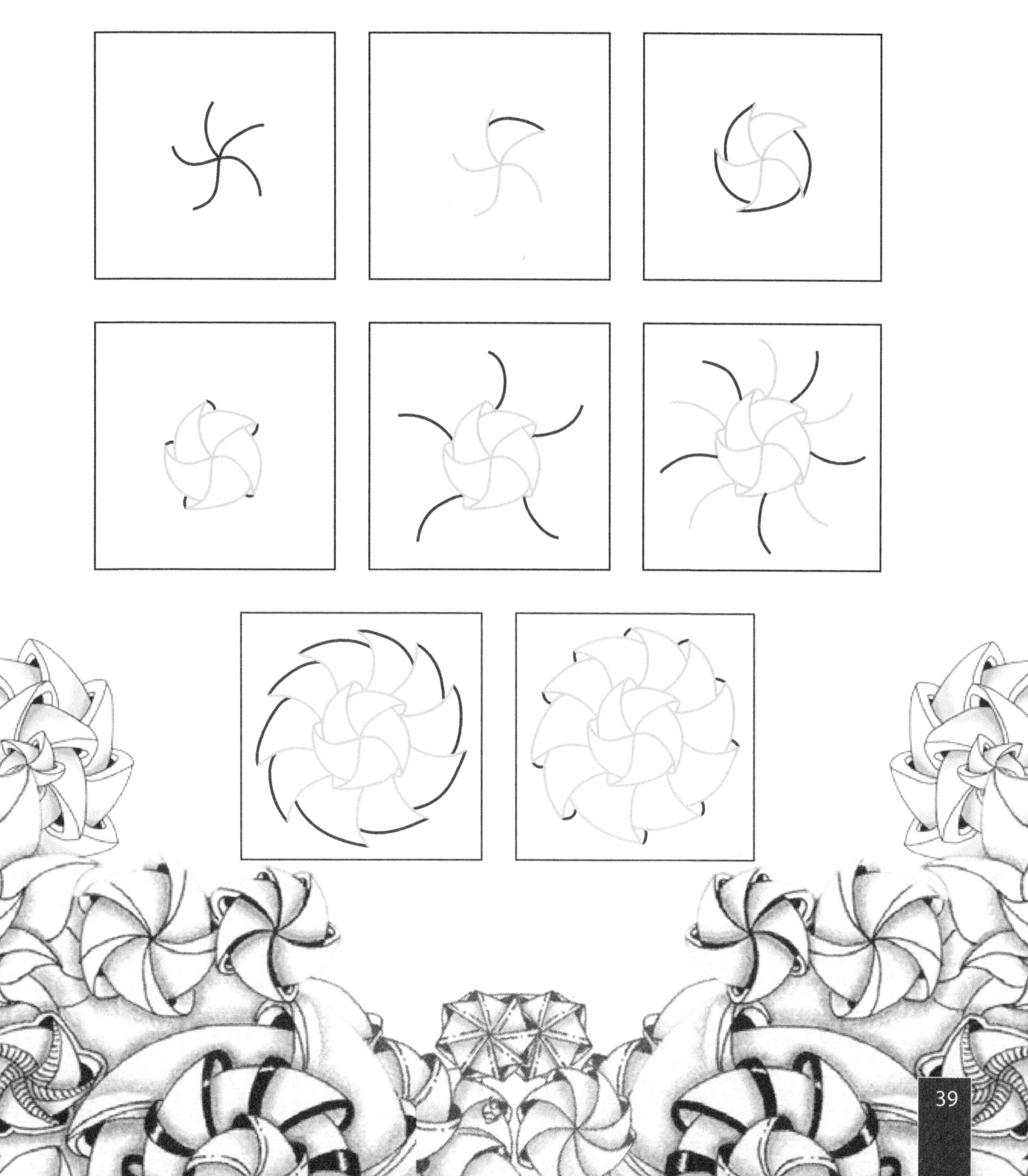

Mythograph

Official Zentangle Pattern

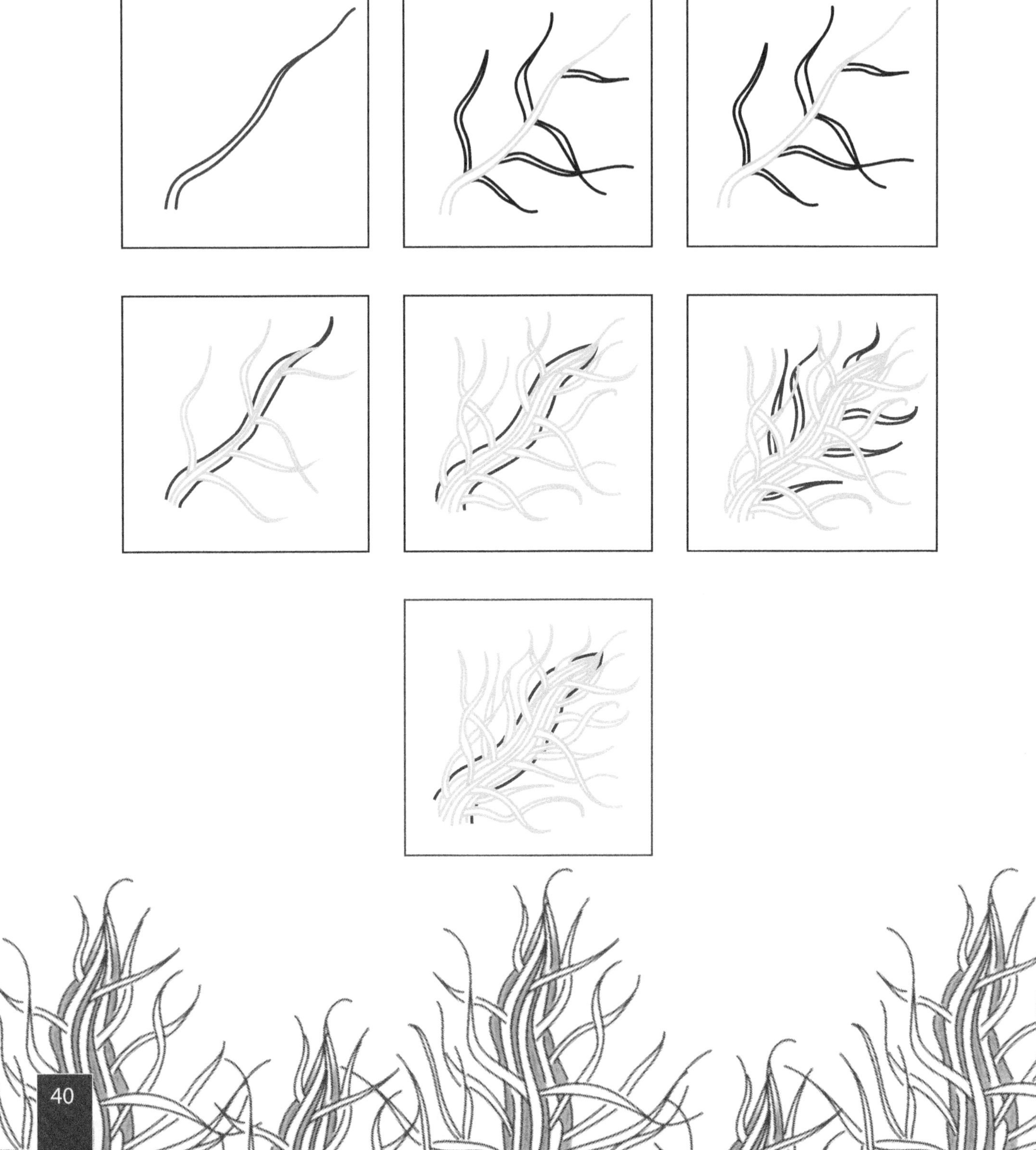

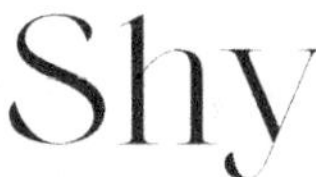

Shy

Suchitra CZT

Cluster

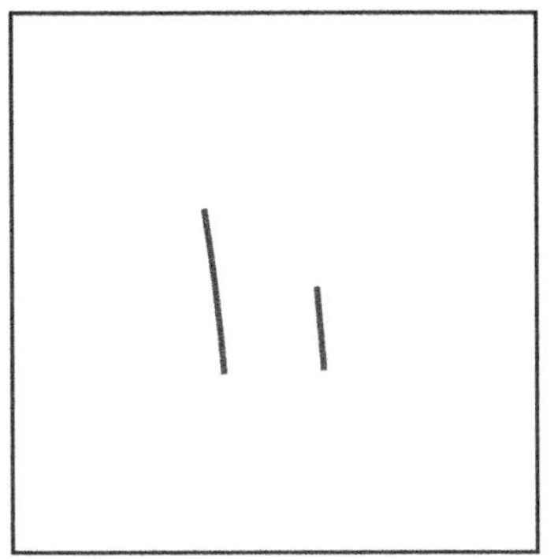

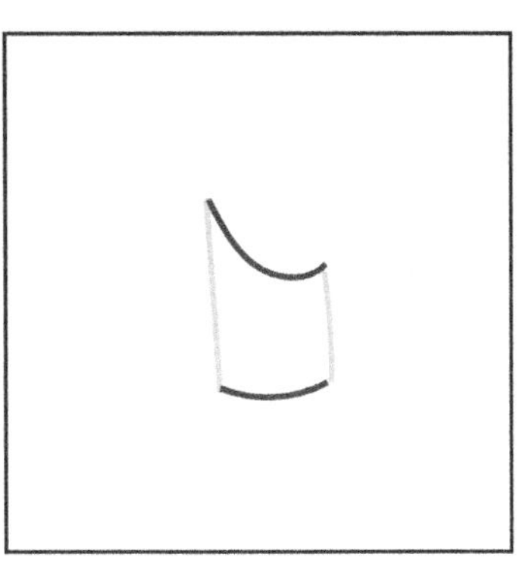

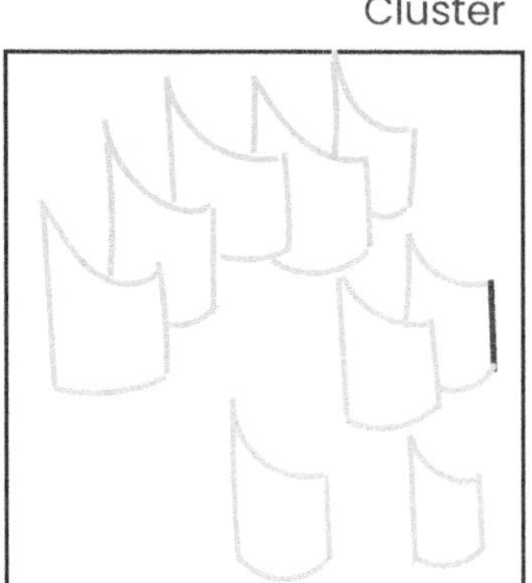

Reticula

Embelish

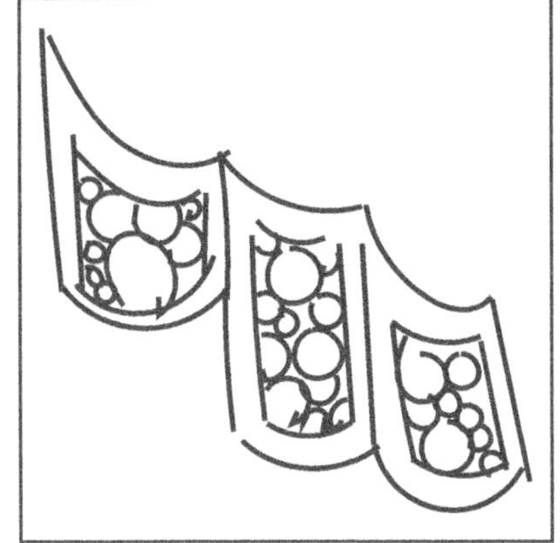

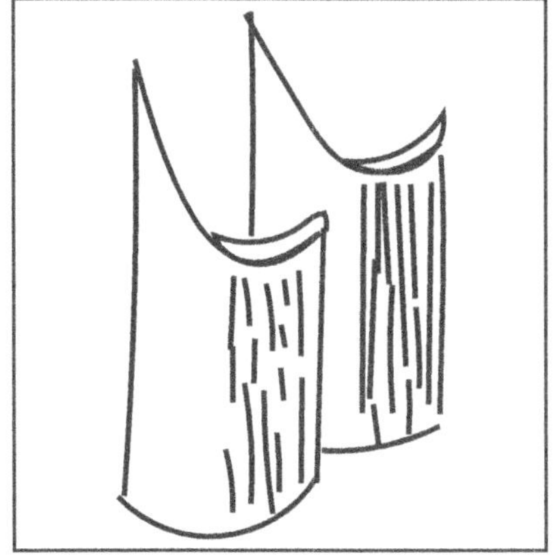

Blossoming

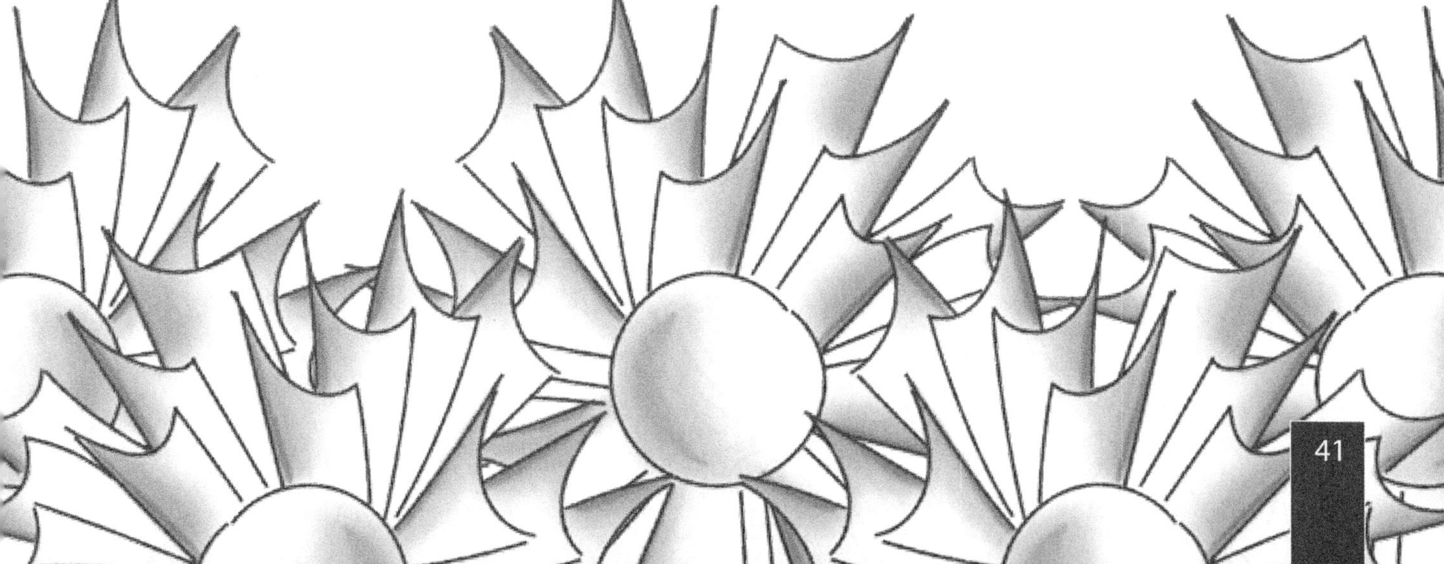

Starlight

Debbie Raaen CZT

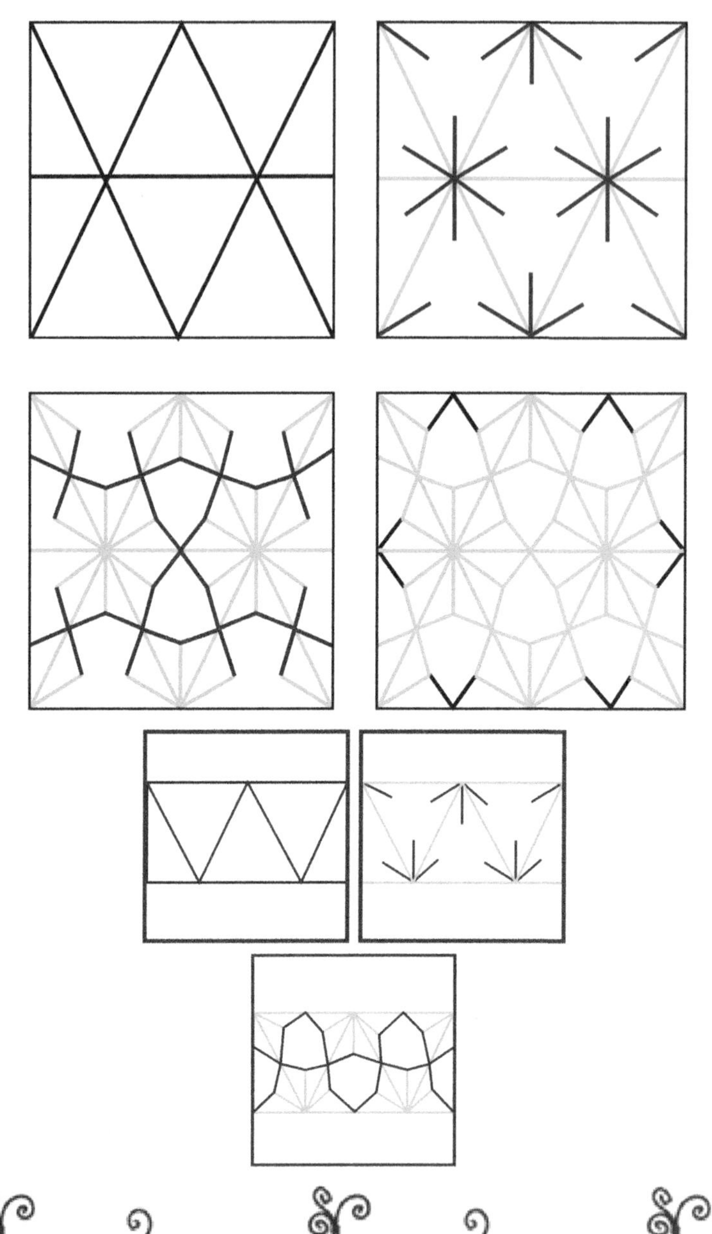

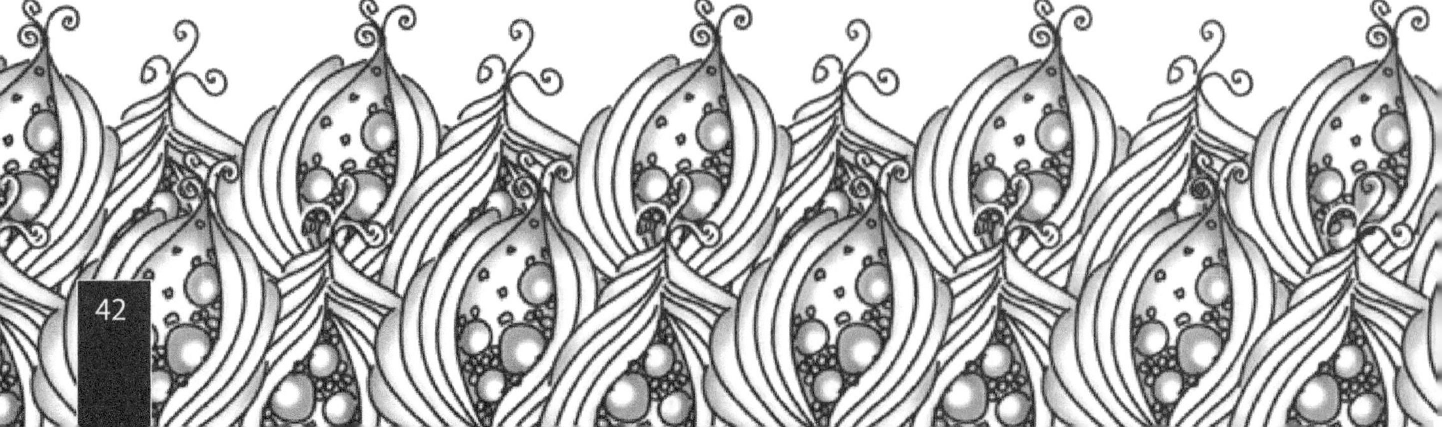

Merryadd

Barbara Duel Johnson CZT

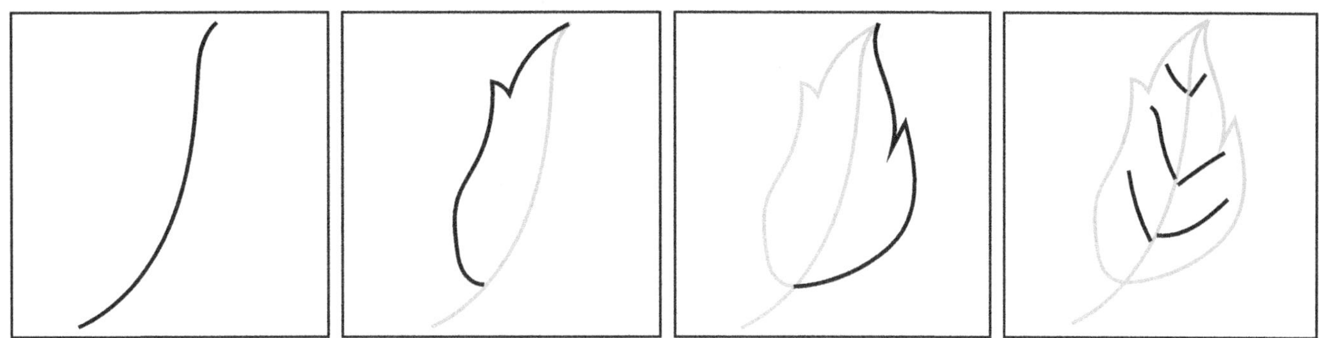

Star Aniz

Carla Jooren CZT

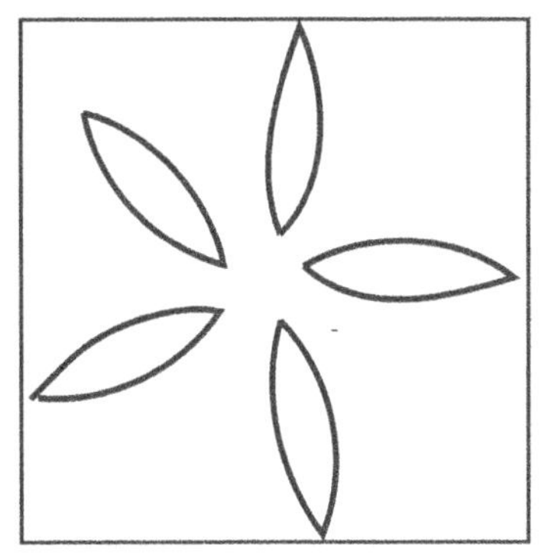
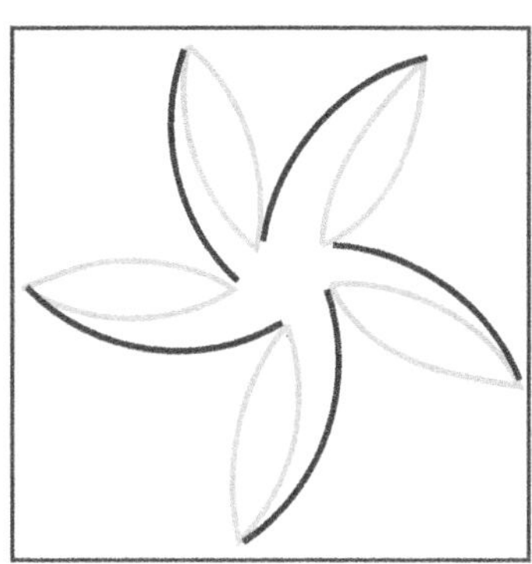
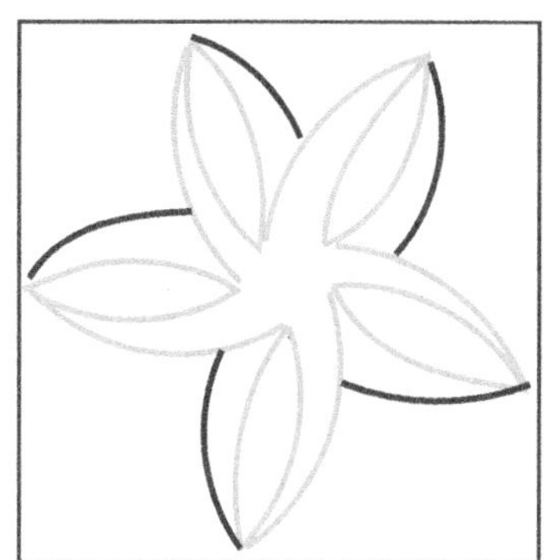

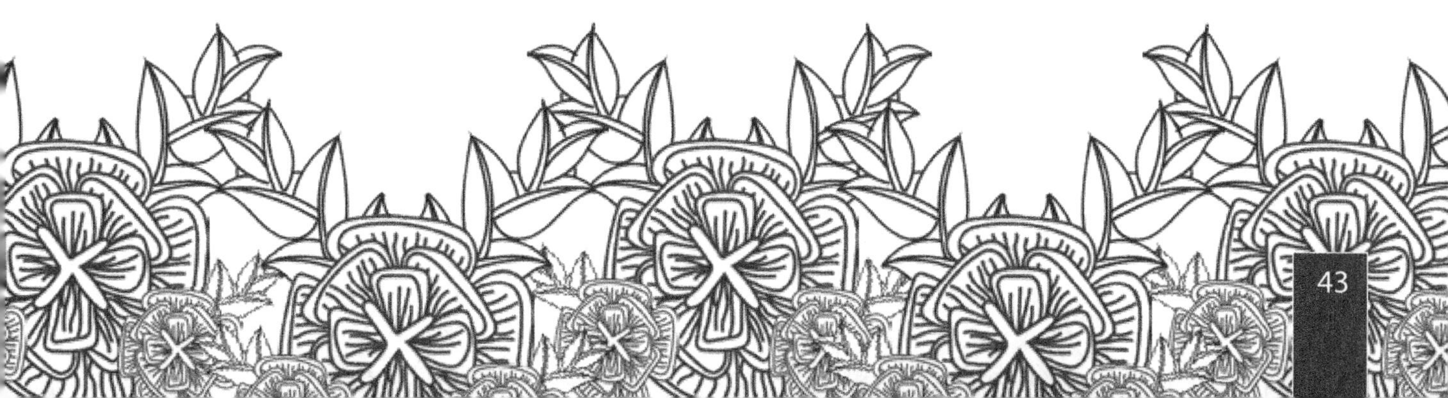

Aihsd

Theresa Fessler CZT

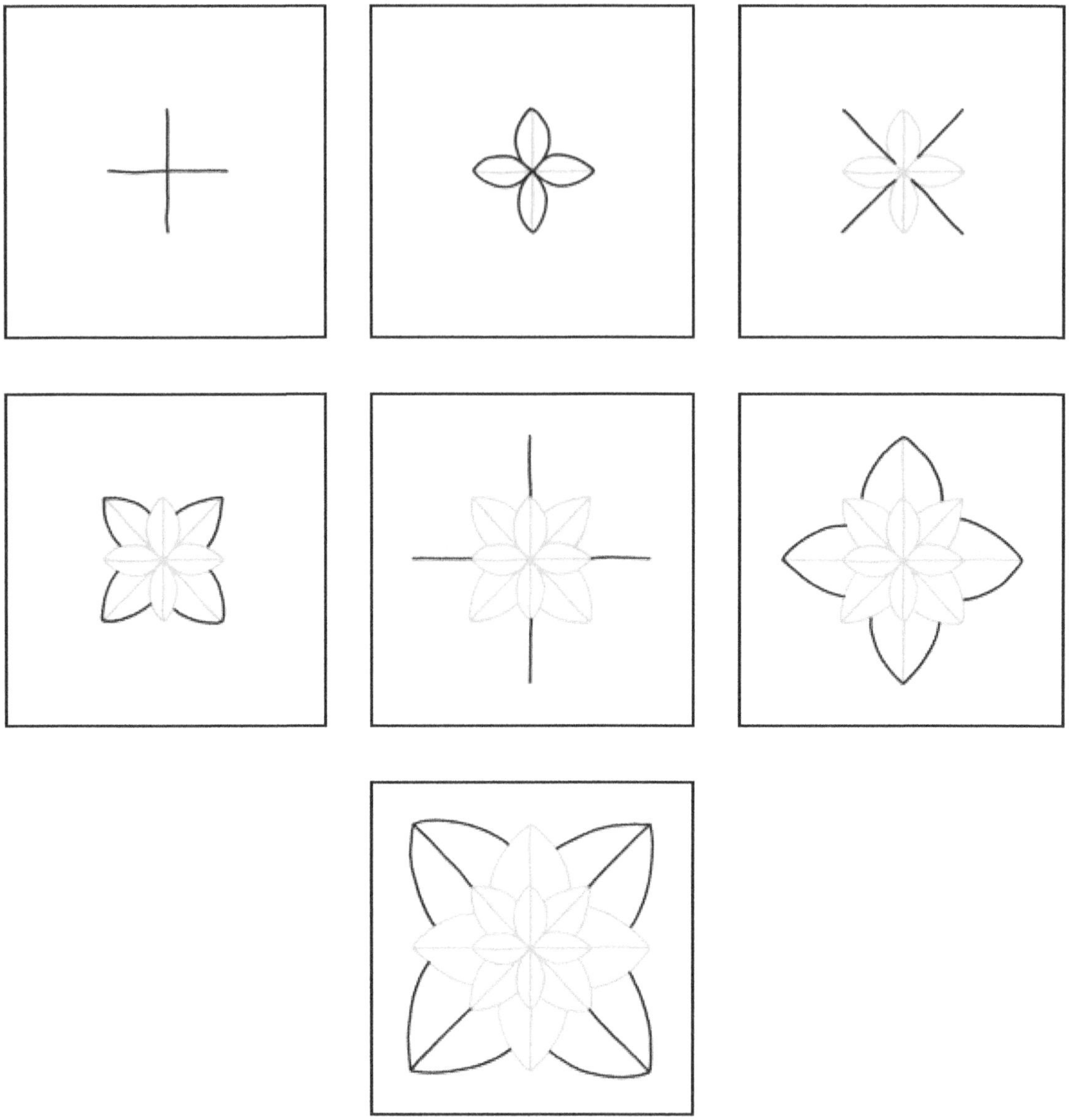

Aihsd (Variation)

Theresa Fessler CZT

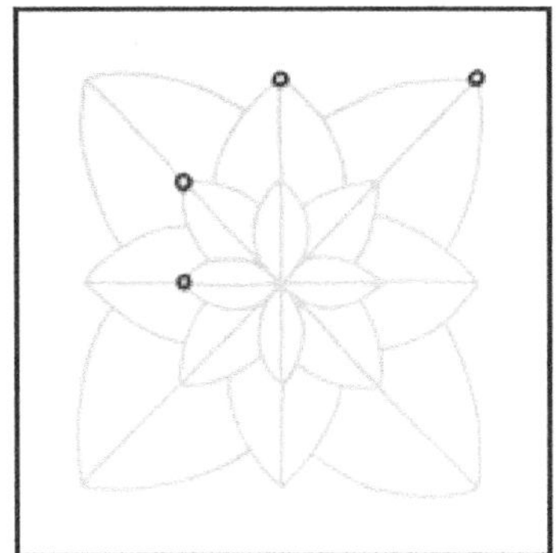
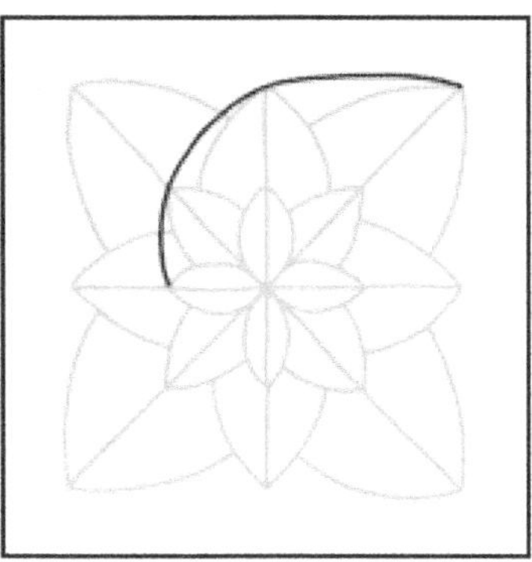
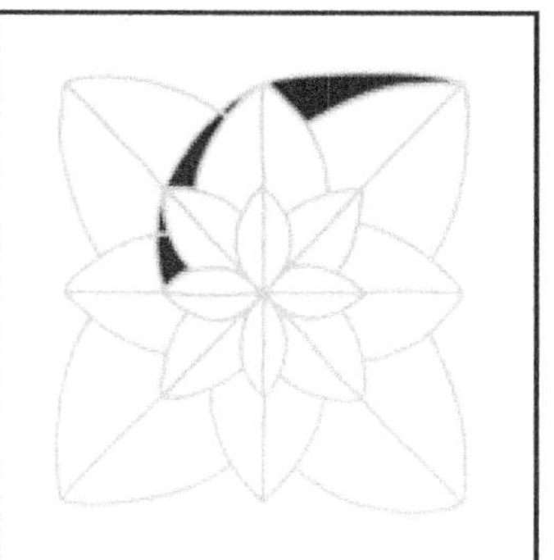
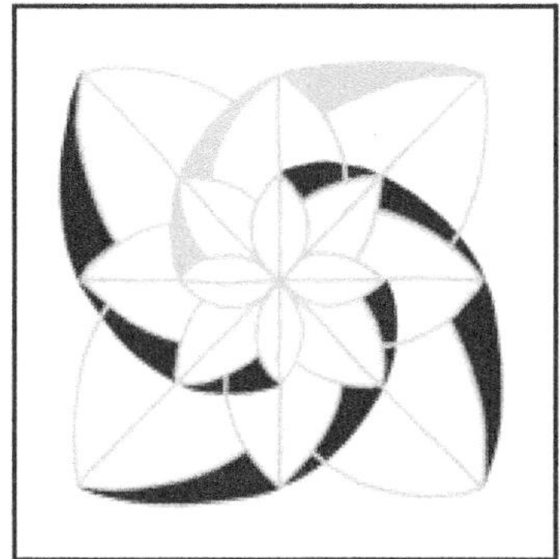
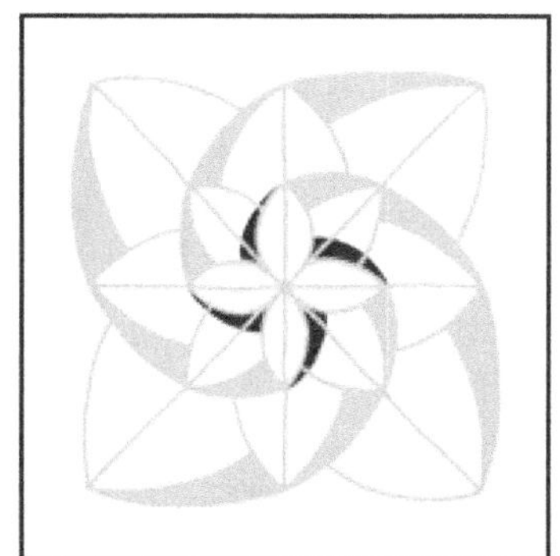
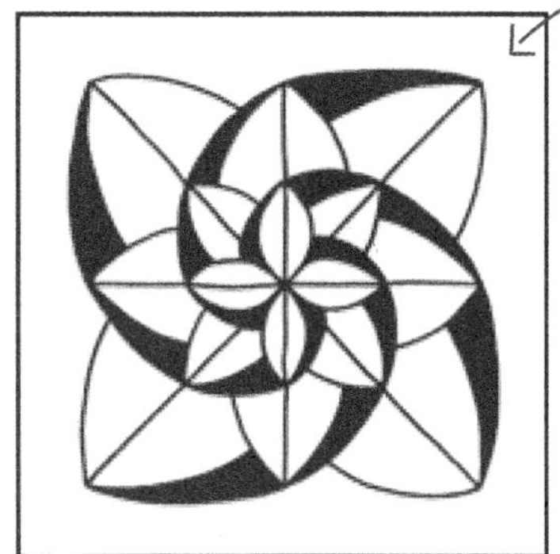

Variation of Basic Aihsd

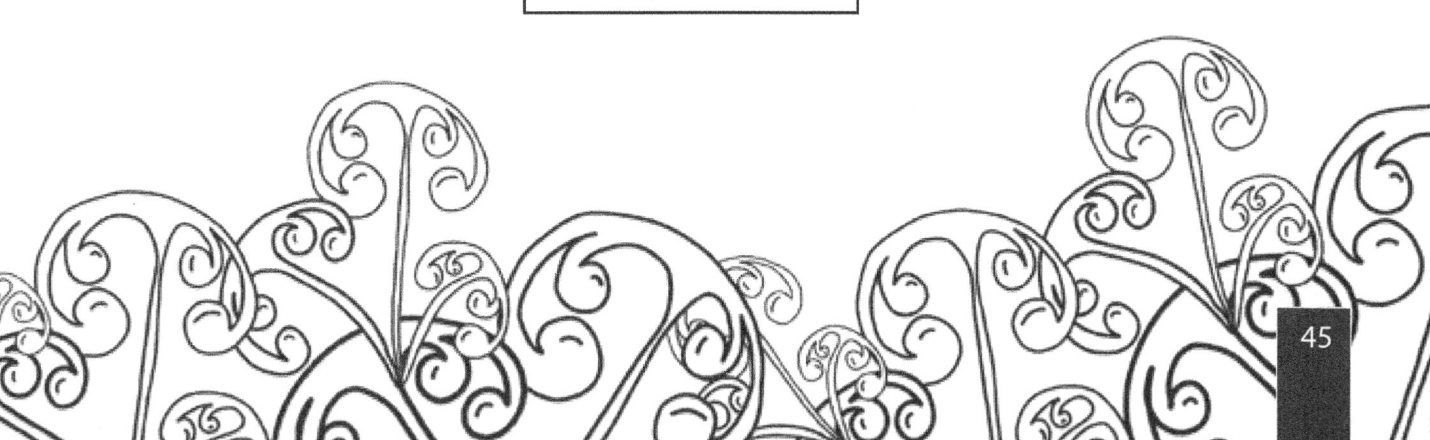

Aihsd Fragment

Theresa Fessler CZT

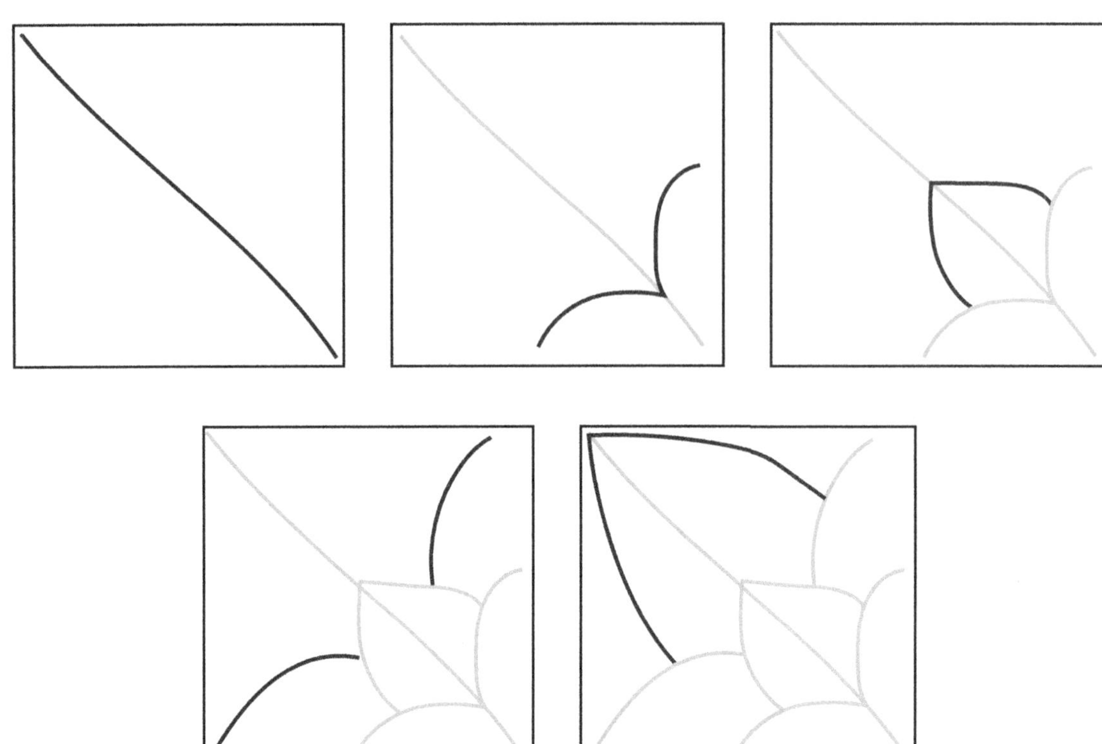

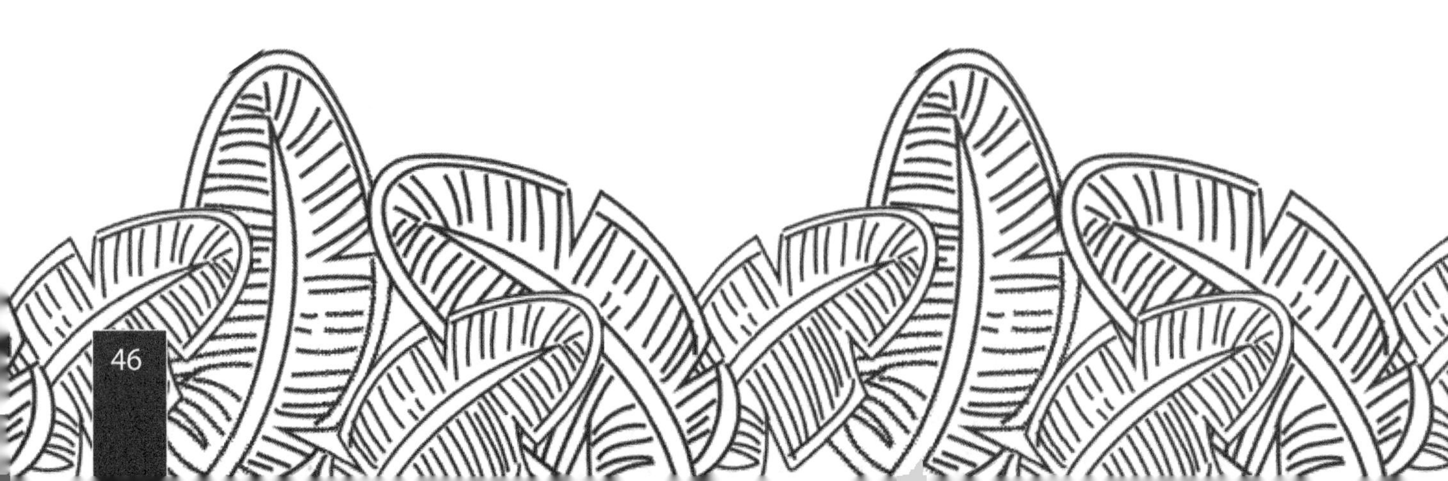

Waving Aihsd

Theresa Fessler CZT

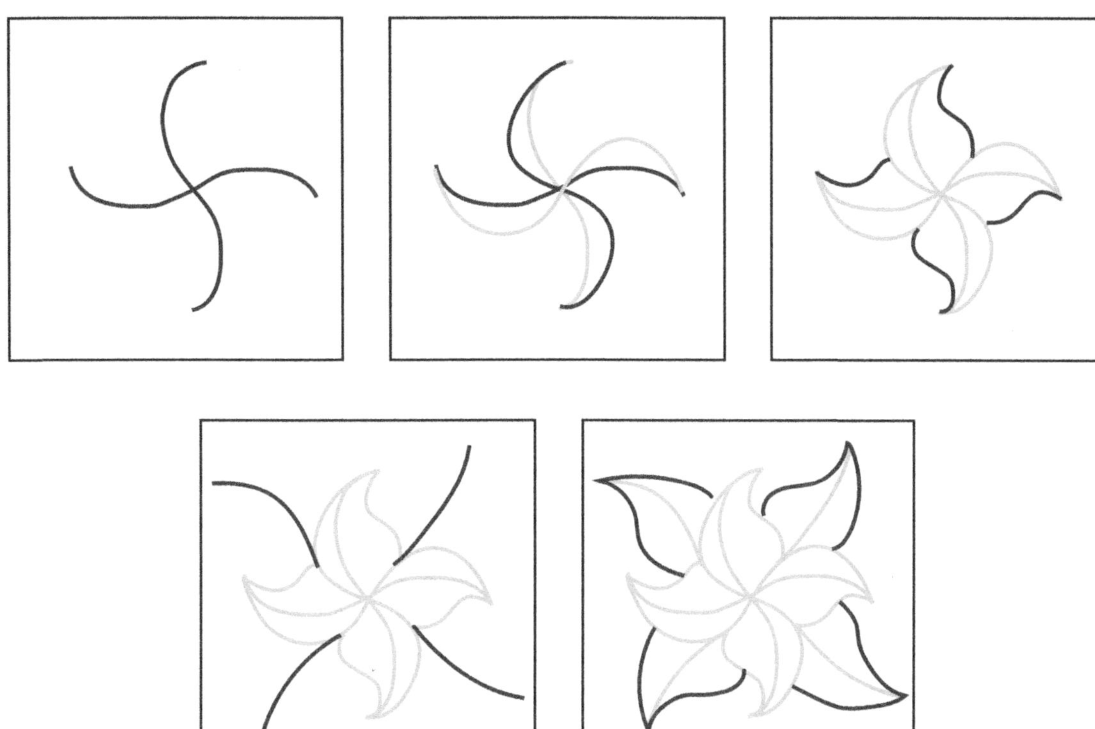

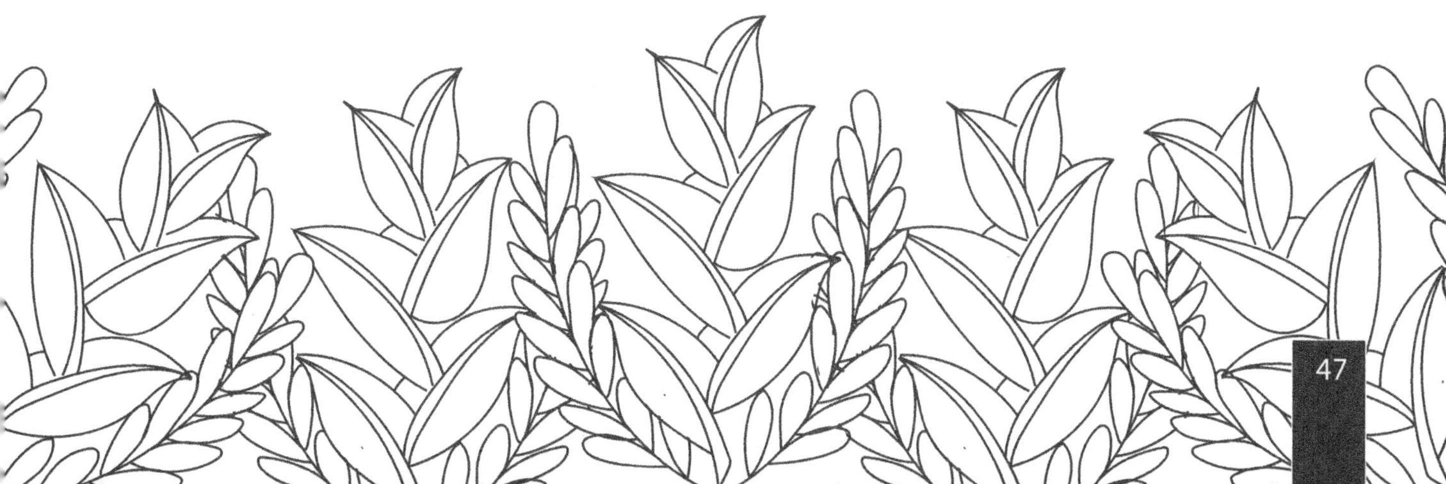

Heartfelt

Barbara Duel Johnson CZT

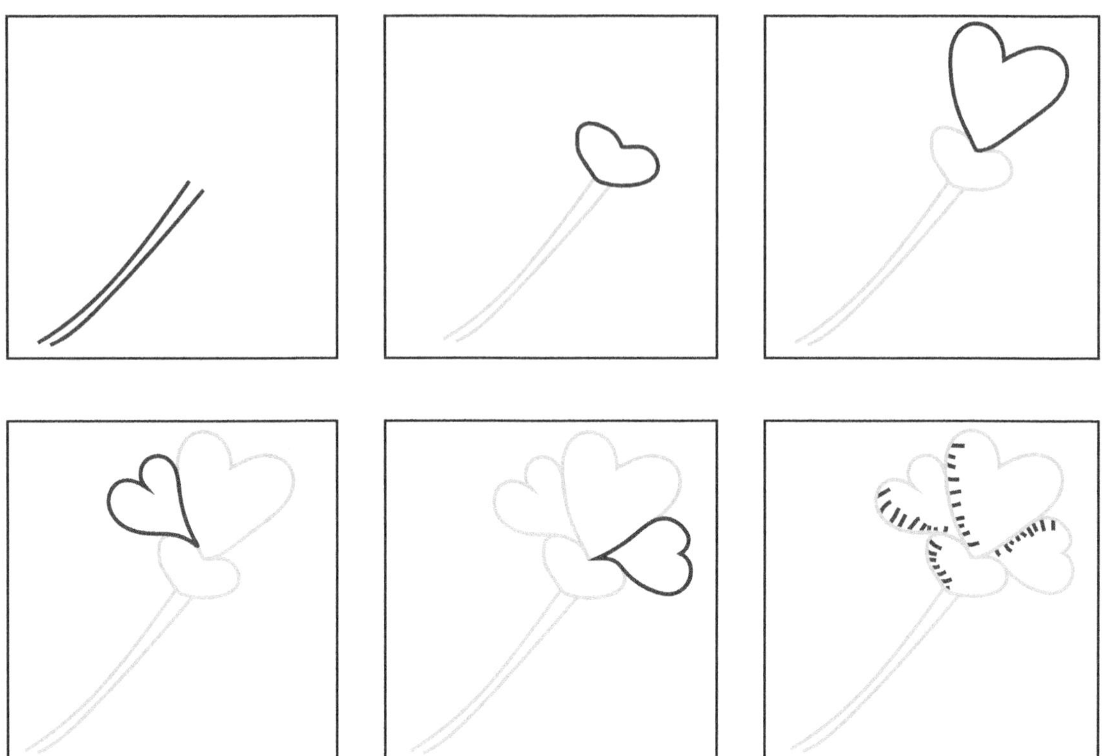

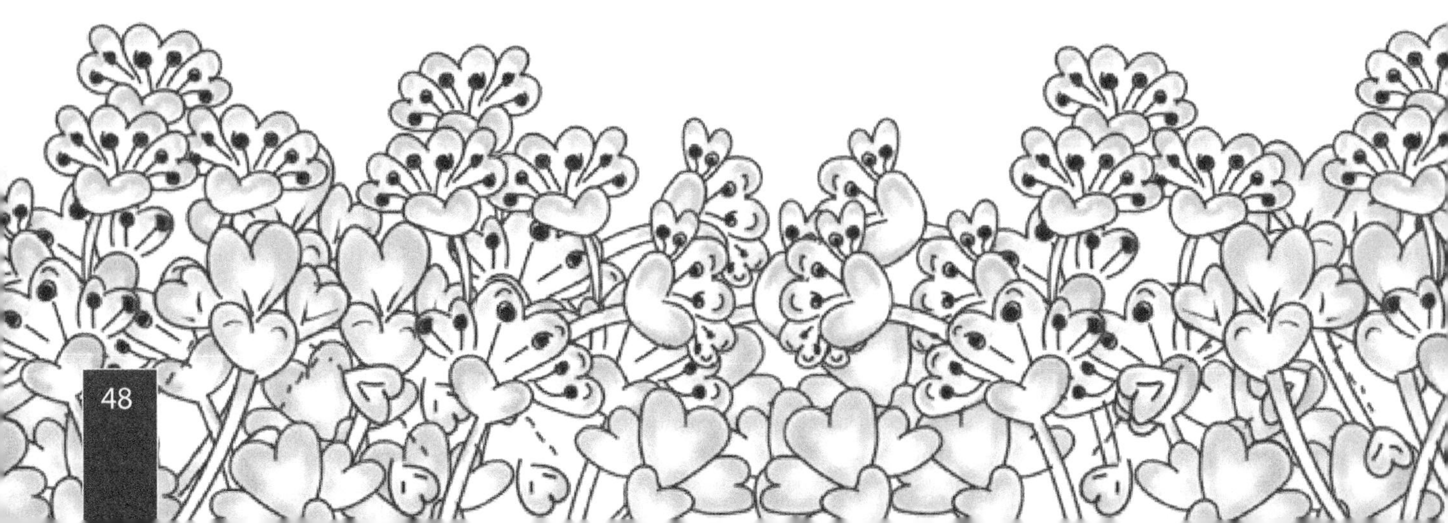

Cloud Tree

Dolly Bolen CZT

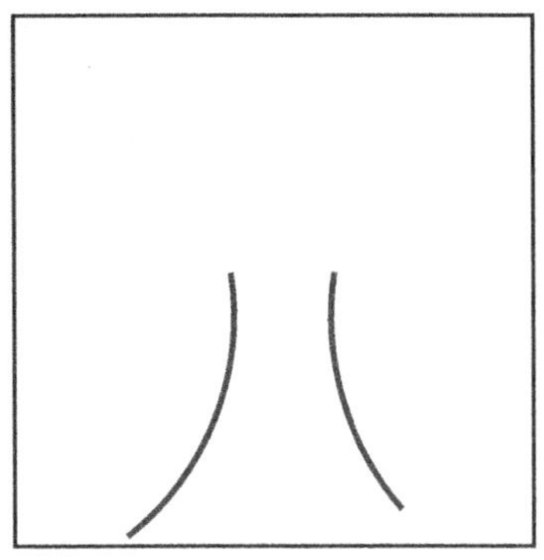
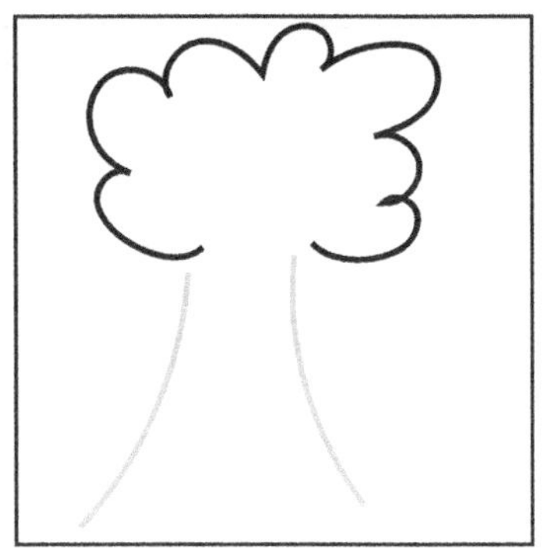
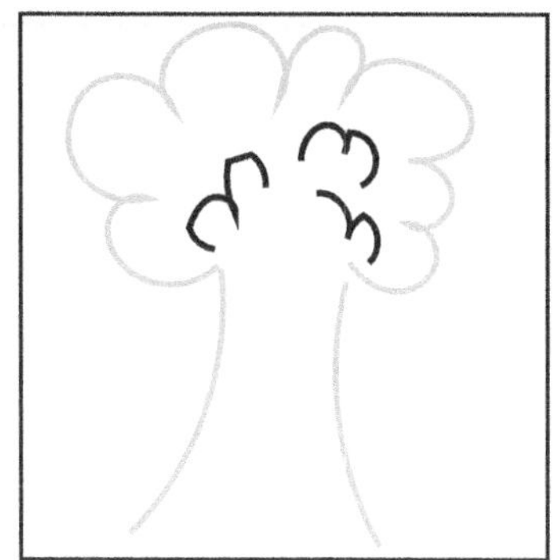

Maggie May

Dolly Bolen CZT

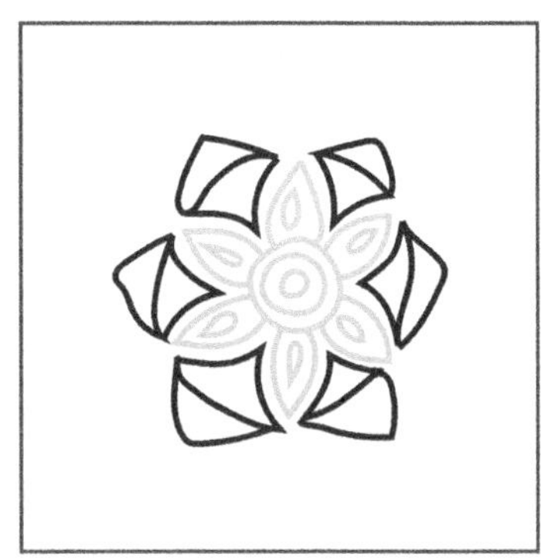

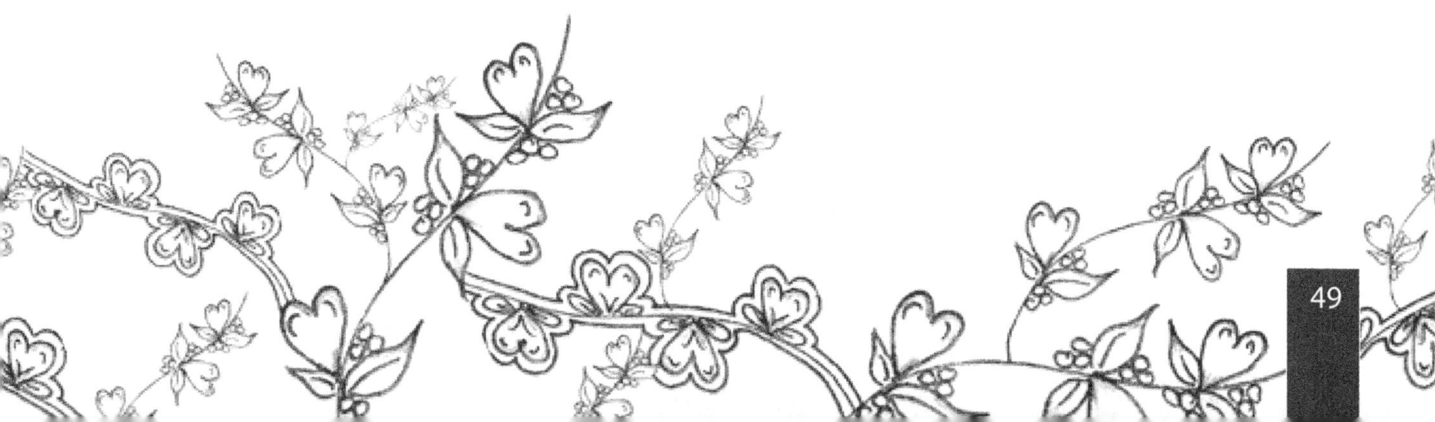

Heartflow

Barbara Duel Johnson CZT

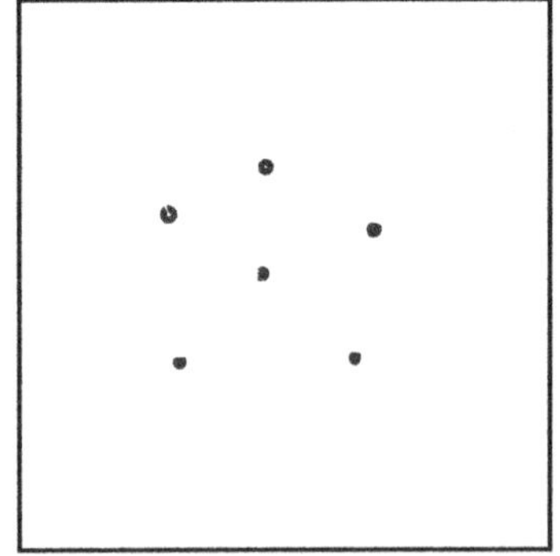

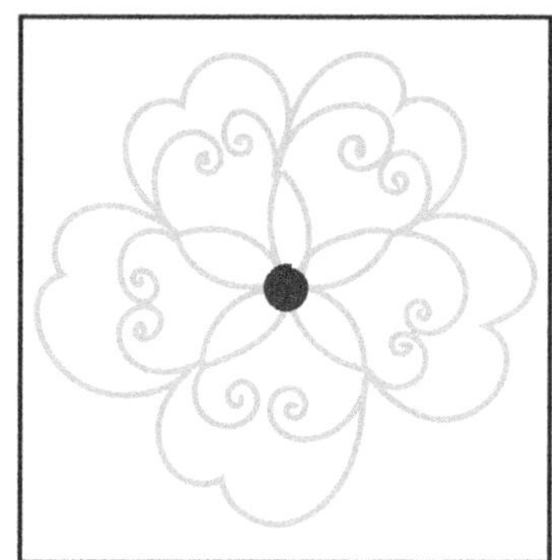
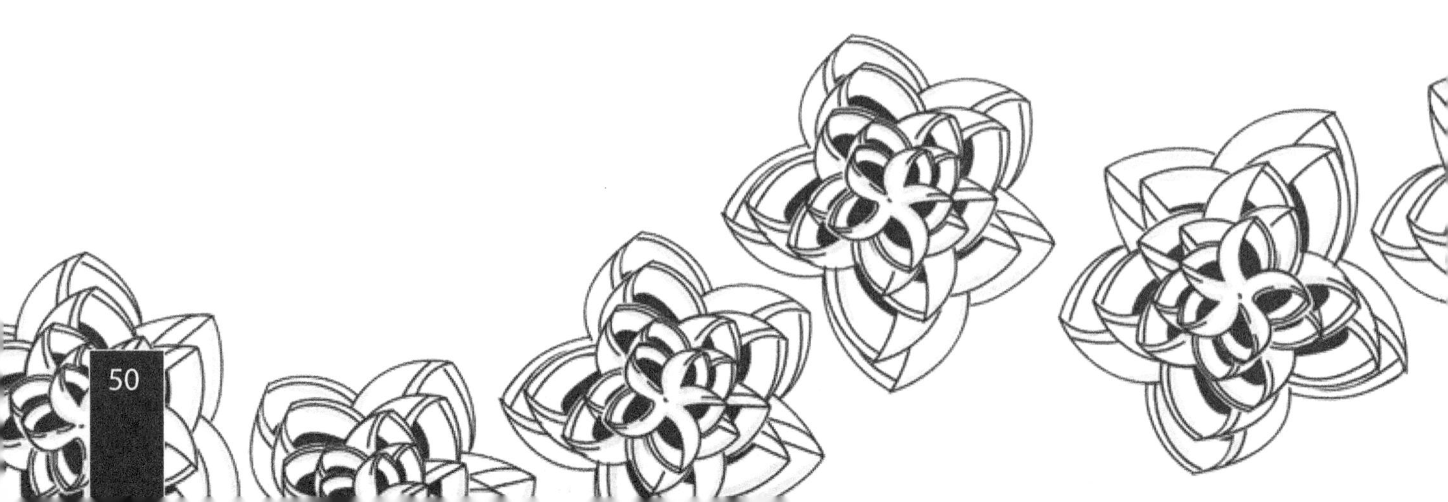

Crescent Leaves

Miranda Gerber CZT

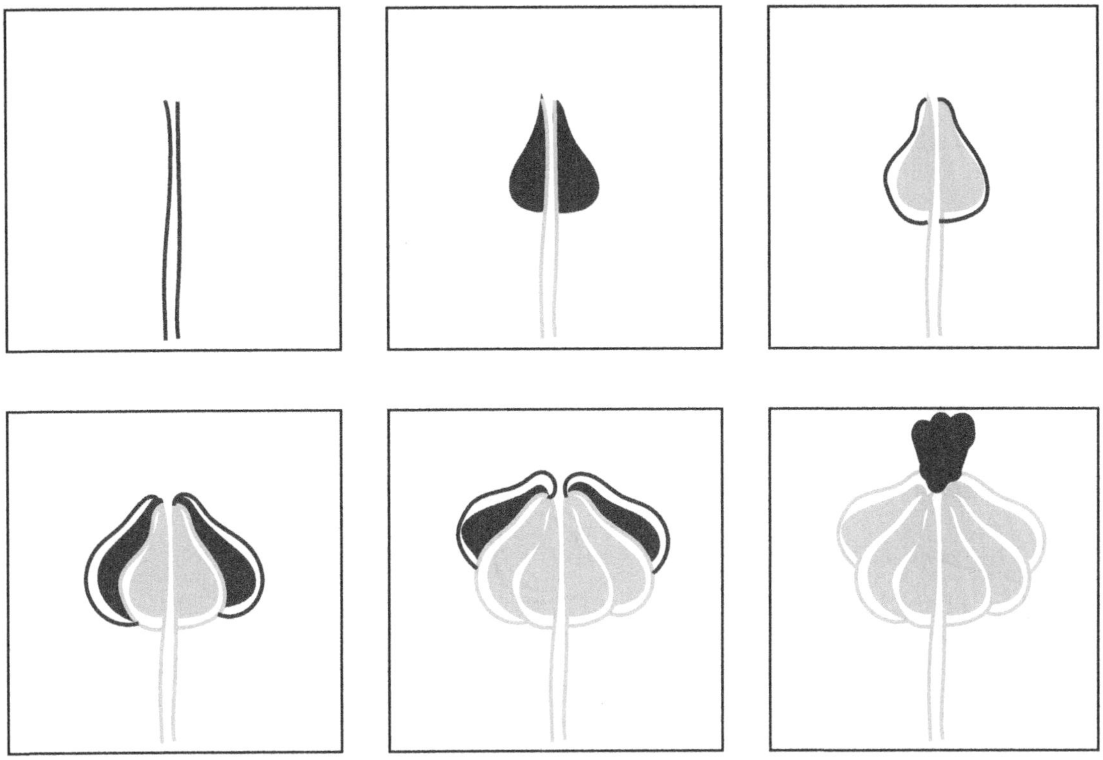

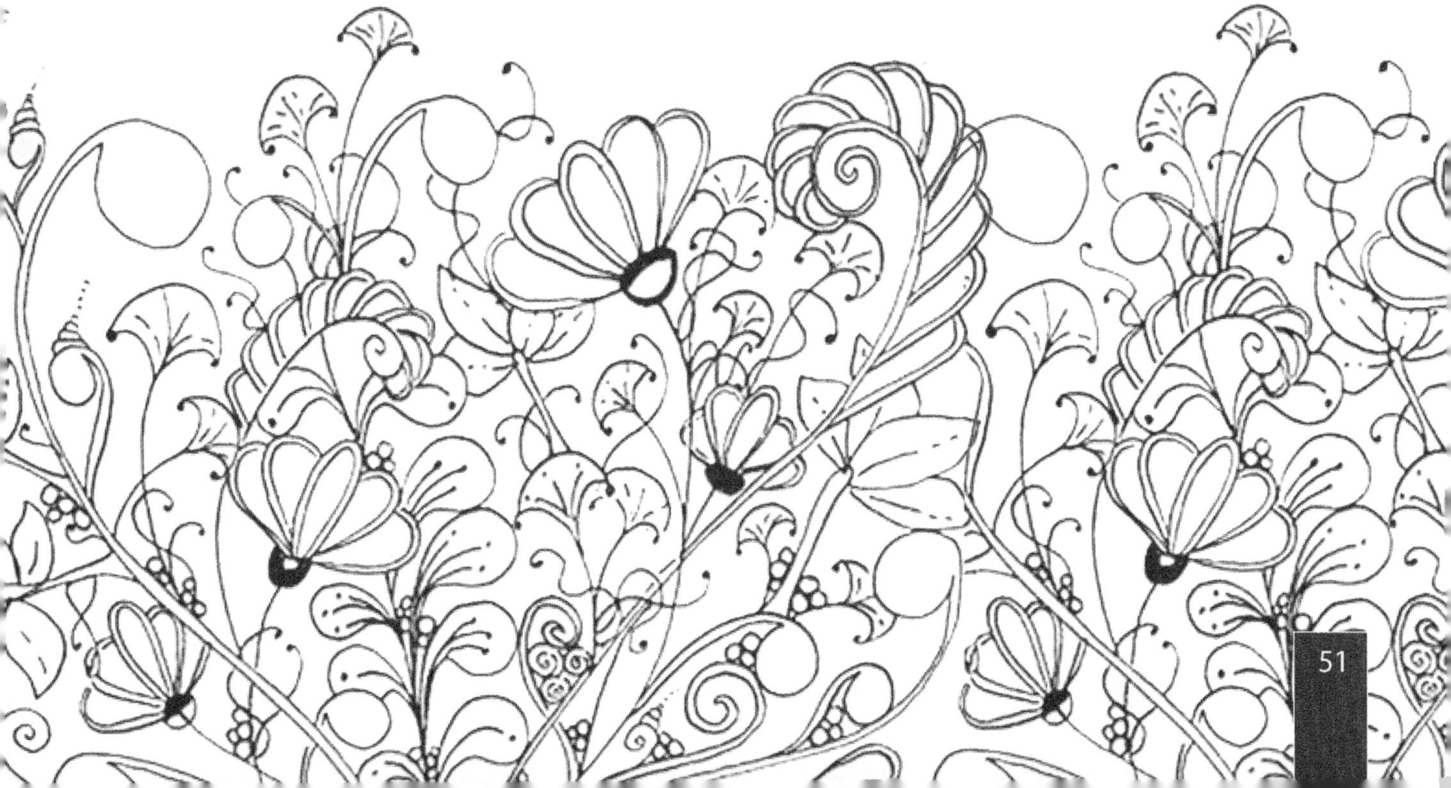

Leaf Chain

Barbara Duel Johnson CZT

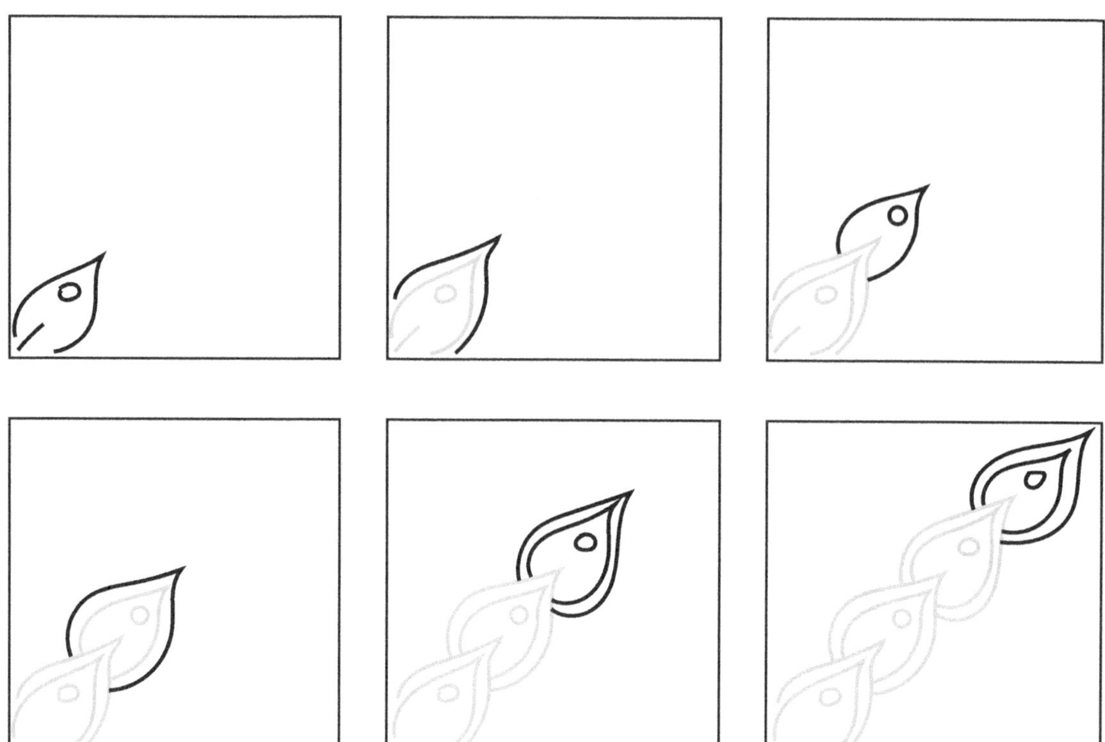

Ple-A

Apple Lim CZT

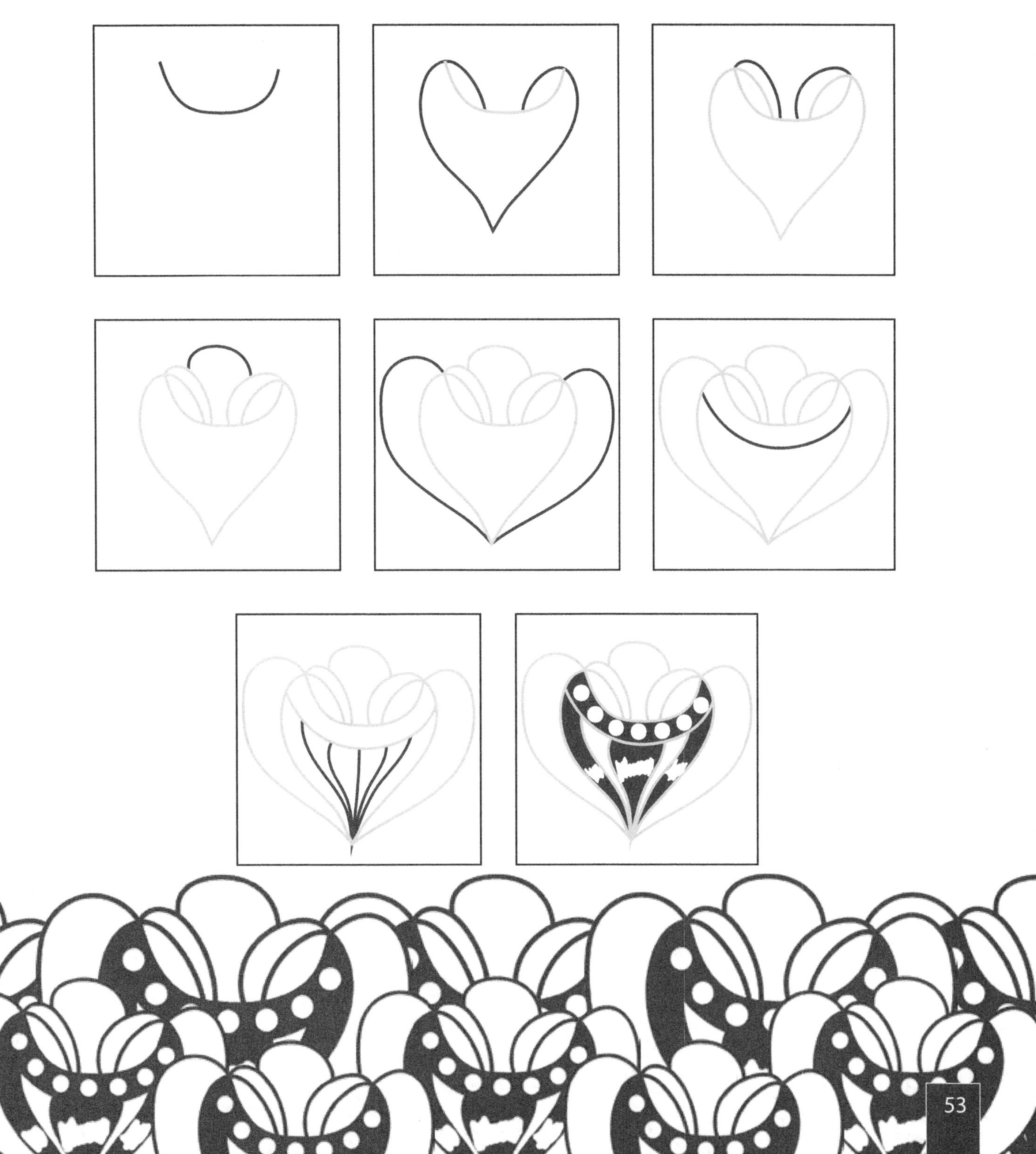

Toodlis

Miranda Gerber CZT

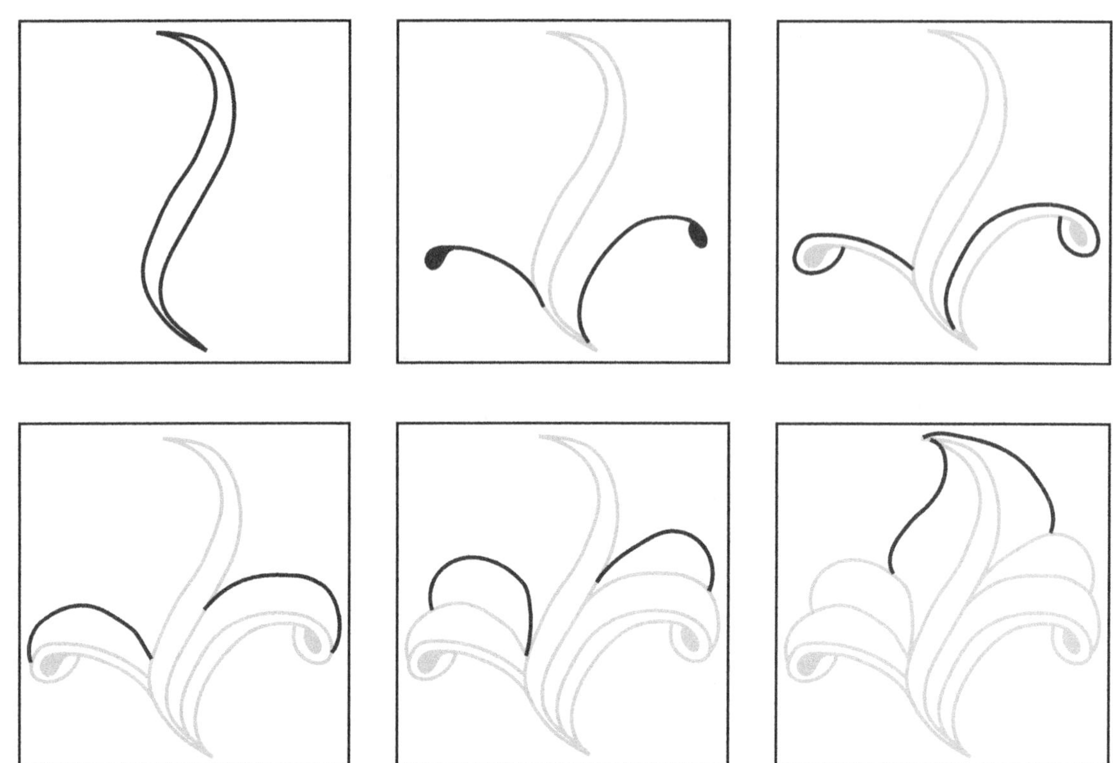

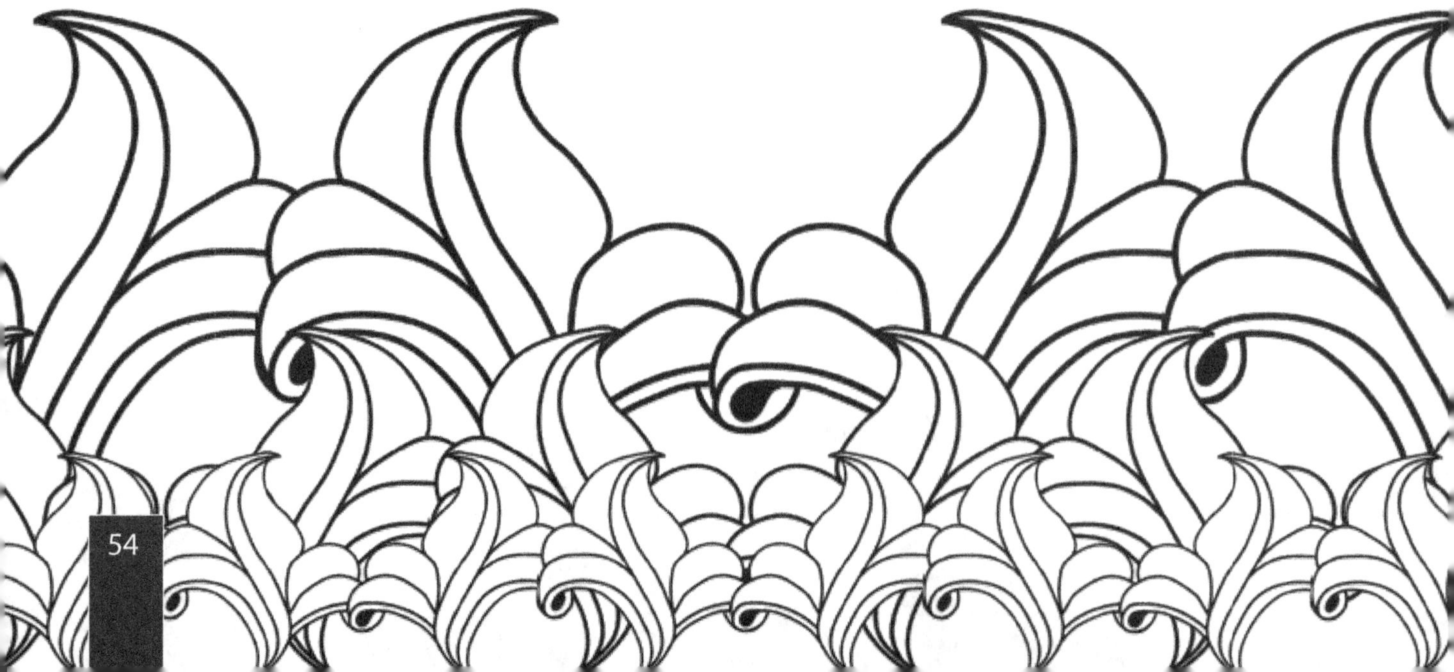

Toodli (2)

Miranda Gerber CZT

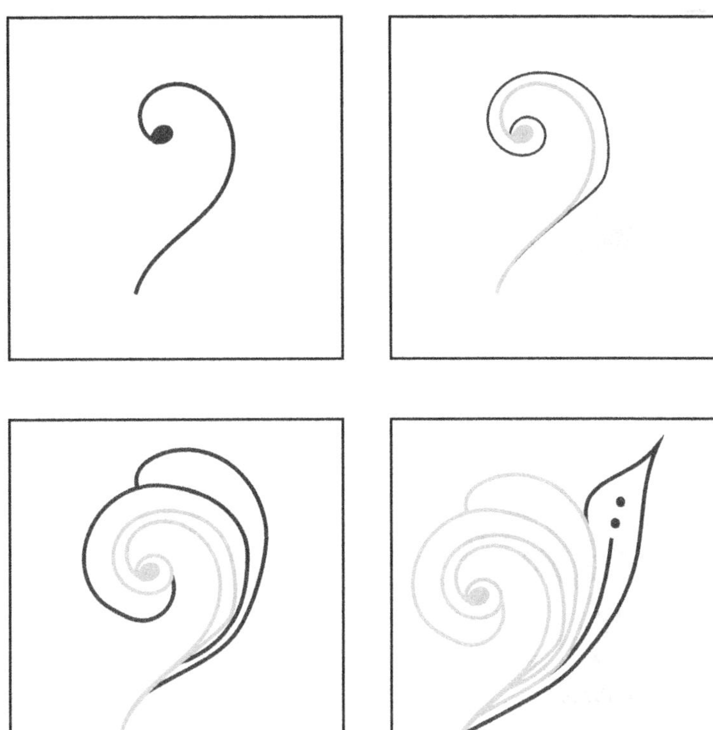

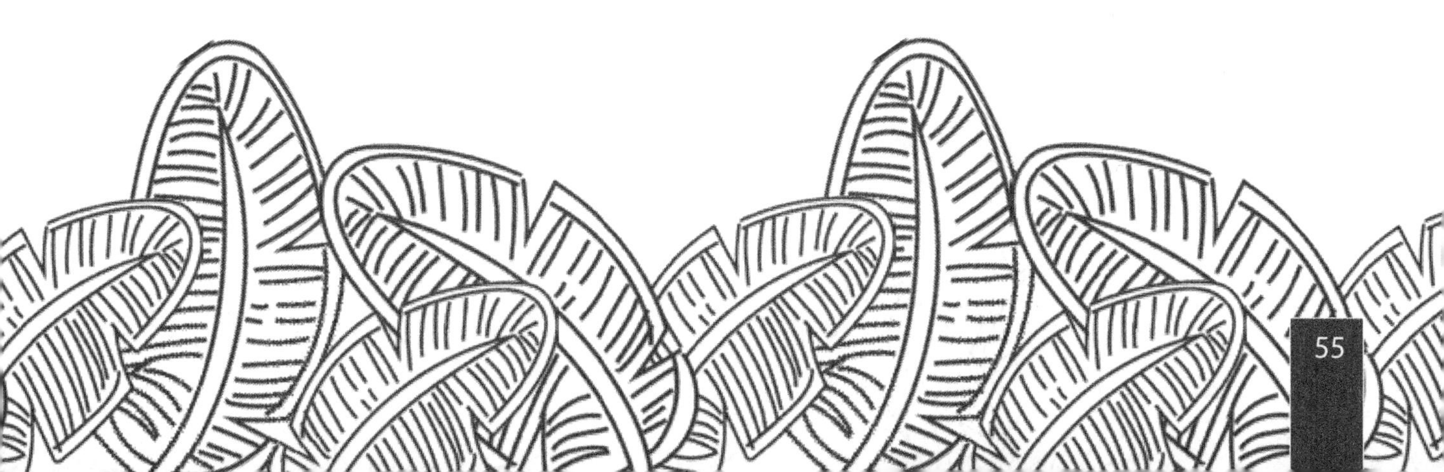

Pouyang

Official Zentangle Pattern

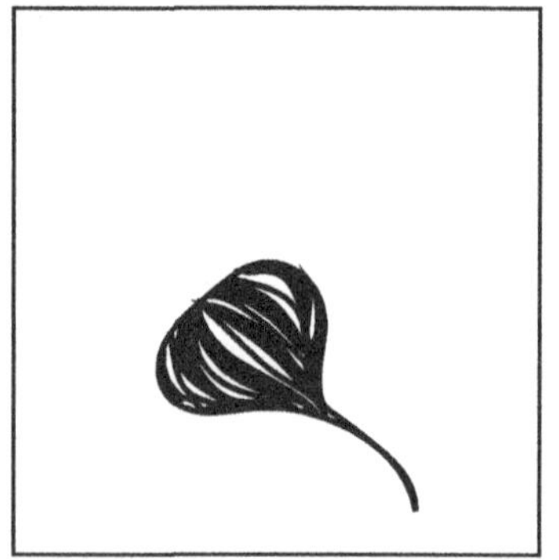

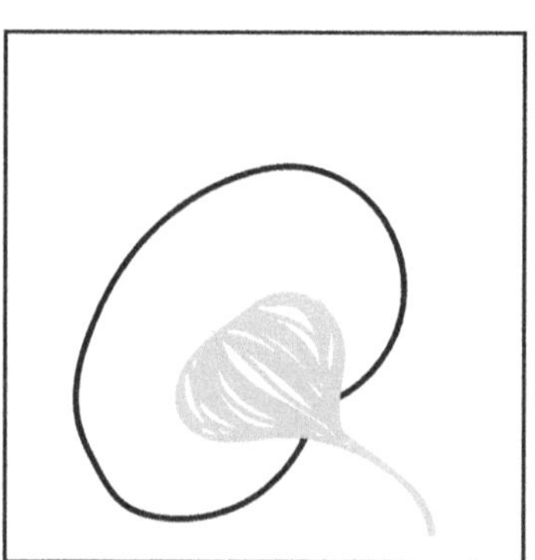

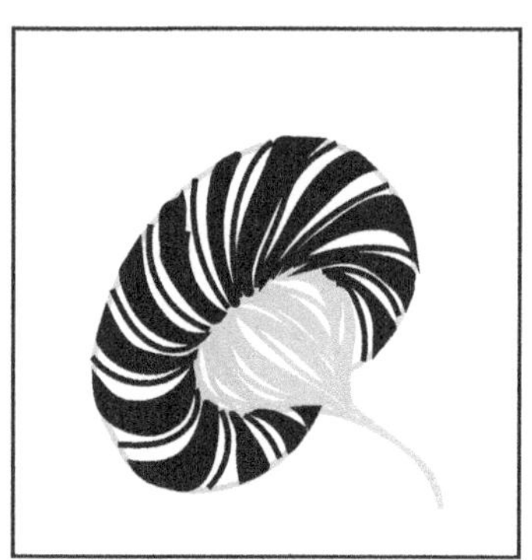

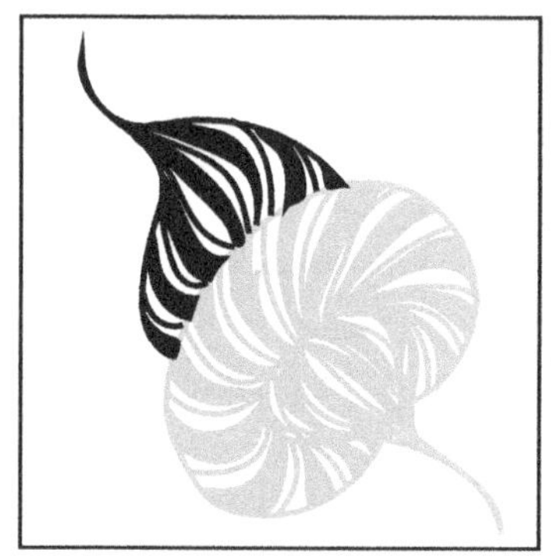

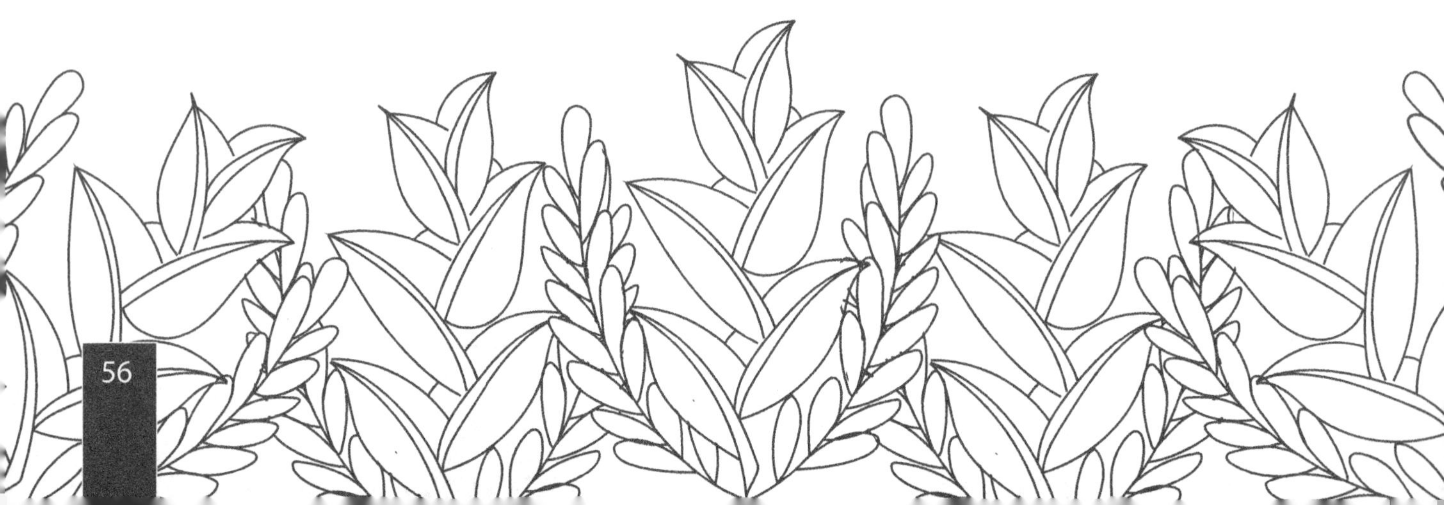

SiRos

Simone Menzel CZT

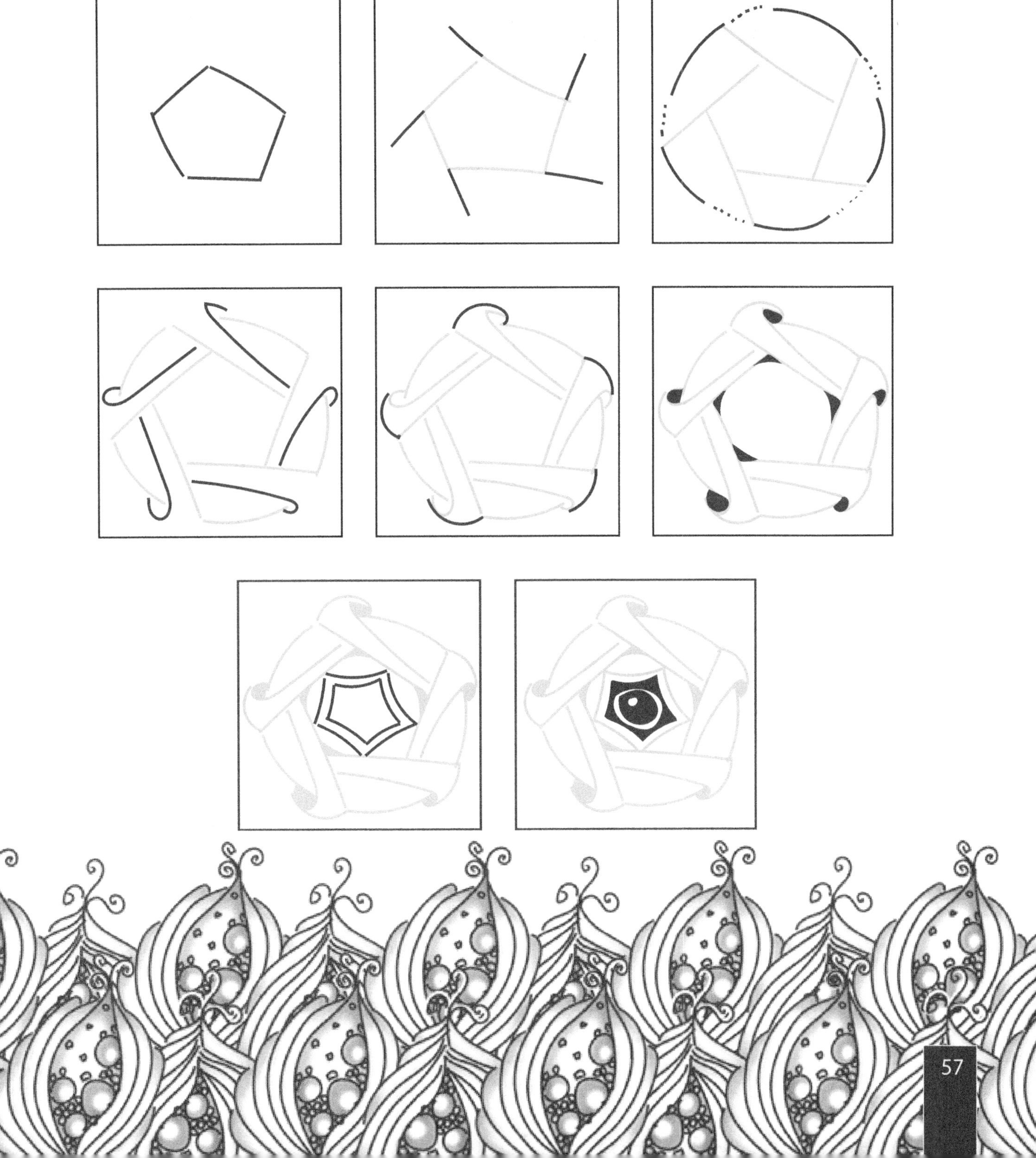

Toodles

Official Zentangle Pattern

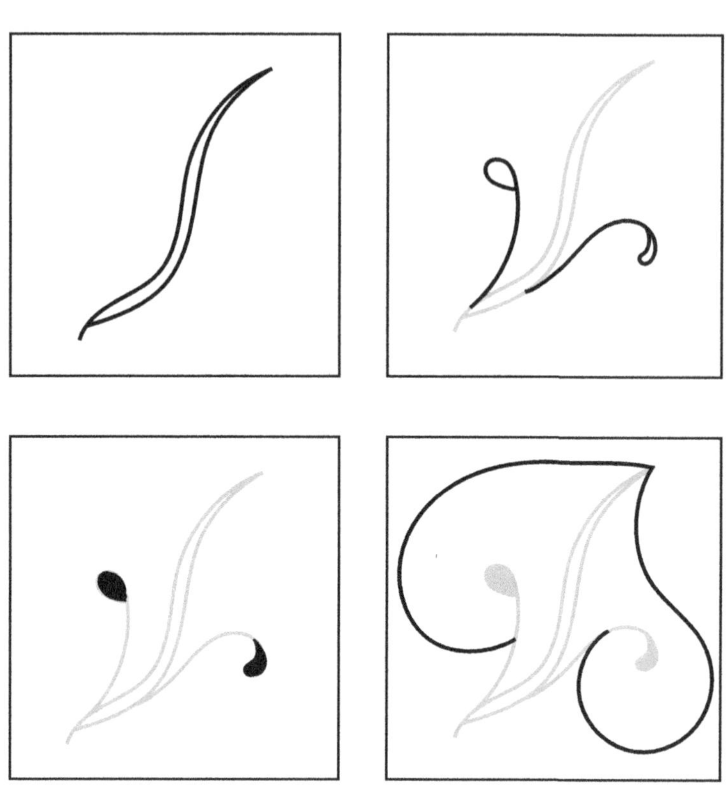

Snowangel

Suzanne Crisafi CZT

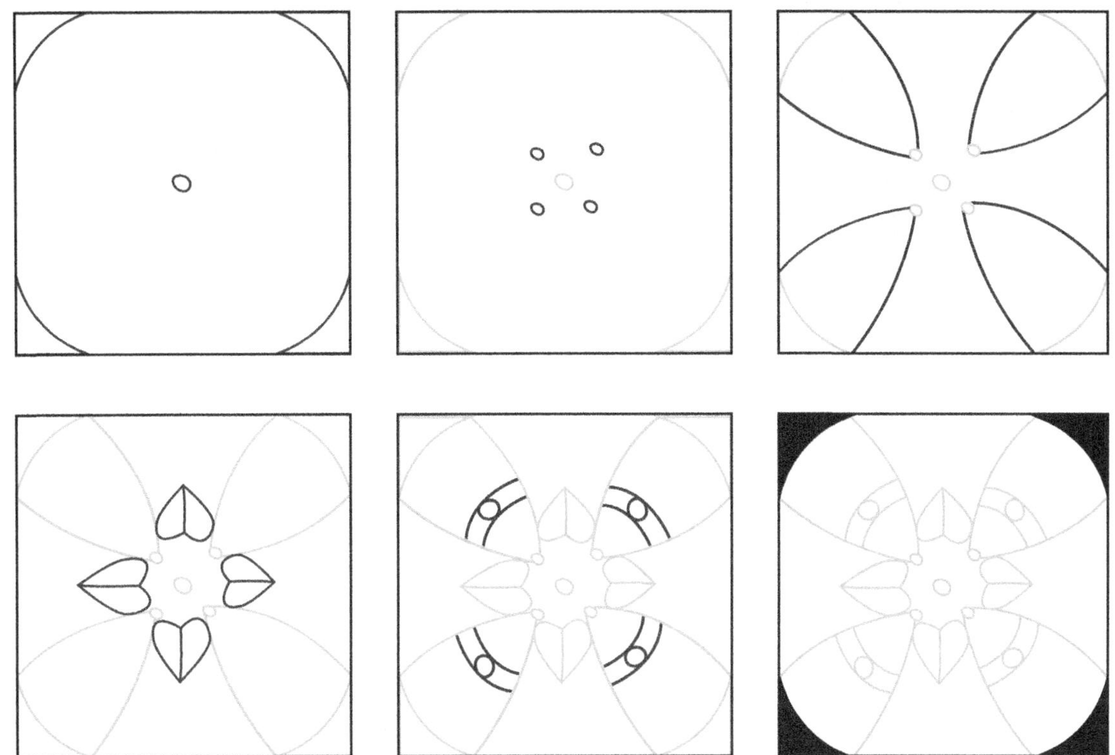

Sparkle Web Marquis

Dolly Bolen CZT

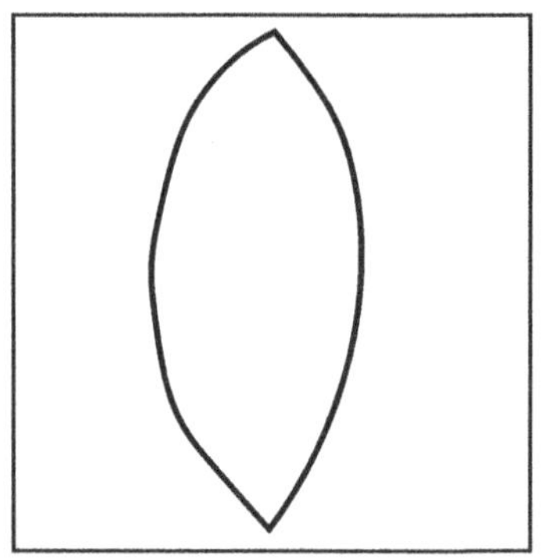

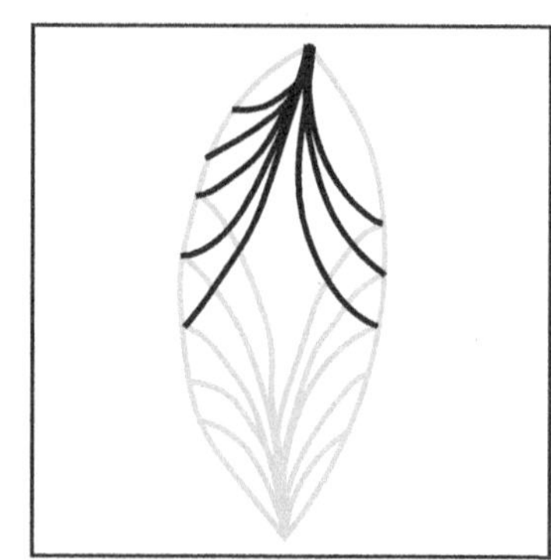

Hip Rose

Dolly Bolen CZT

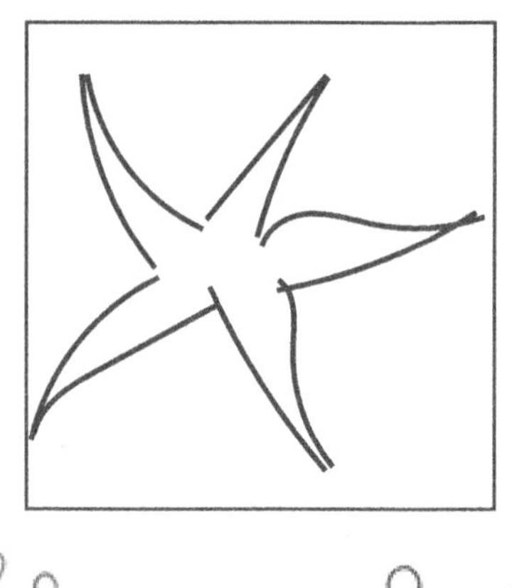
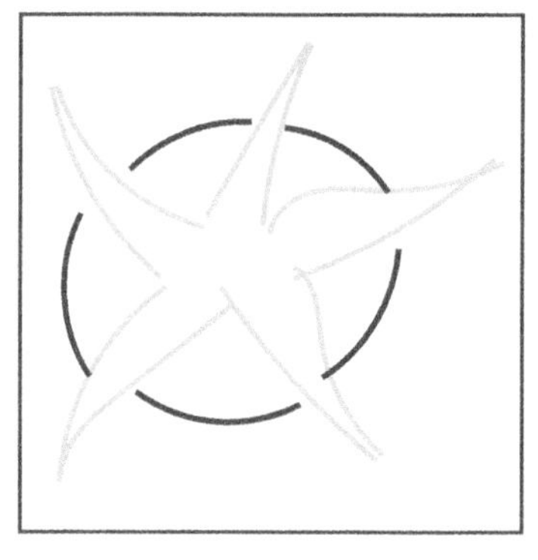
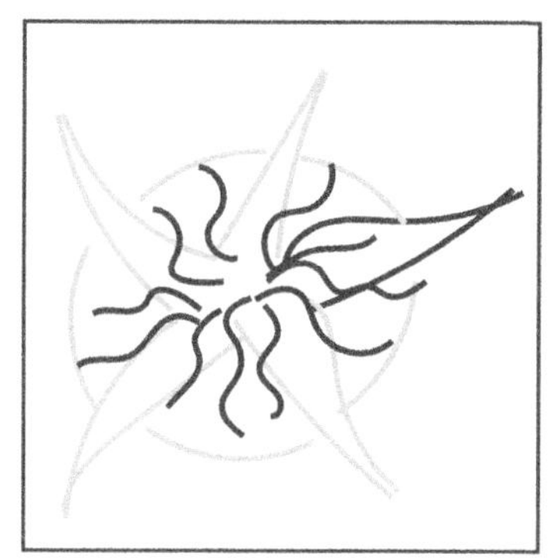

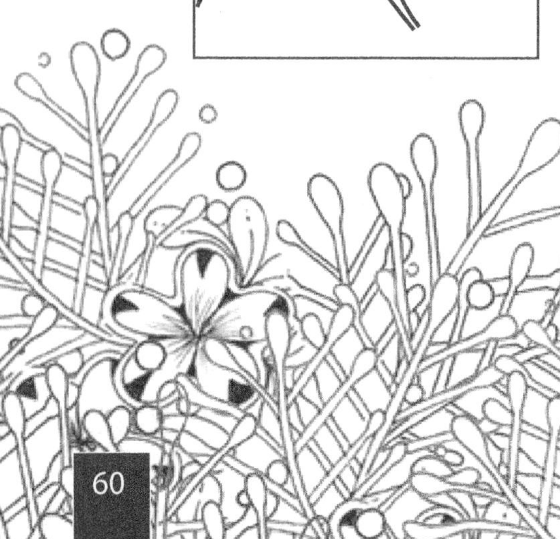
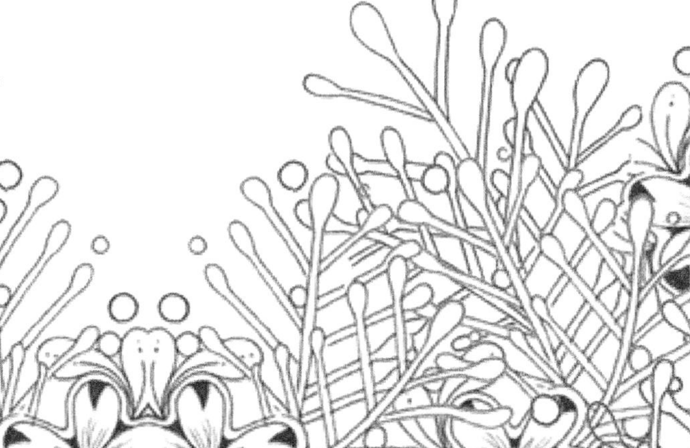

Tulipa

Simone Menzel CZT

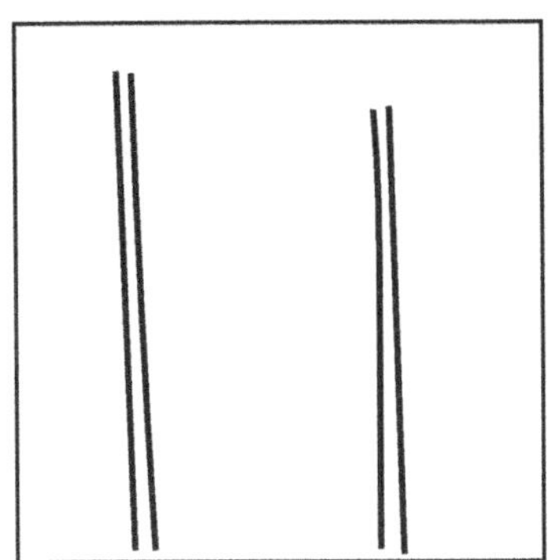
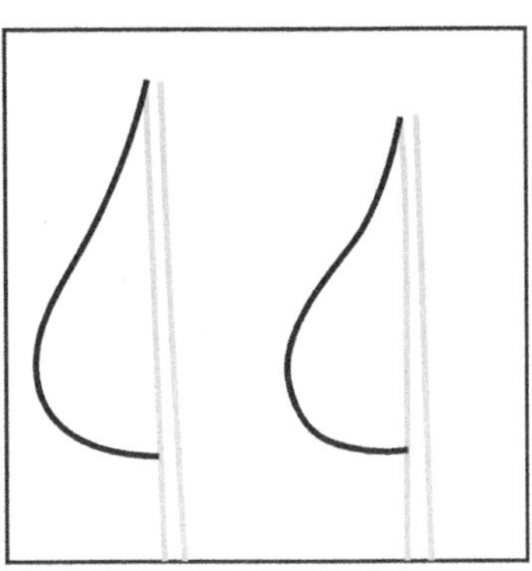
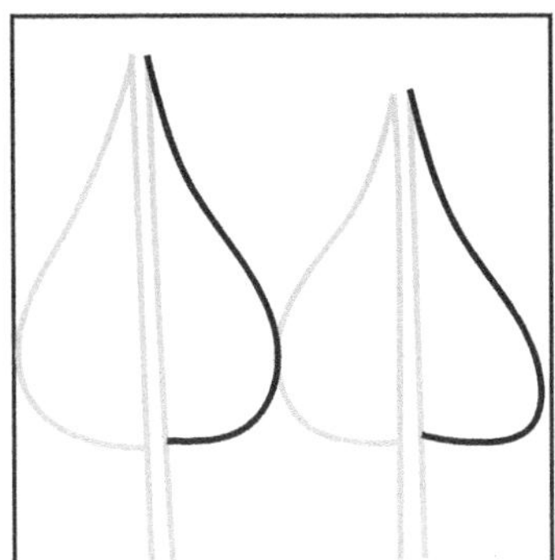

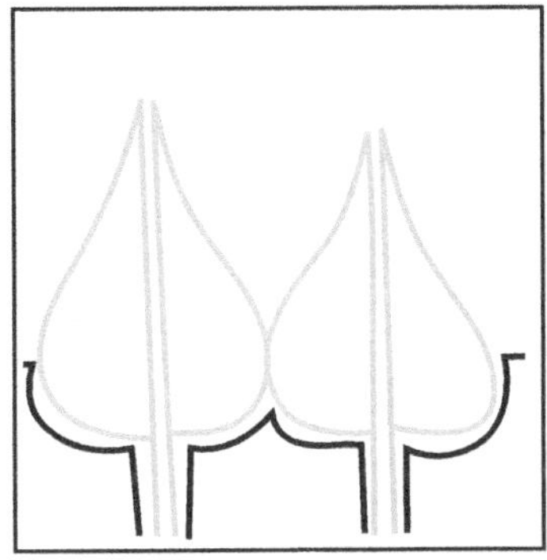
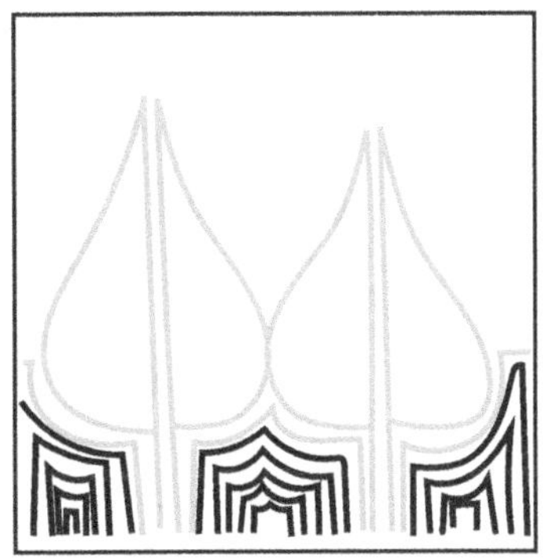

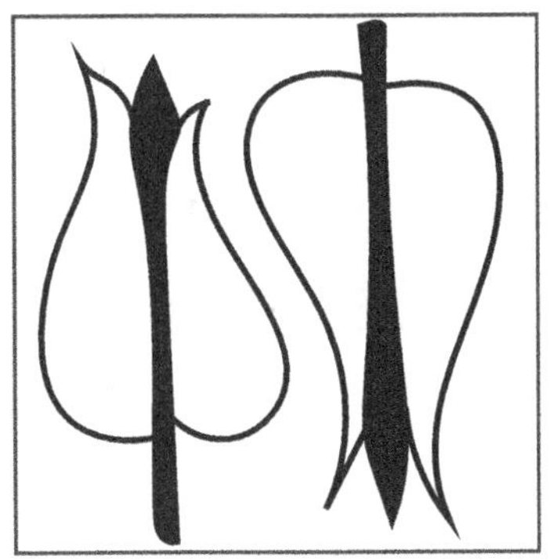

Open bud variation

Ravenna

Theresa Fessler CZT

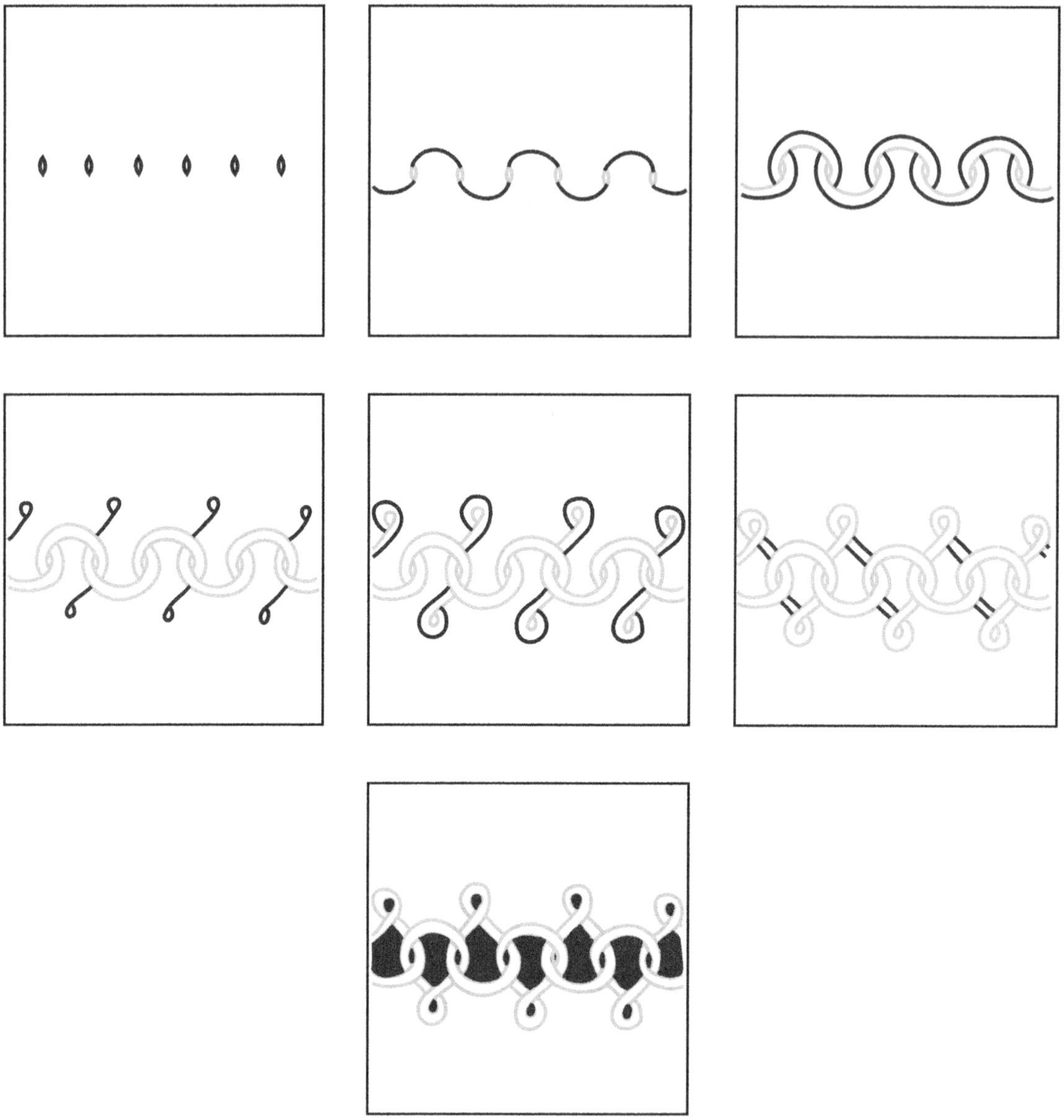

Cyme Lok

Suzanne Crisafi CZT

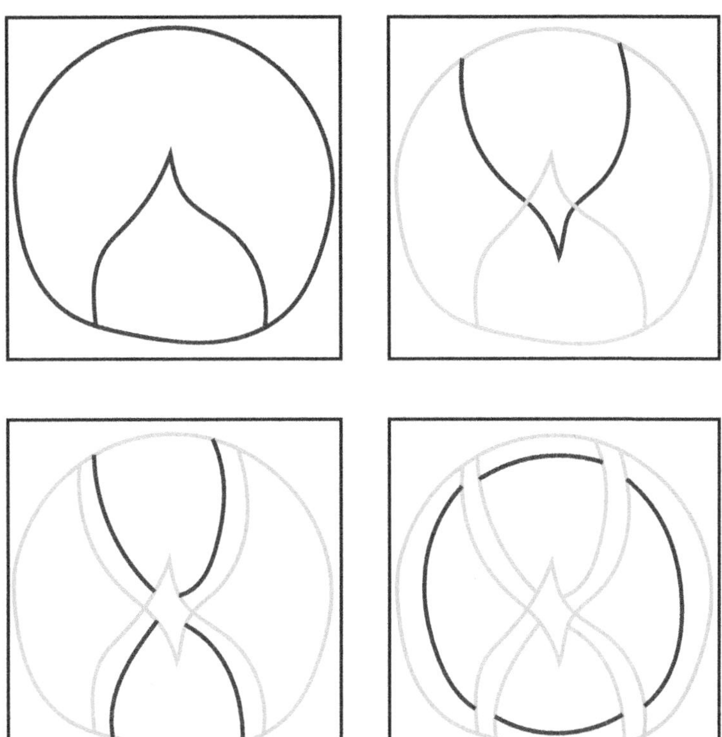

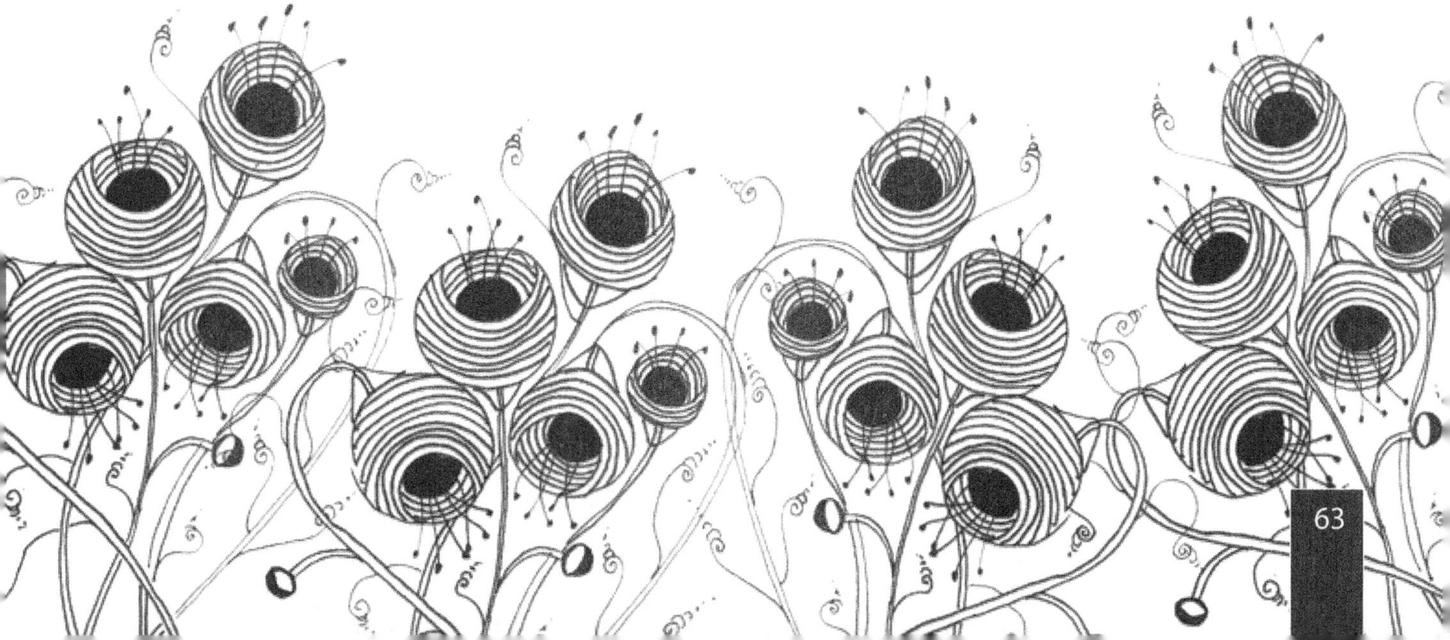

Eze

Emiko Kaneko CZT

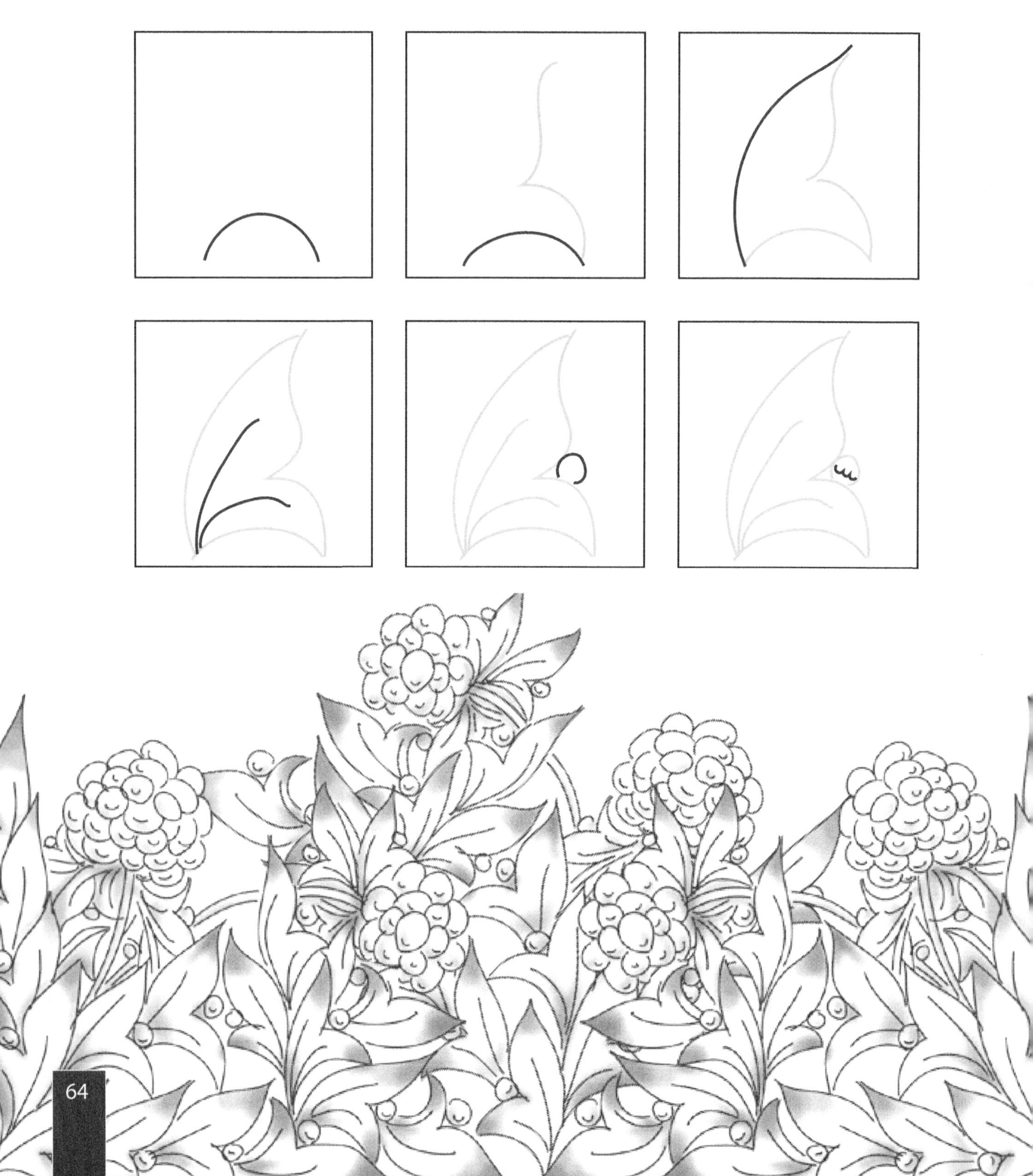

Wumi 1

Miranda Gerber CZT

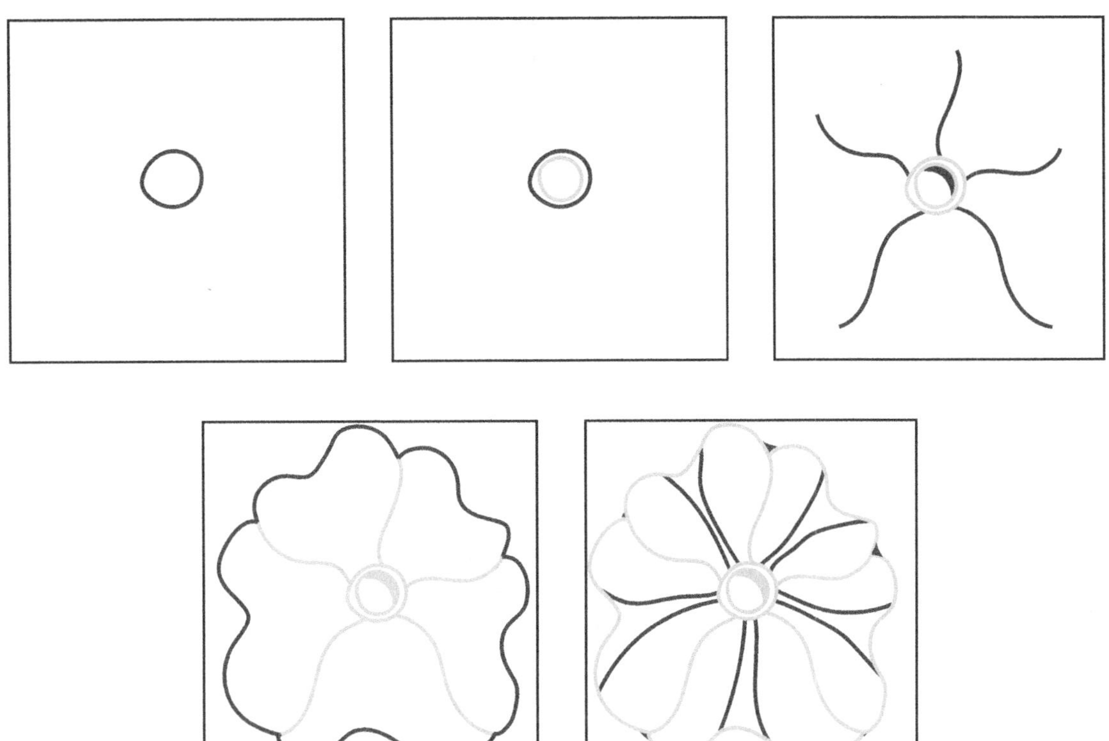

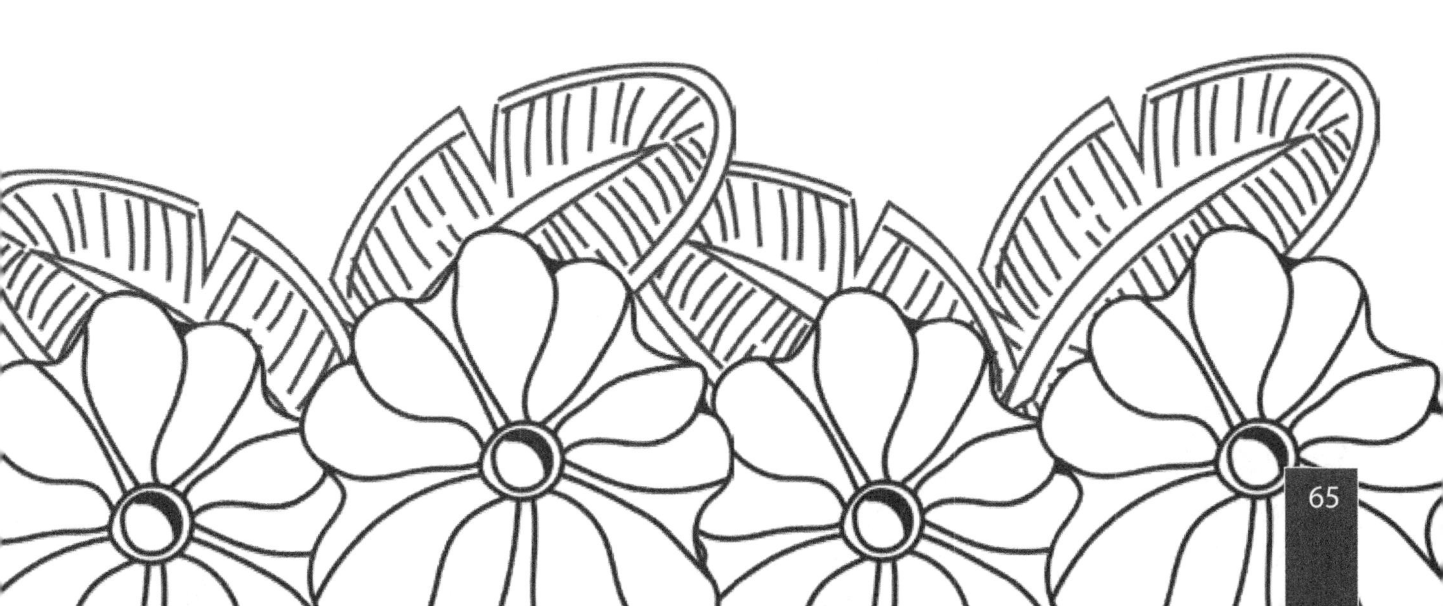

Helter

Debbie Raven CZT

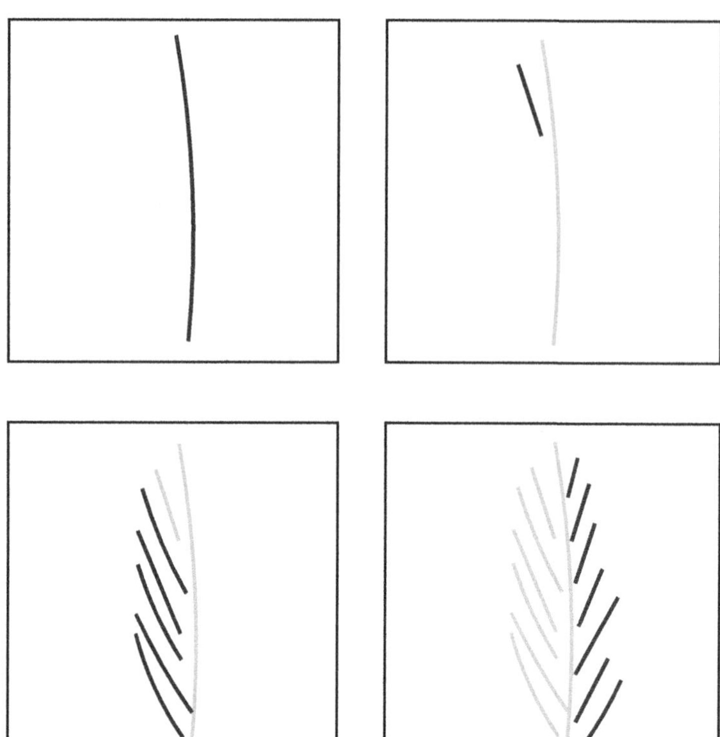

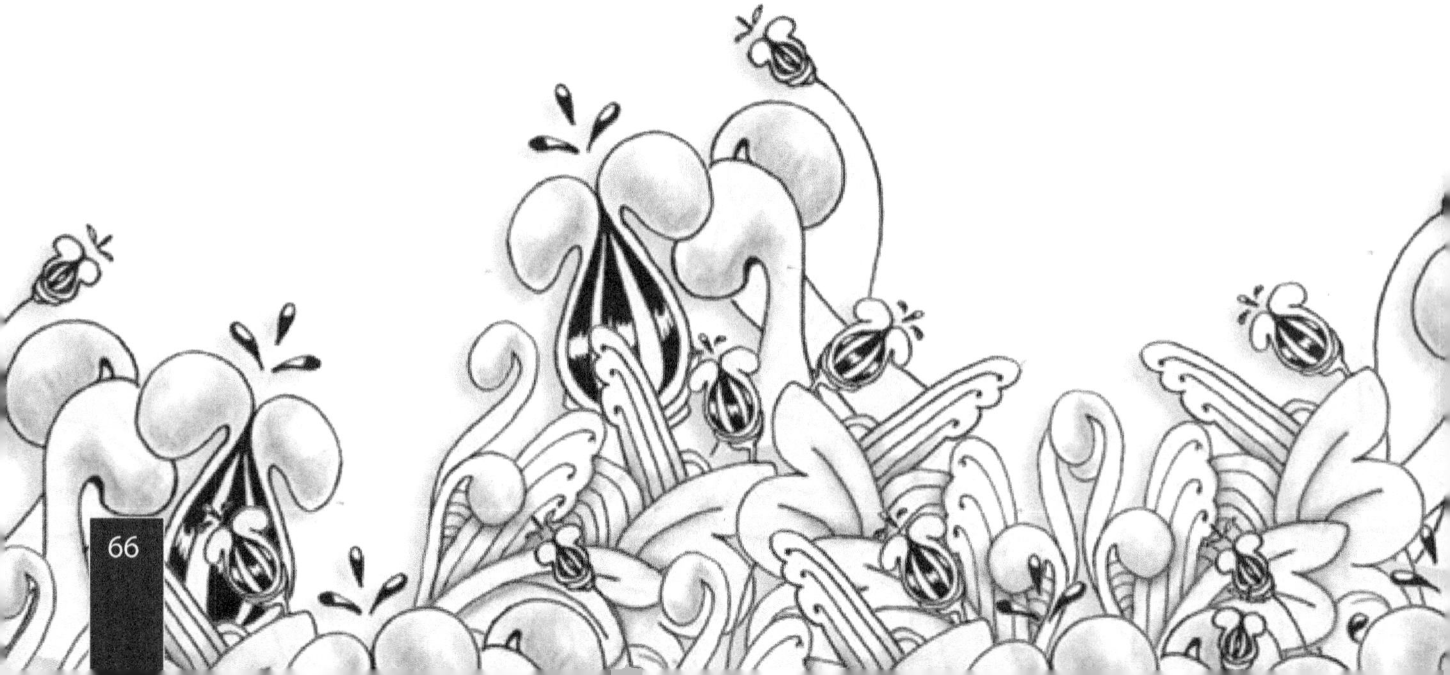

Nodana

Theresa Fessler CZT

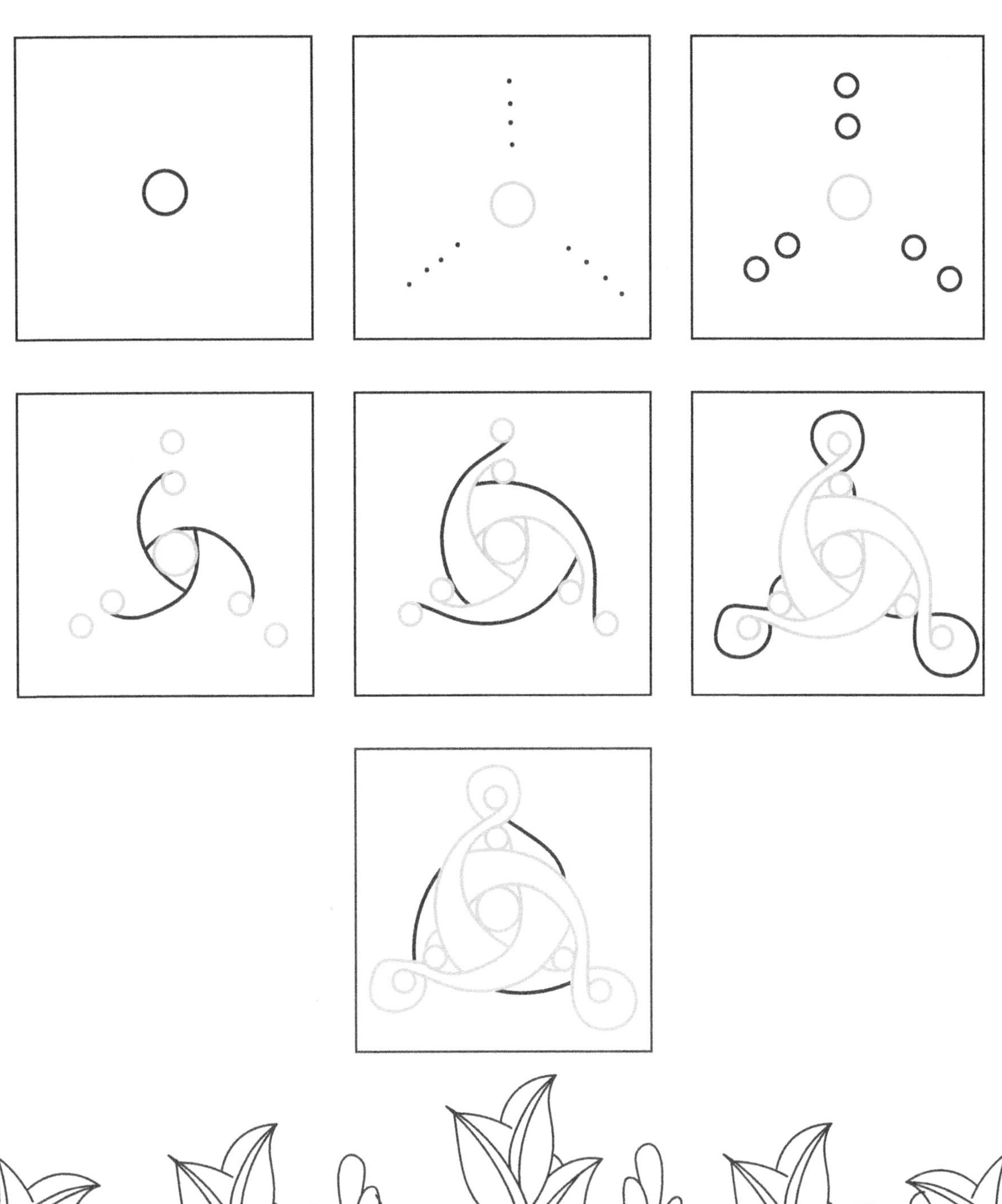

Pennie

Barbara Duel Johnson CZT

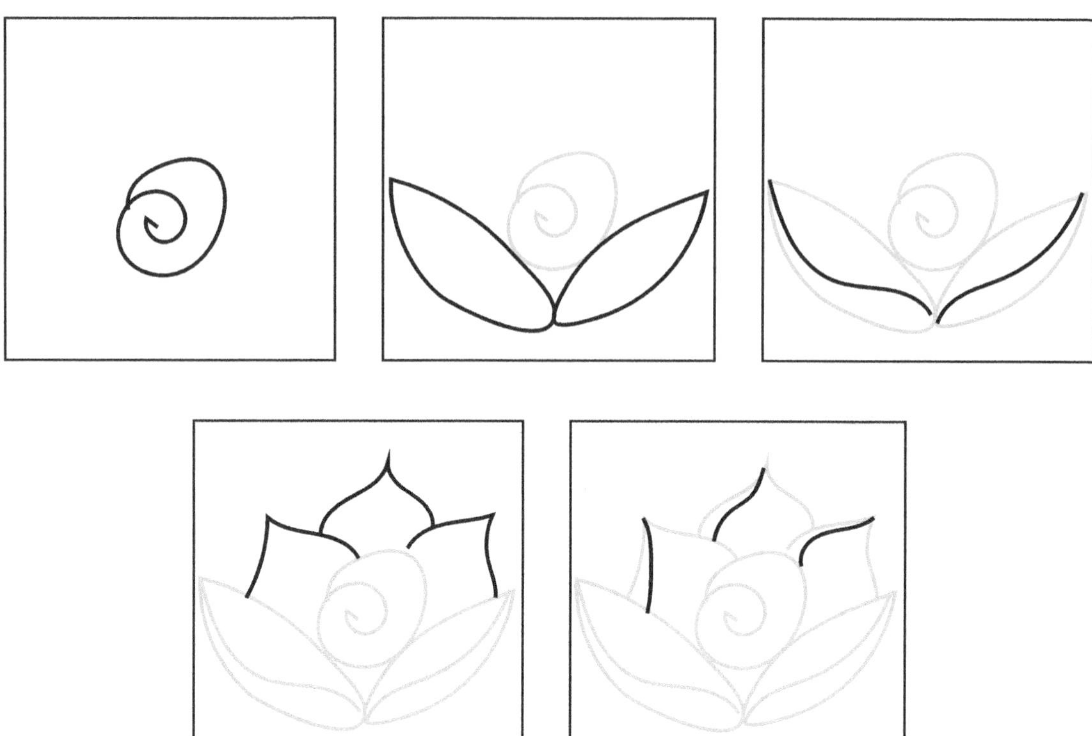

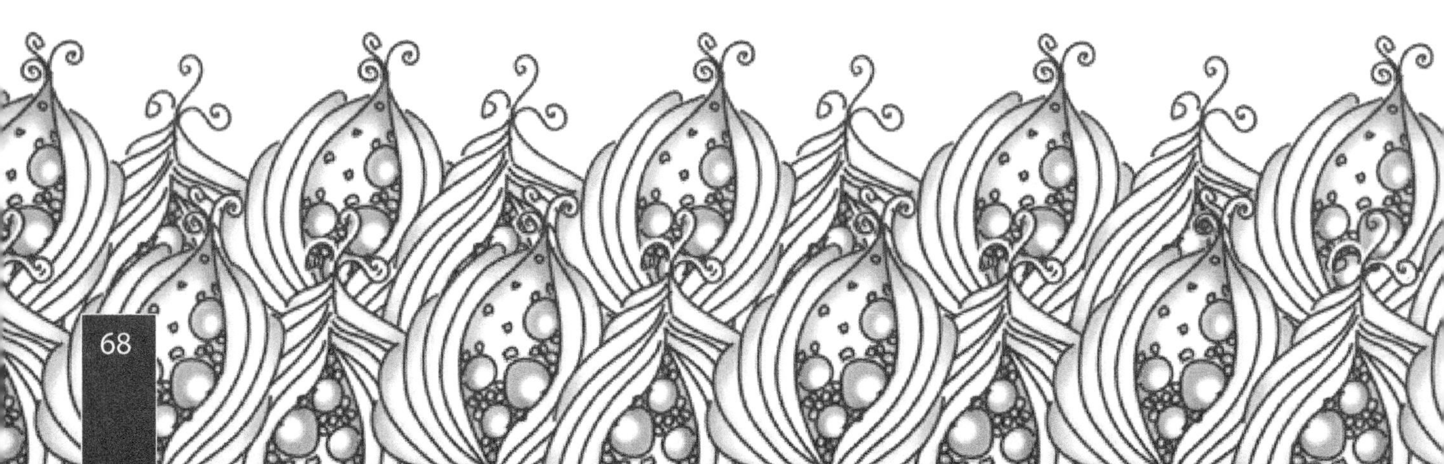

Pipski

Barbara Duel Johnson CZT

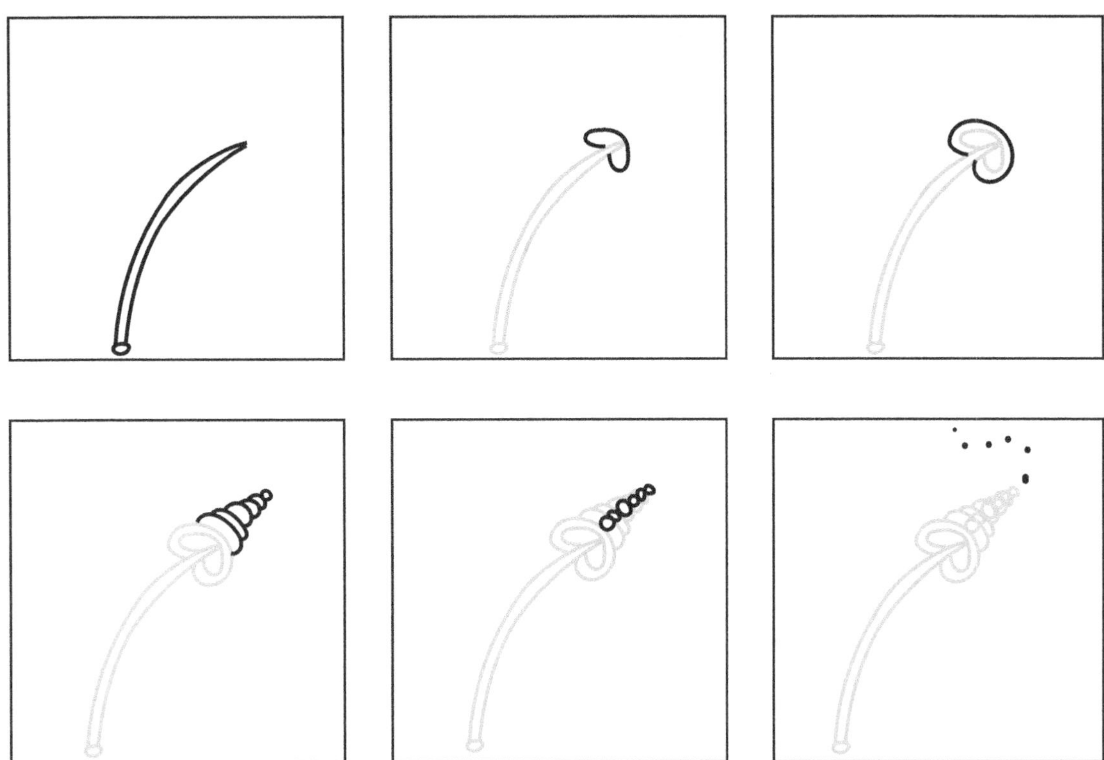

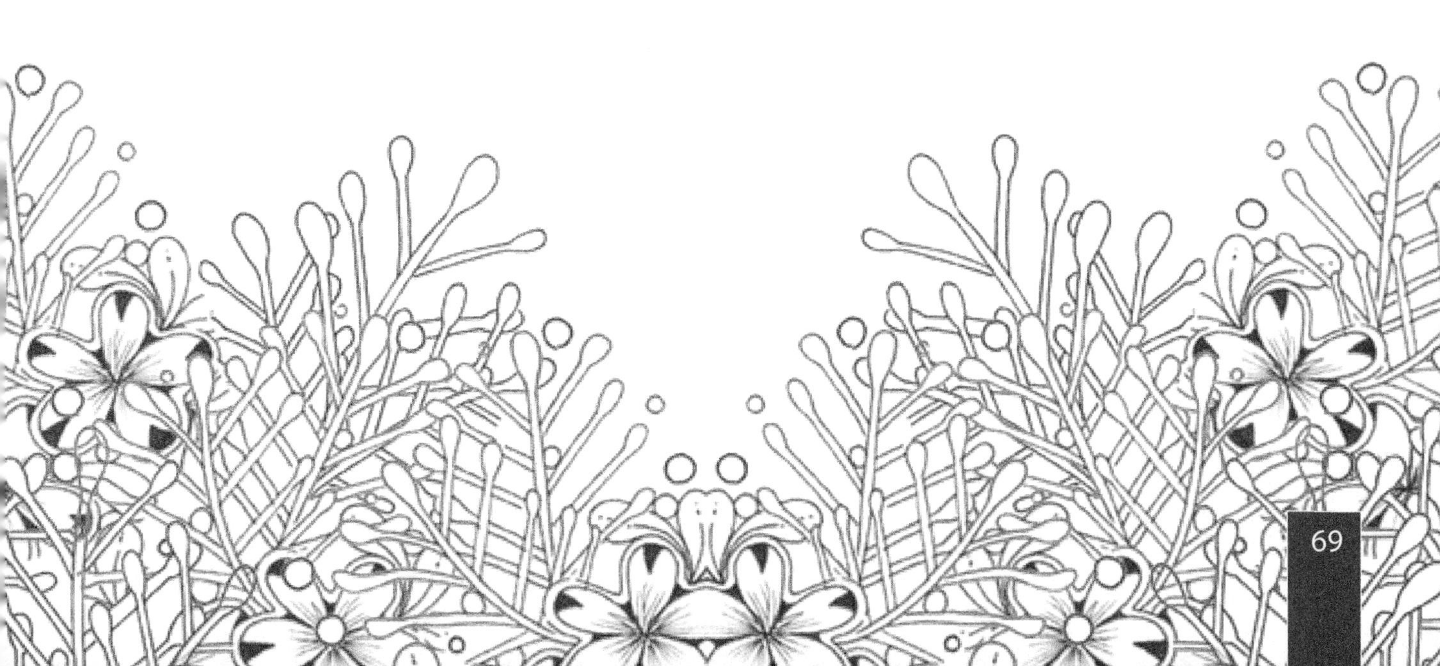

Finegogh

Juliette F CZT

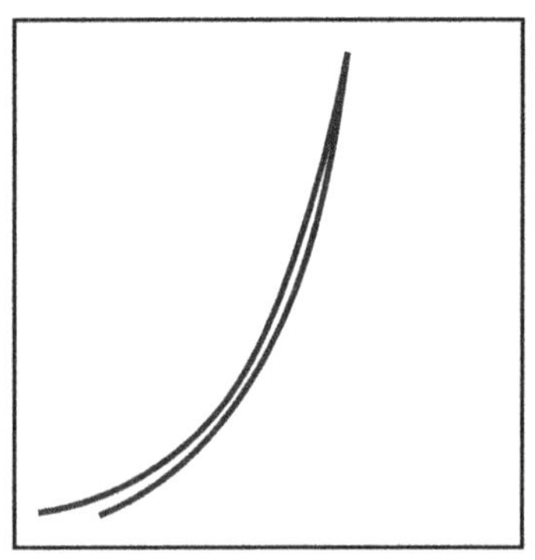
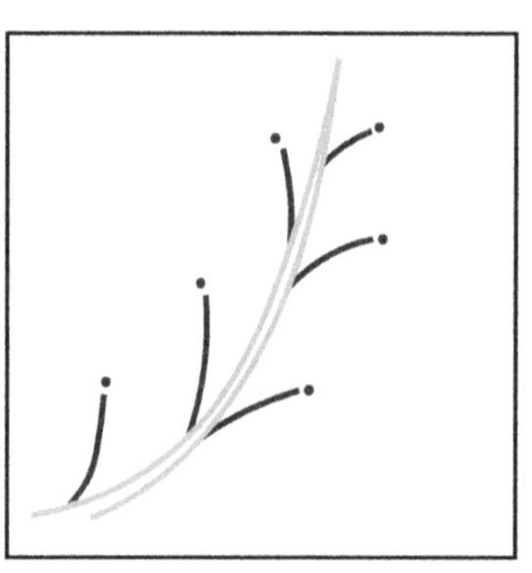
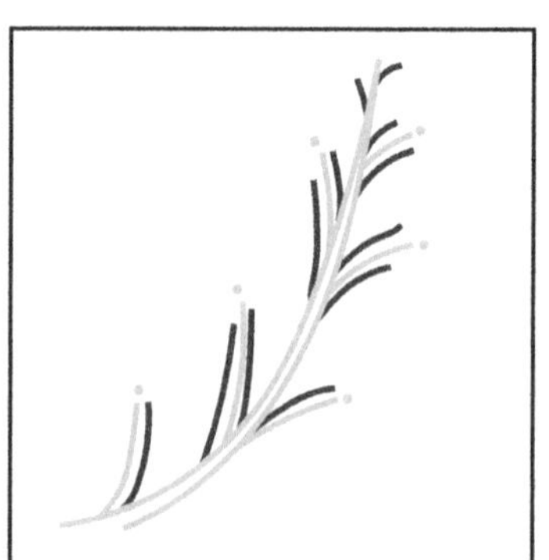
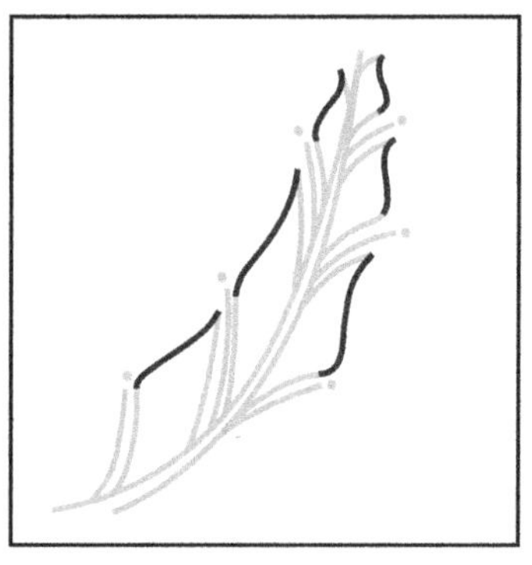
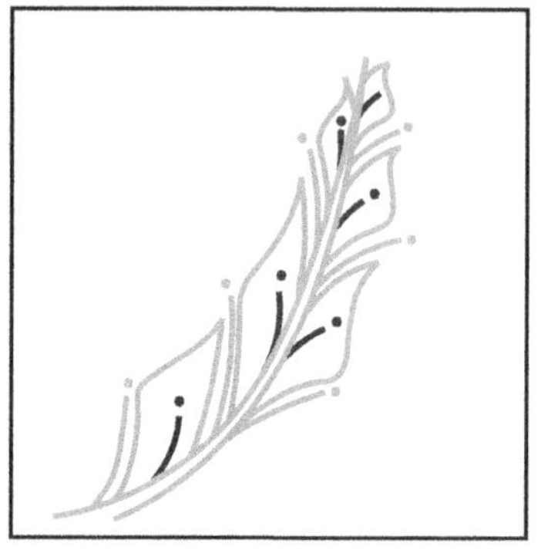

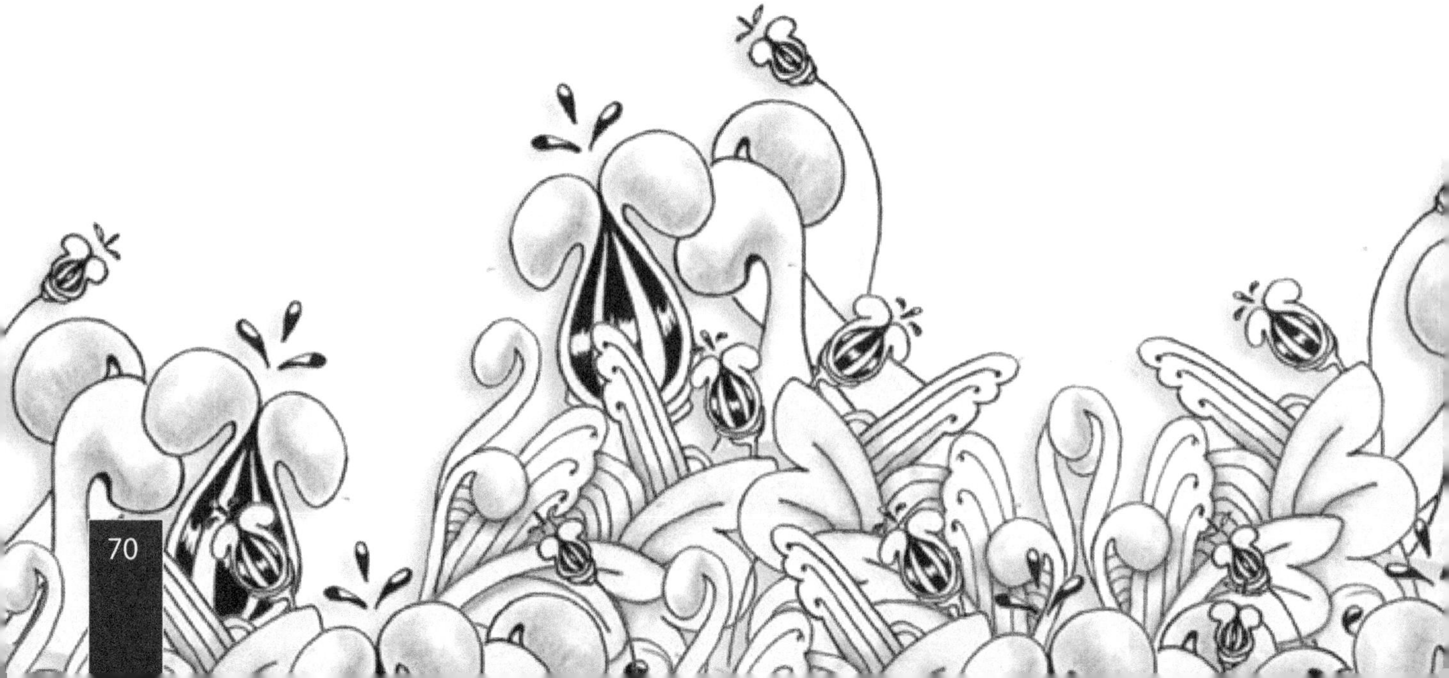

Mimis

Miranda Gerber CZT

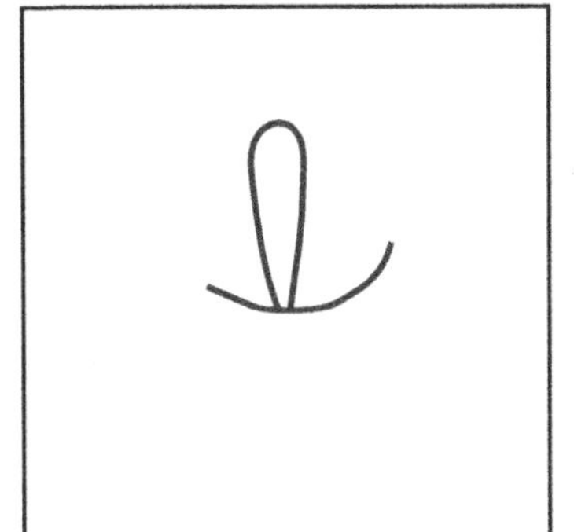
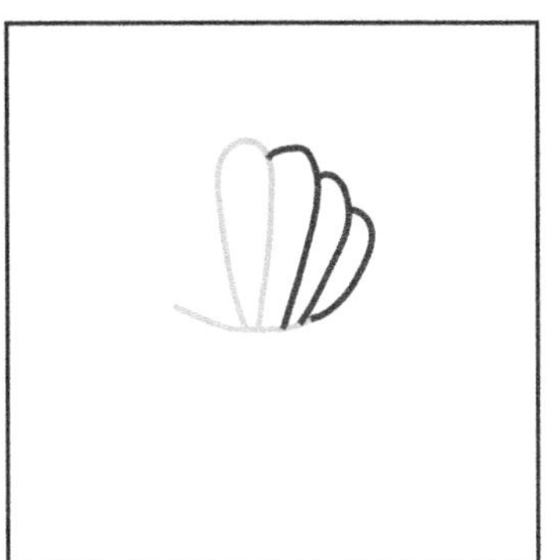
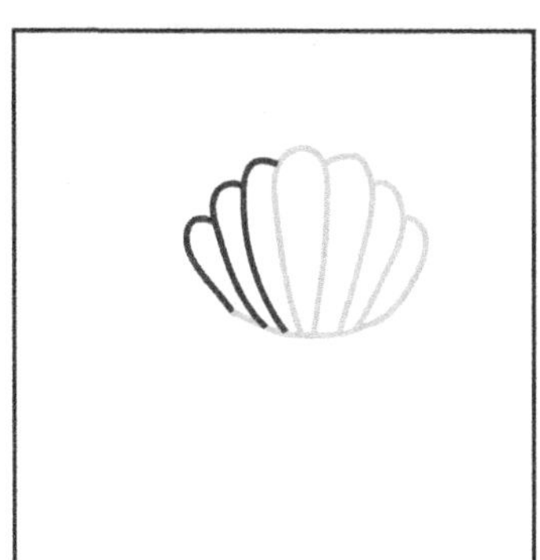
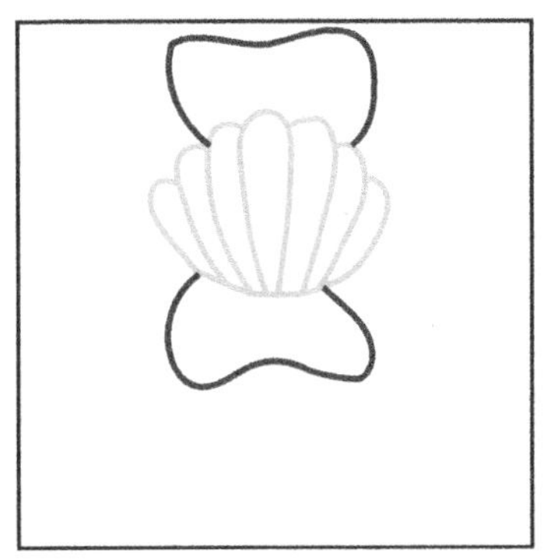
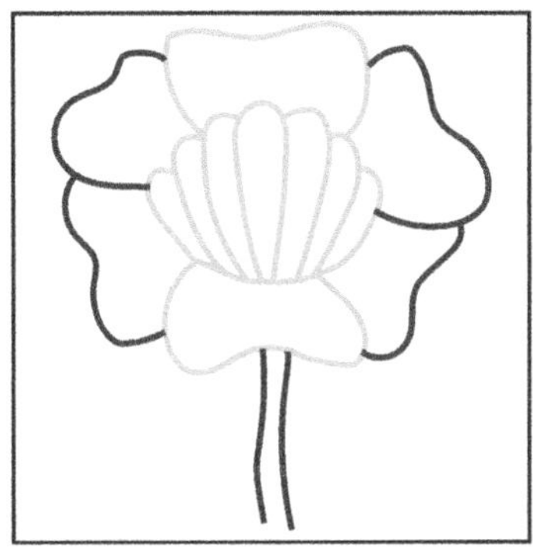
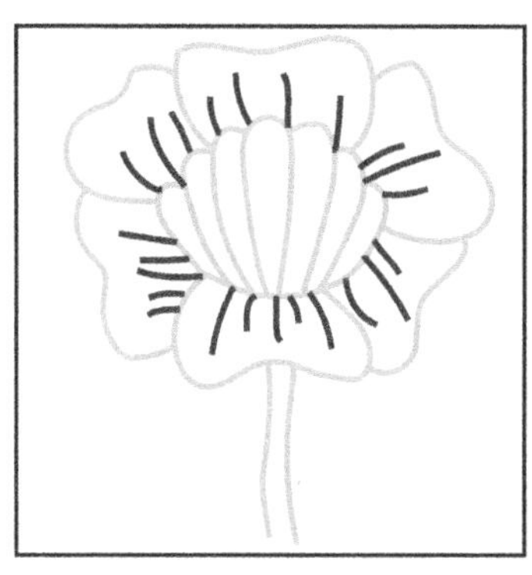

Lyra

Theresa Fessler CZT

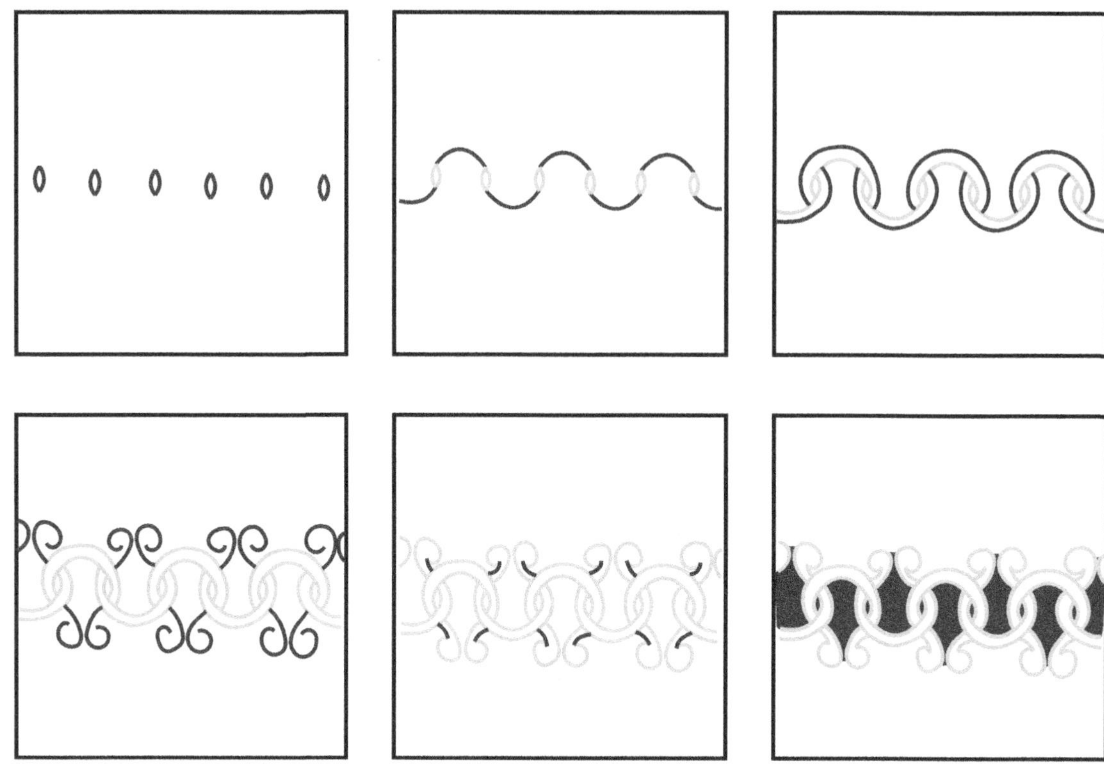

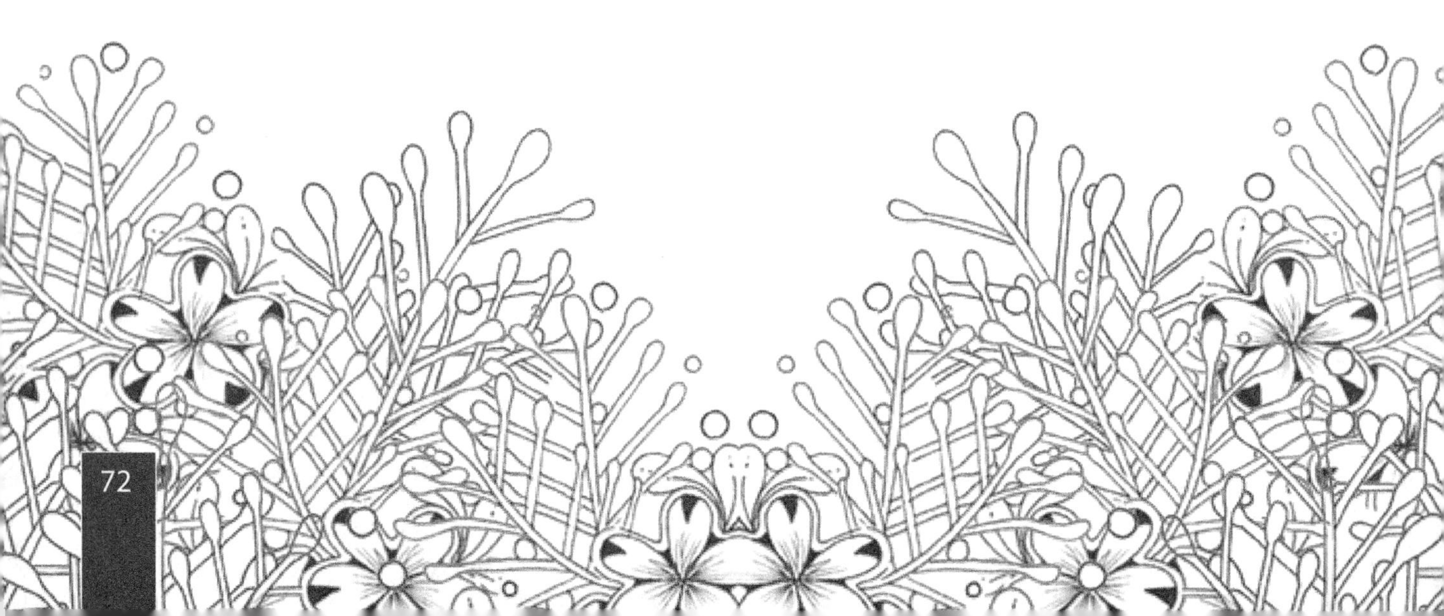

Floatfest

Carole Ohl CZT

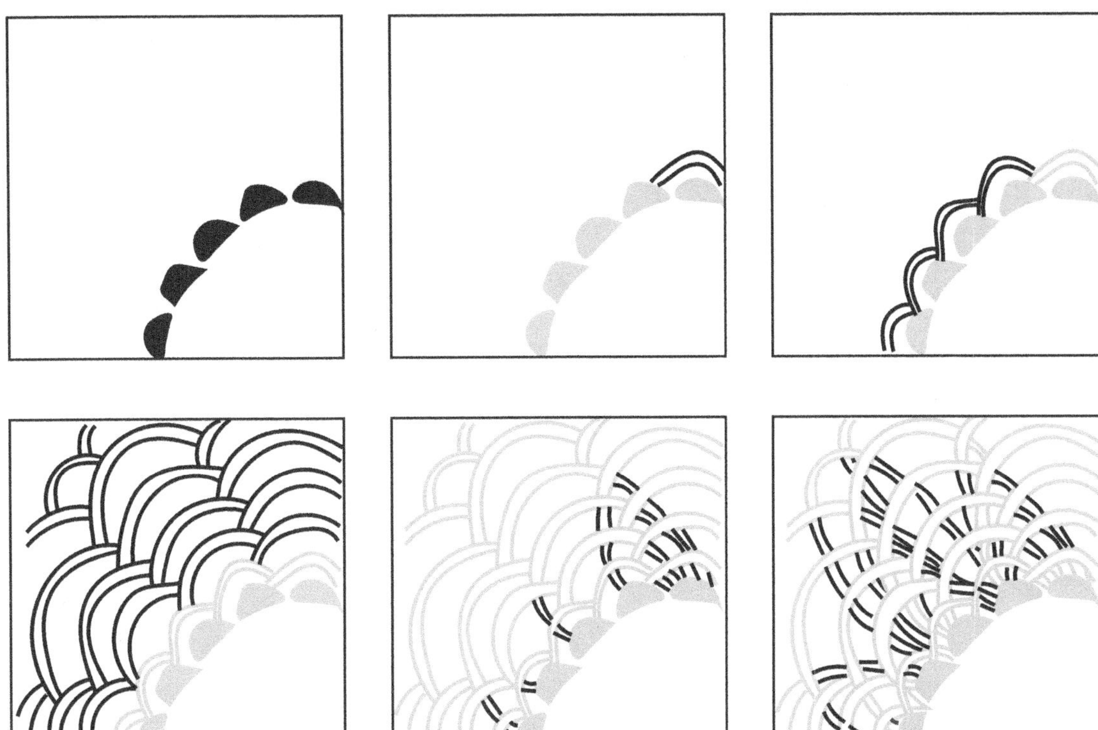

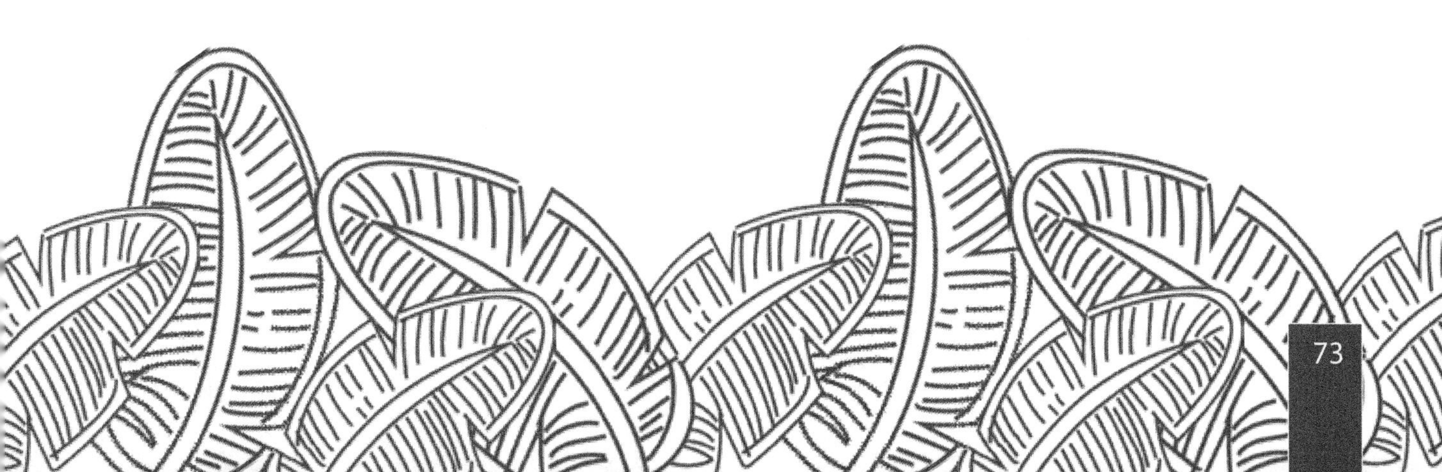

Mazokini

Miranda Gerber CZT

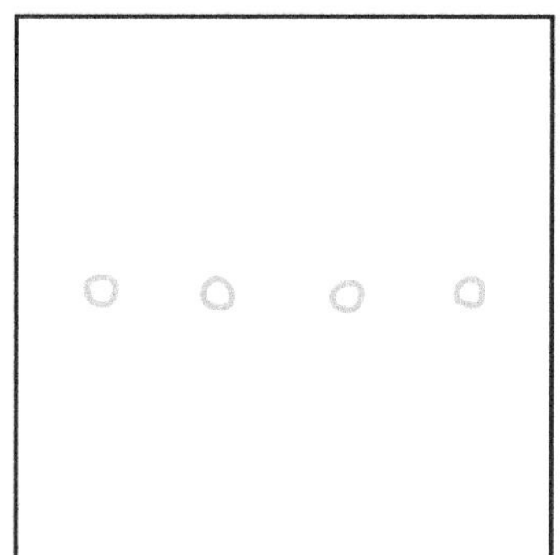
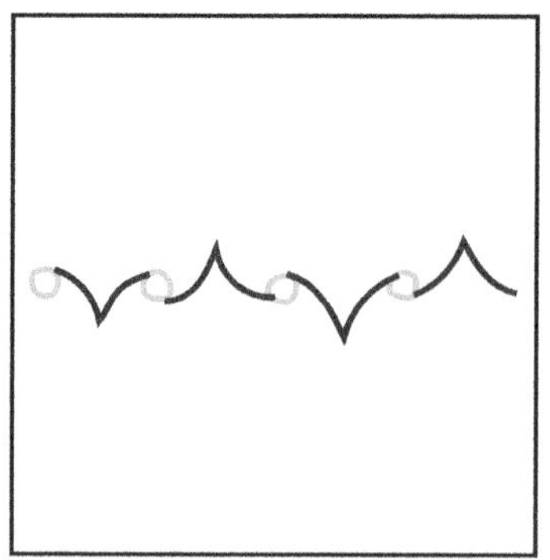
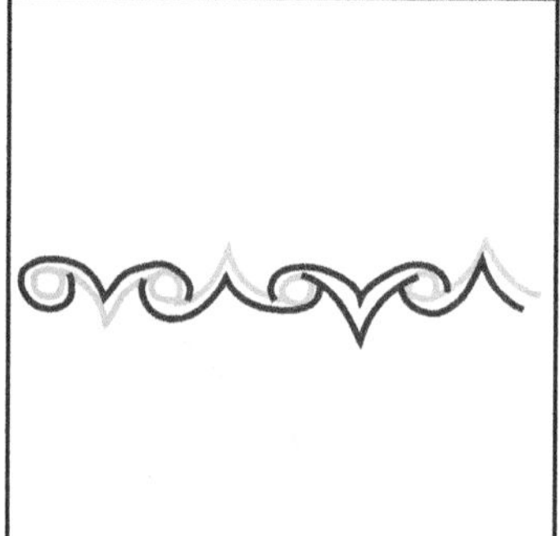
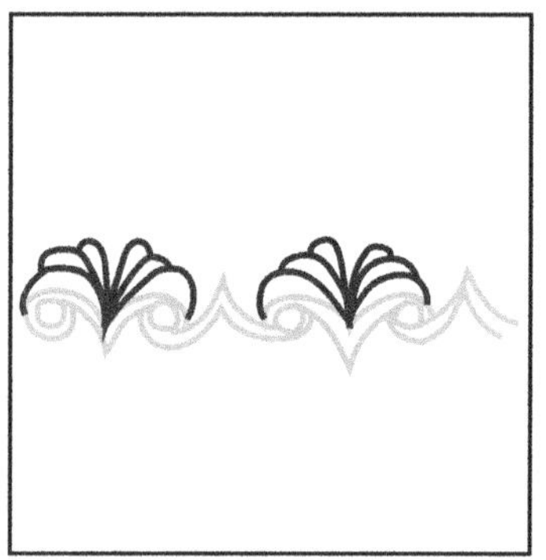
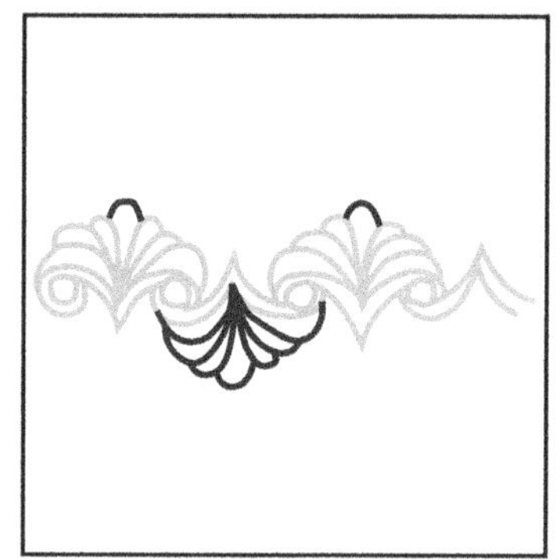
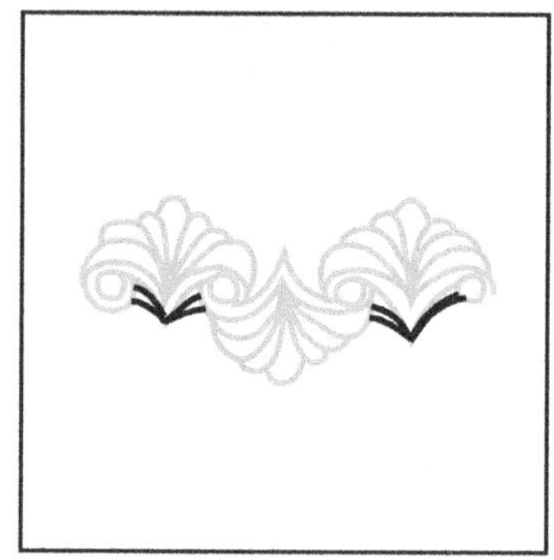

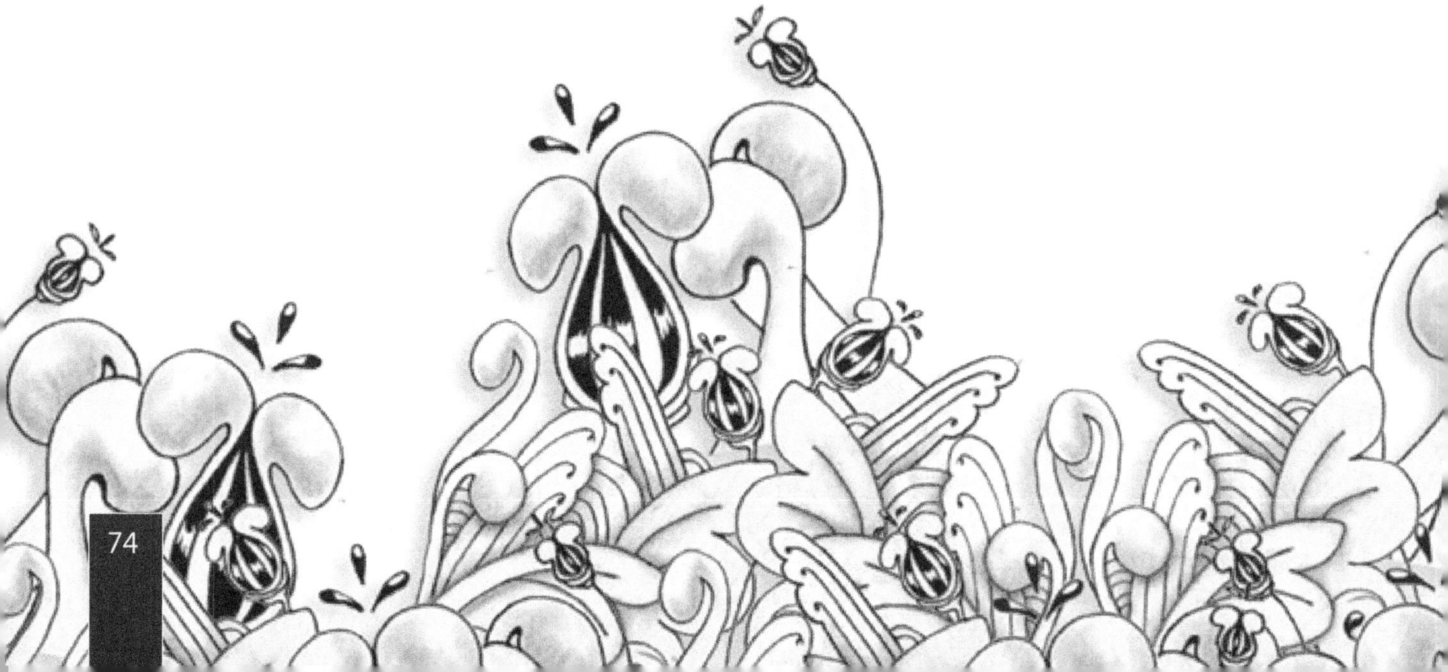

Lockta

Theresa Fessler CZT

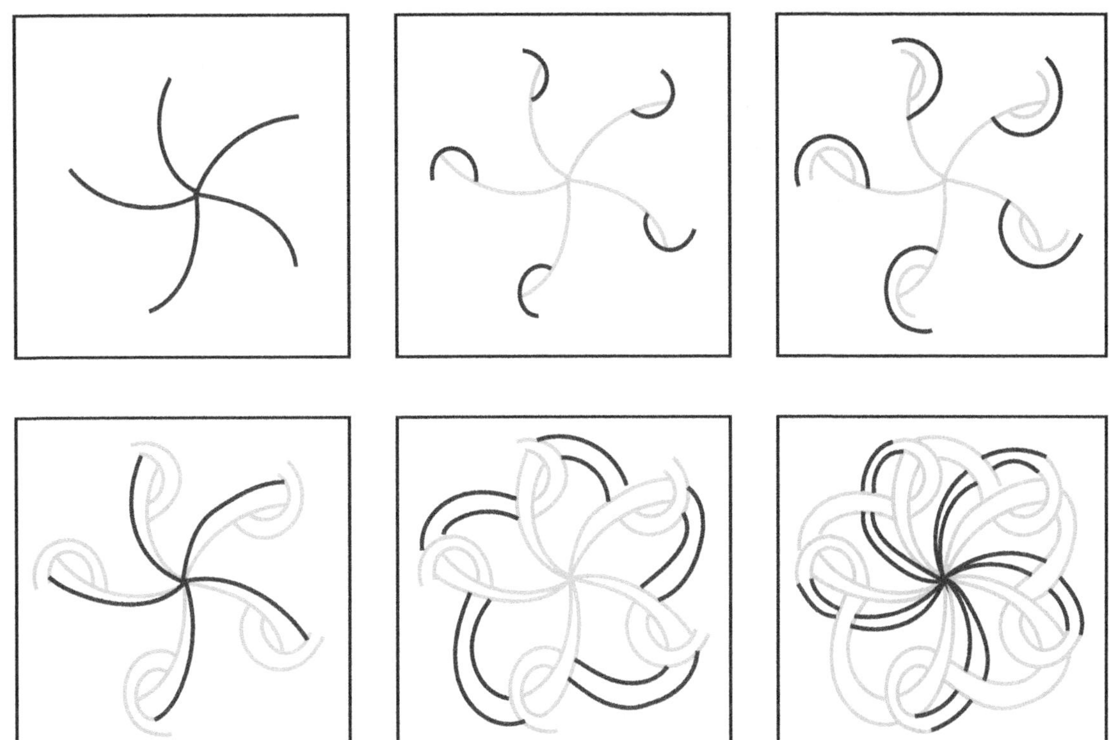

Beach

Barbara Duel Johnson CZT

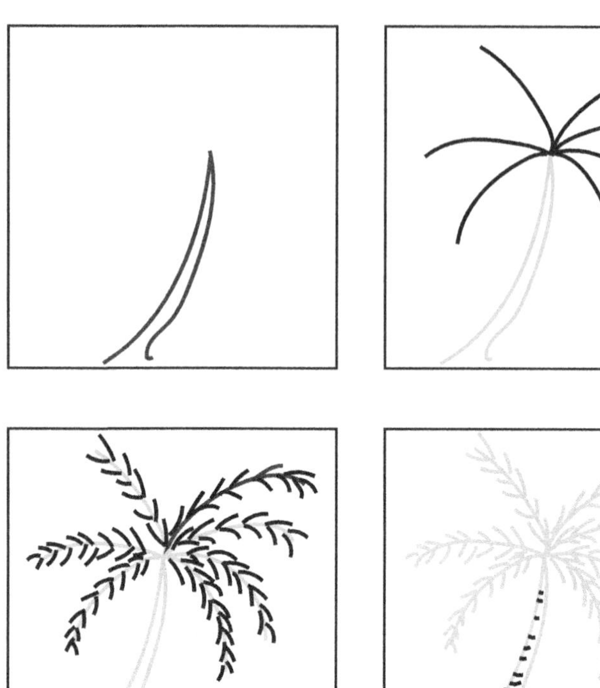

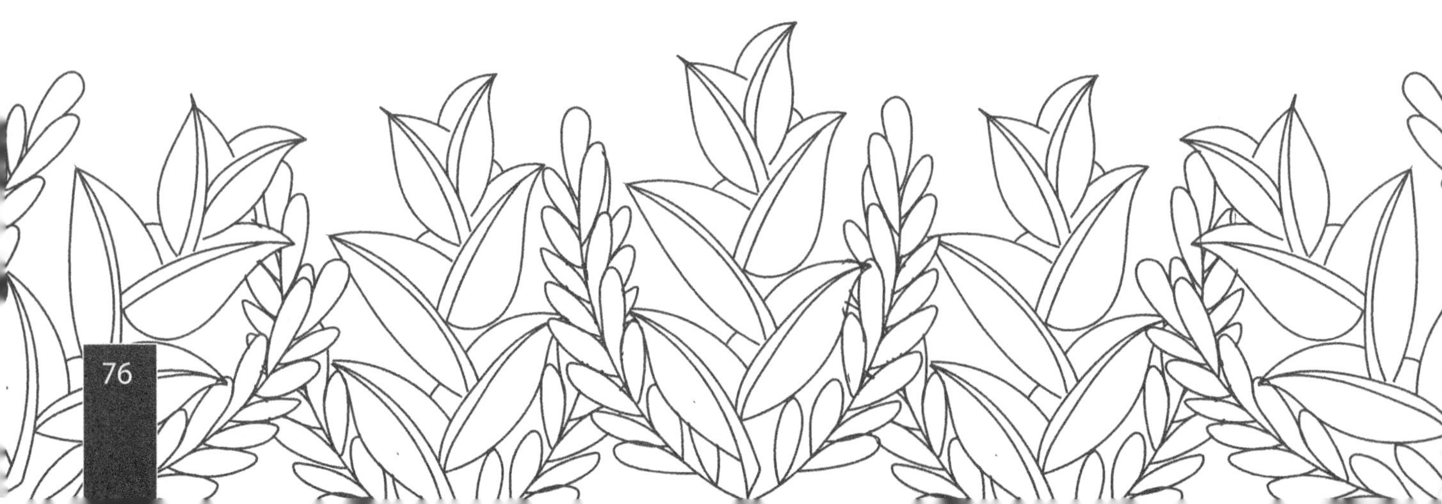

Binx

Carla Jooren CZT

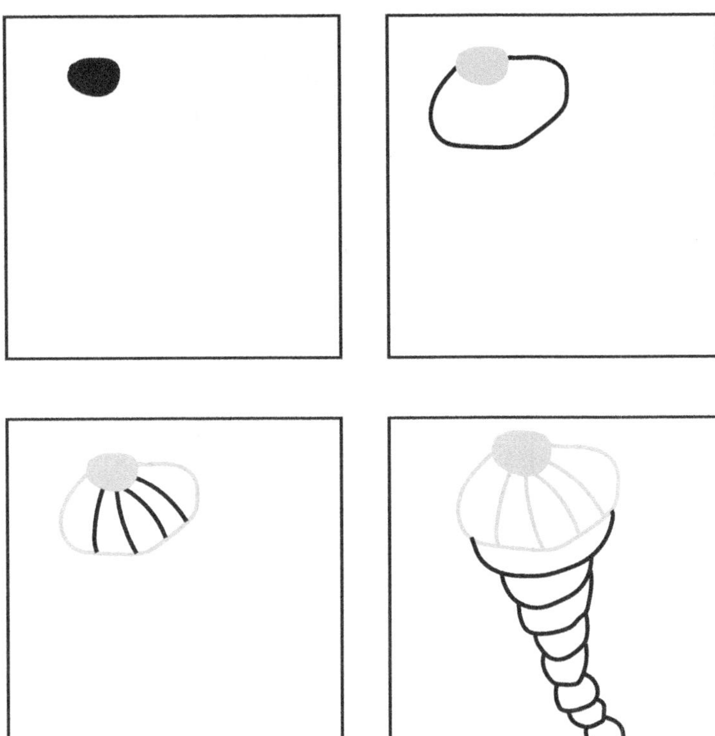

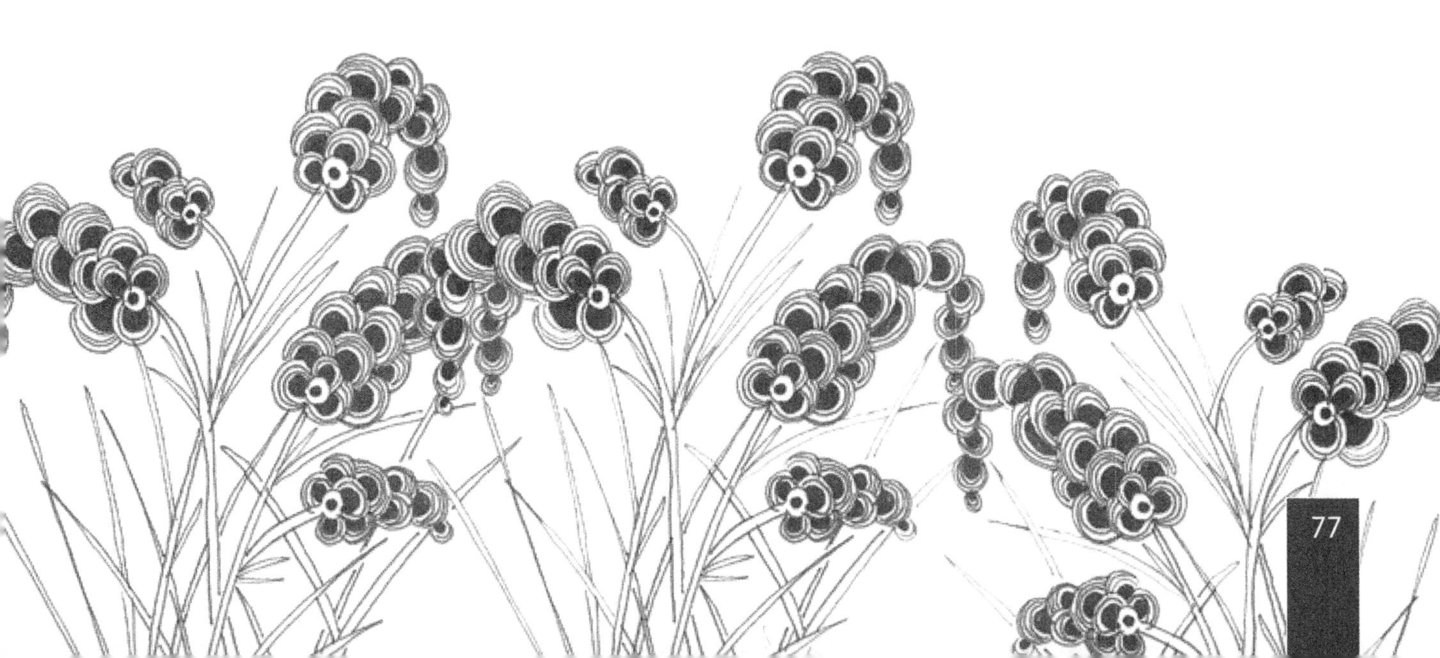

Ionada

Theresa Fessler CZT

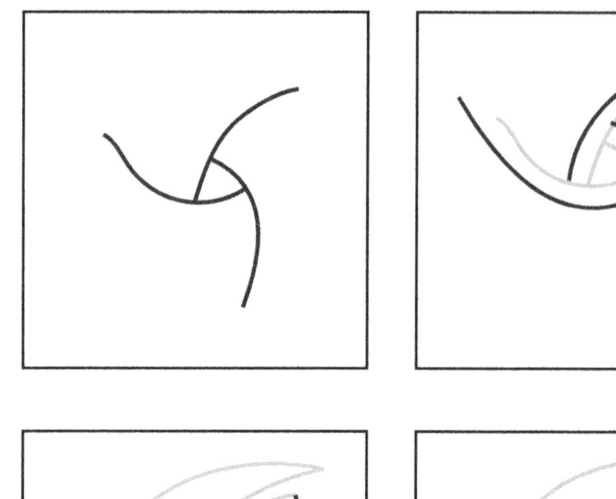

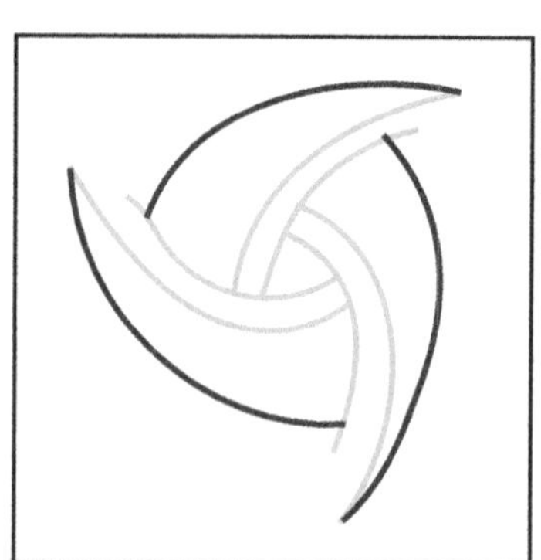

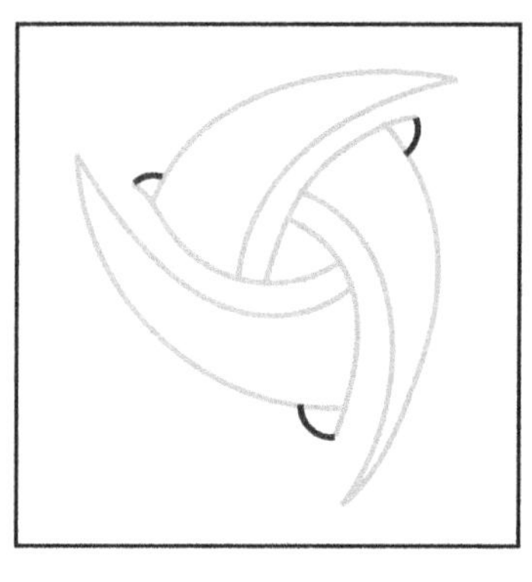

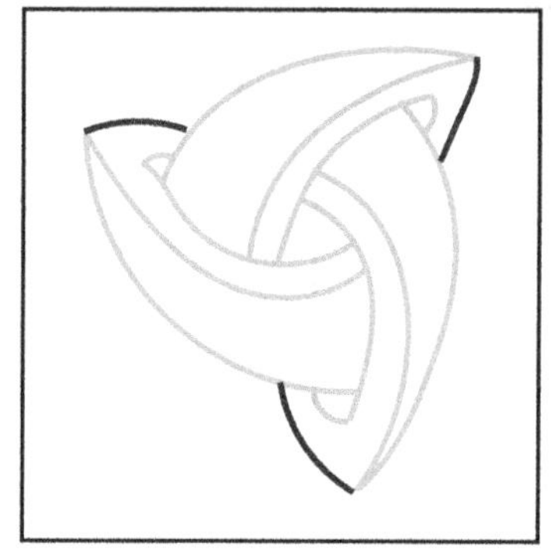

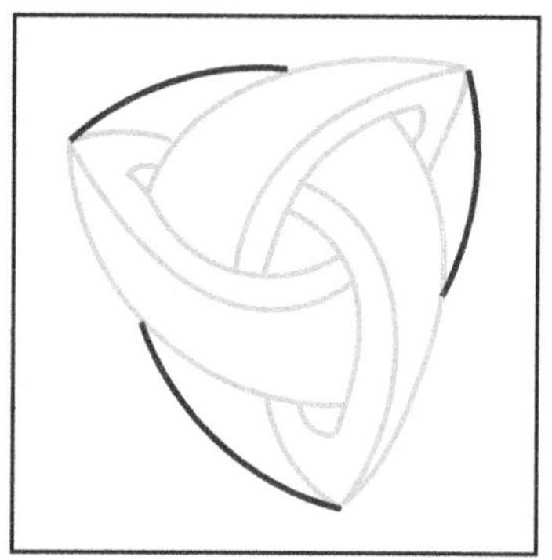

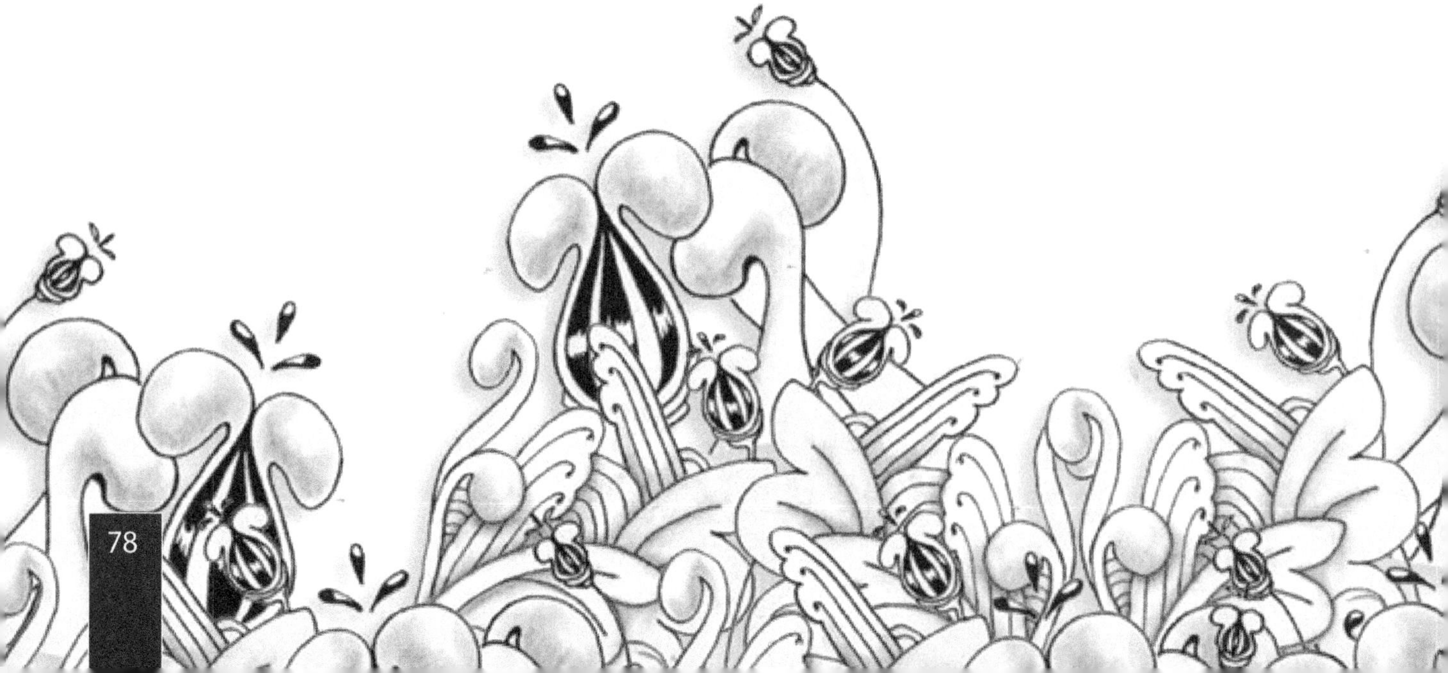

Hearts Content

Barbara Duel Johnson CZT

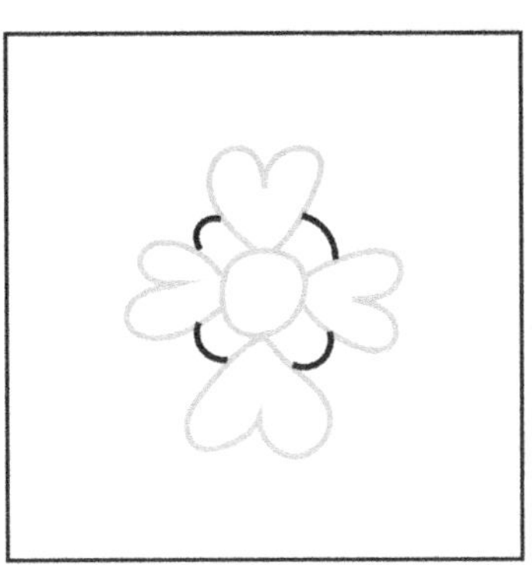

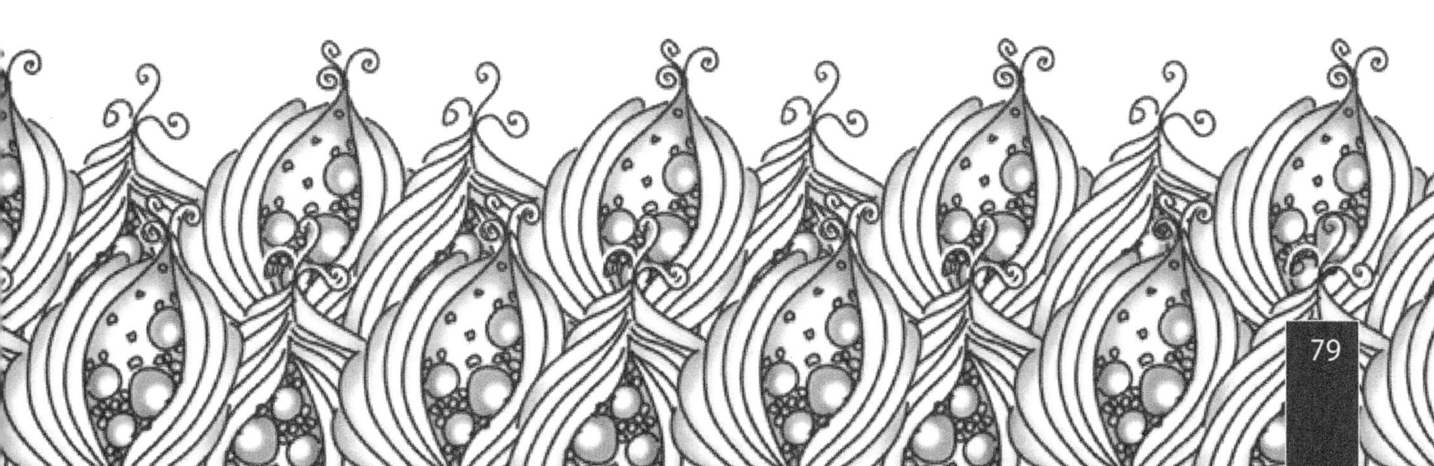

Gilgo

Danielle DePalma - Mabanta CZT

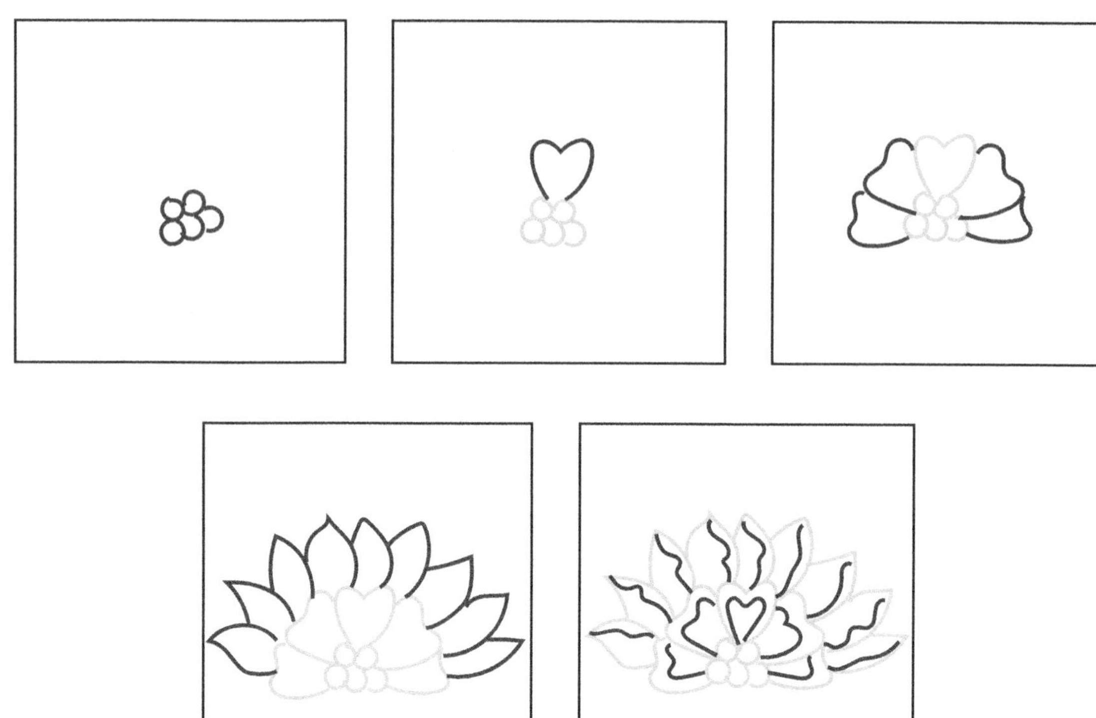

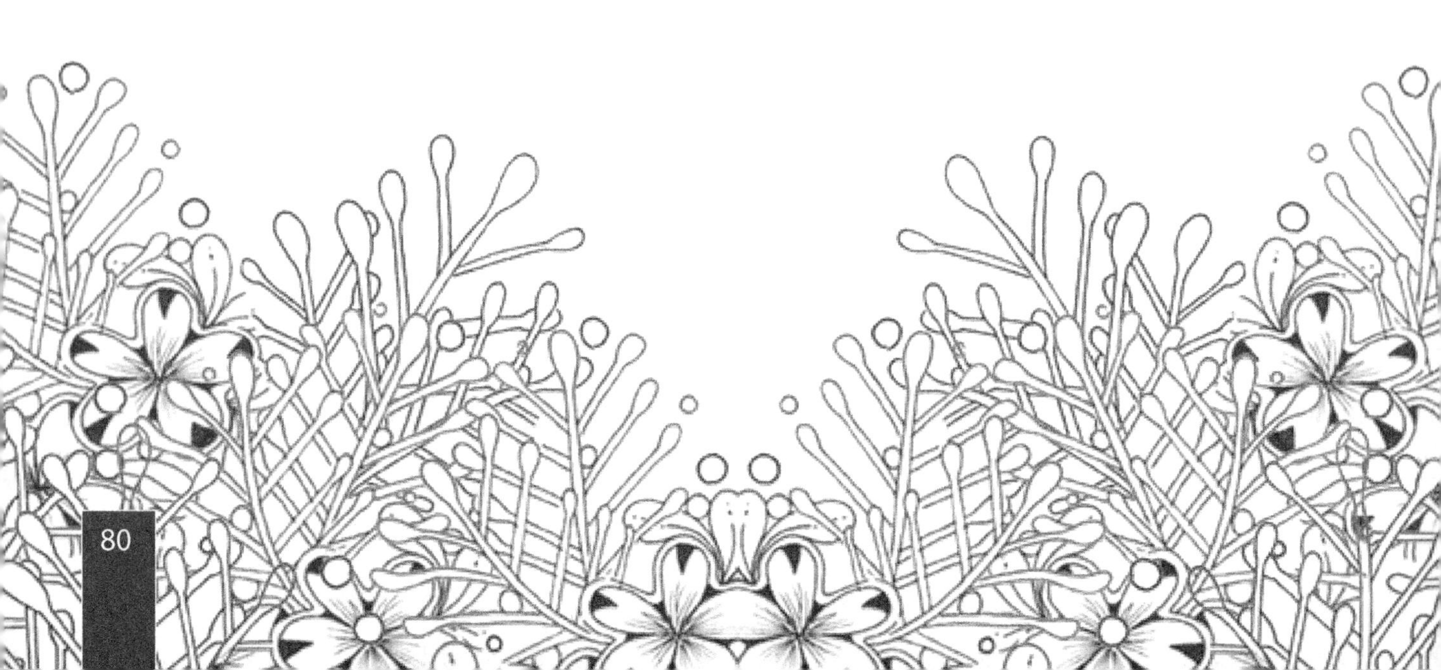

Lilium

Danielle DePalma - Mabanta CZT

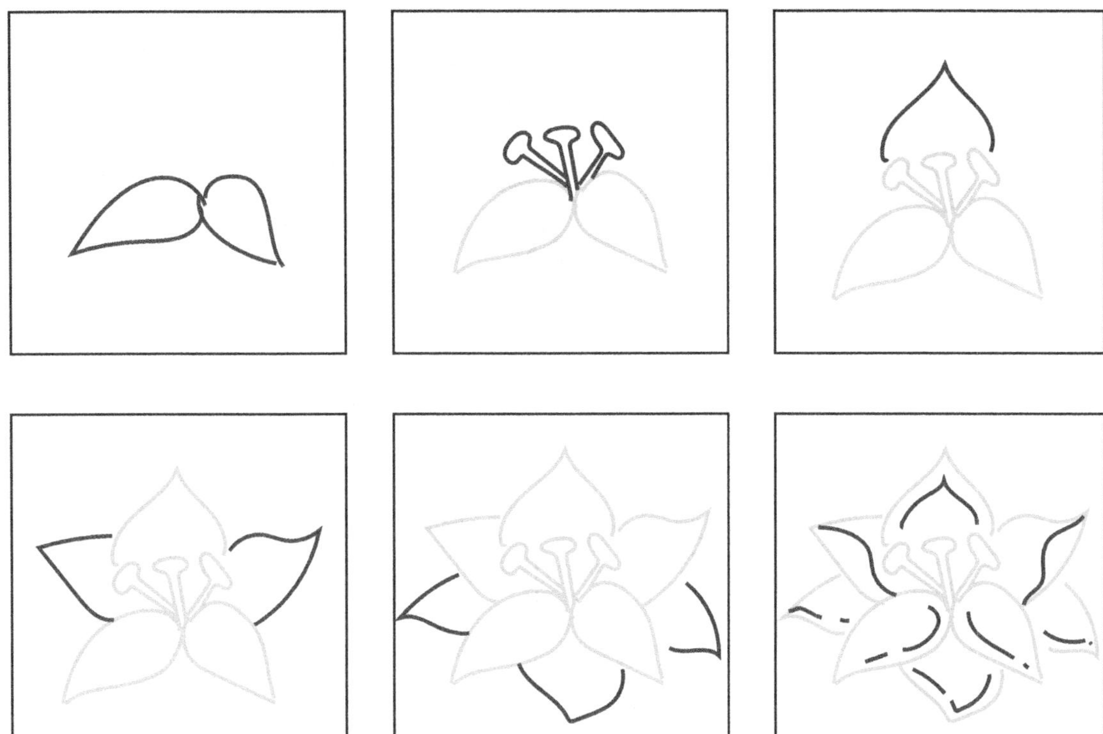

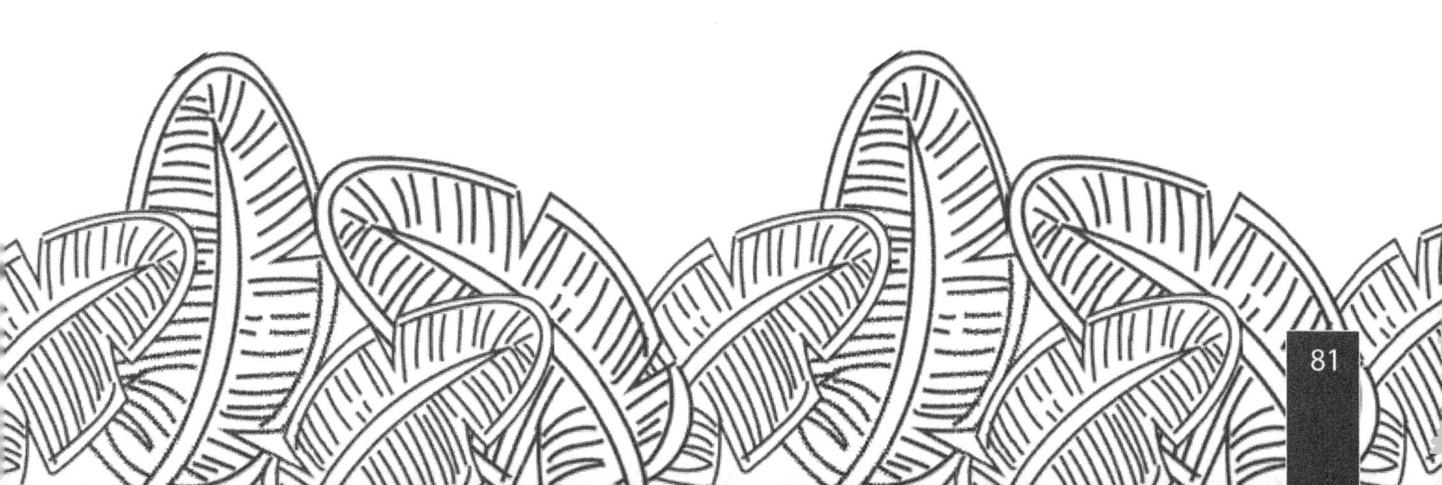

Heartily

Barbara Duel Johnson CZT

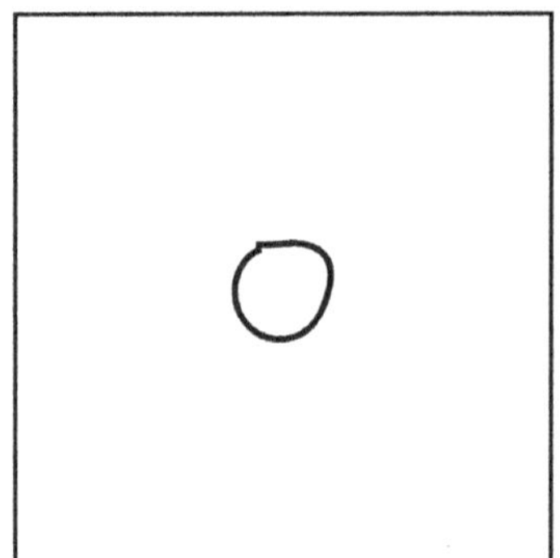
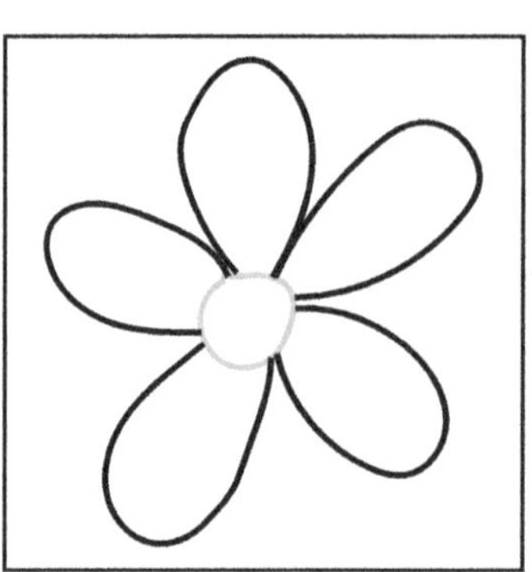

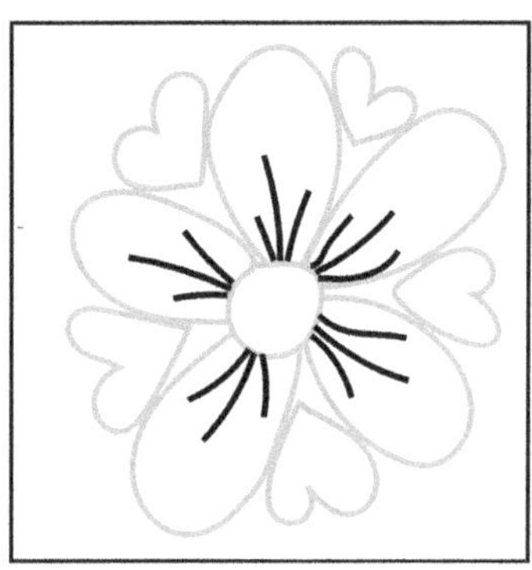
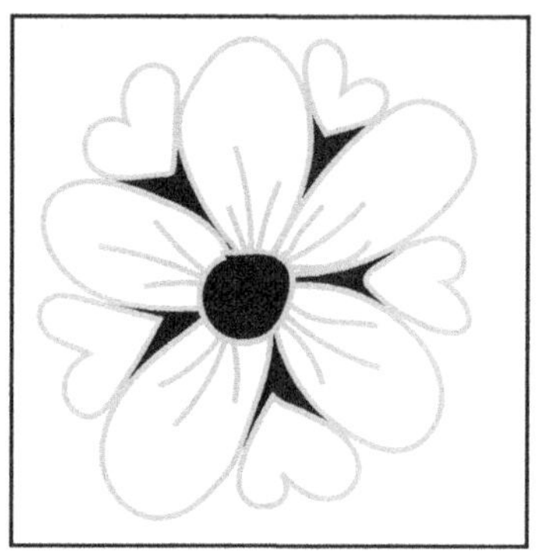

Crown Leaves

Miranda Gerber CZT

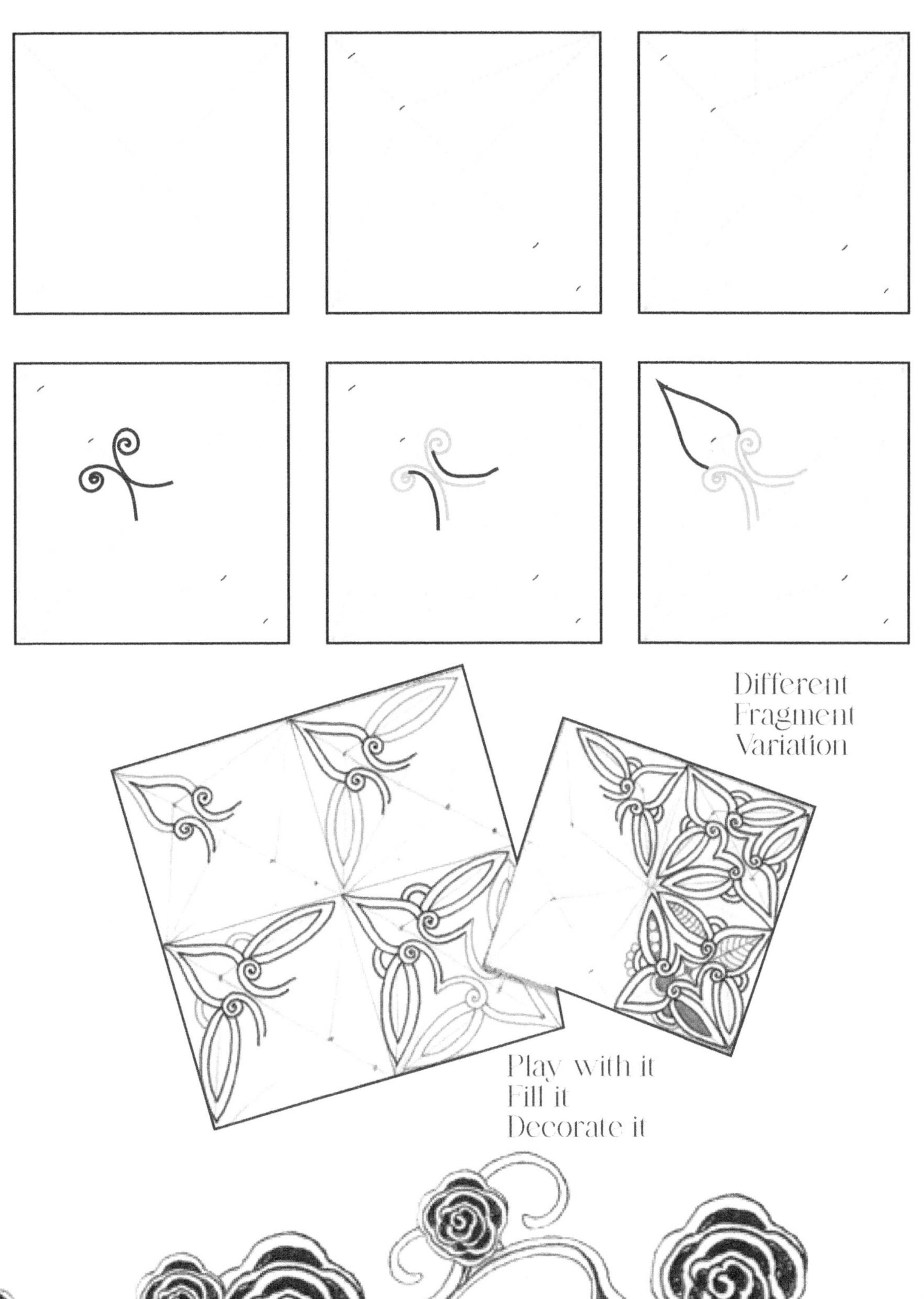

Rambles

Official Zentangle Pattern

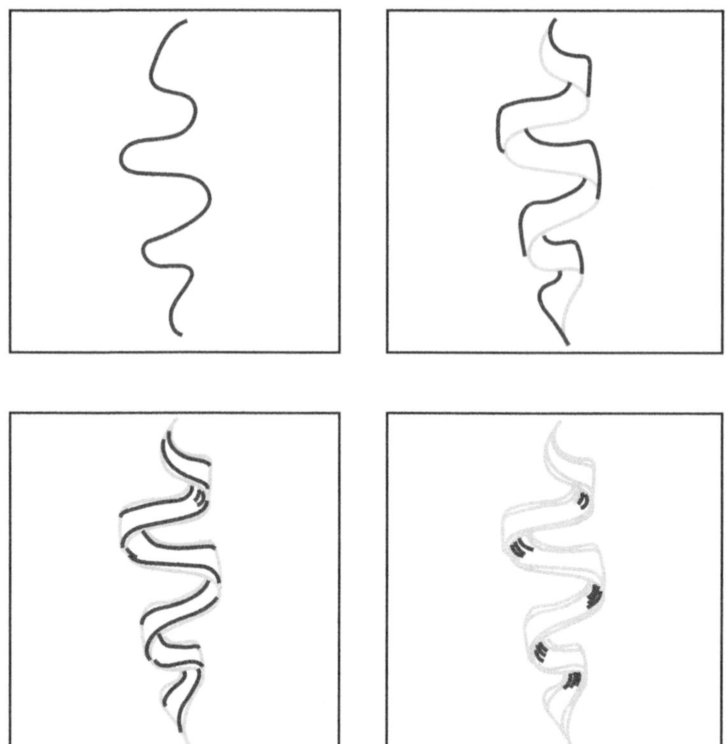

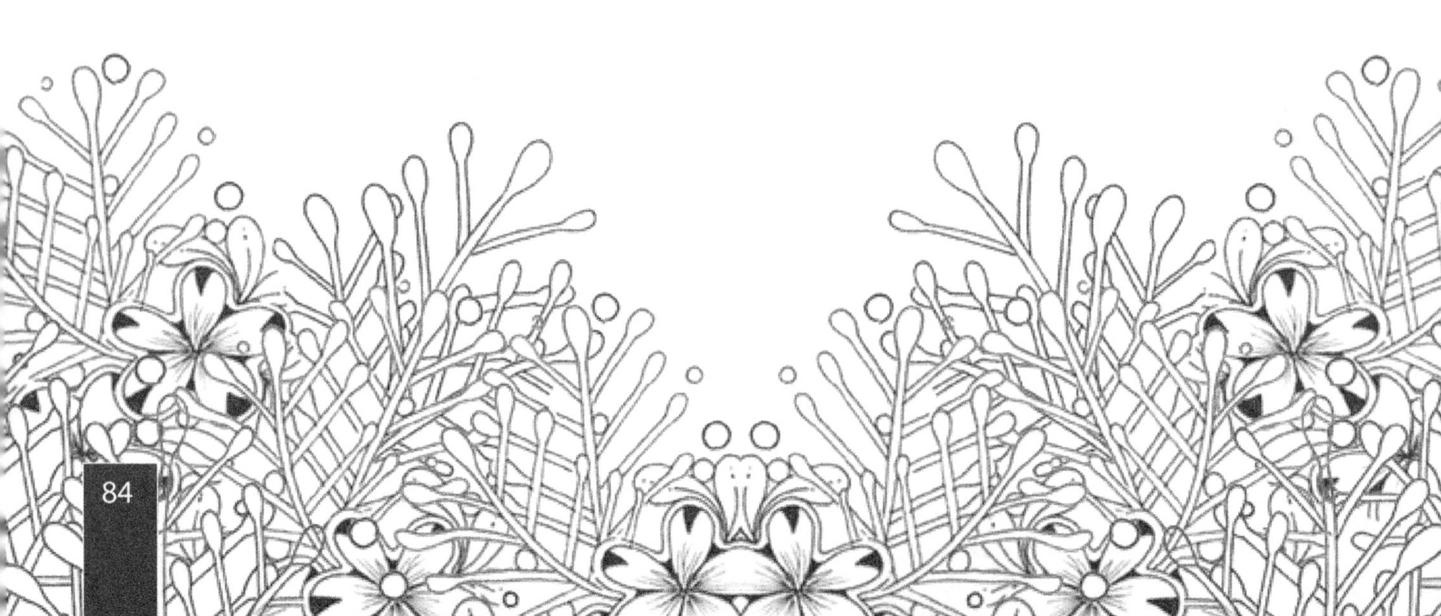

Spray

Barbara Duel Johnson CZT

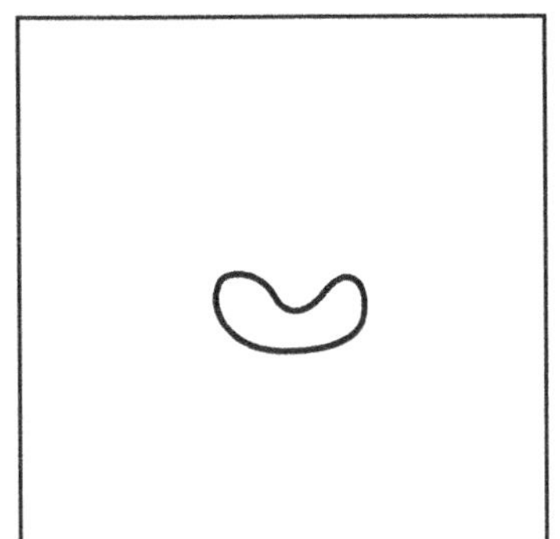

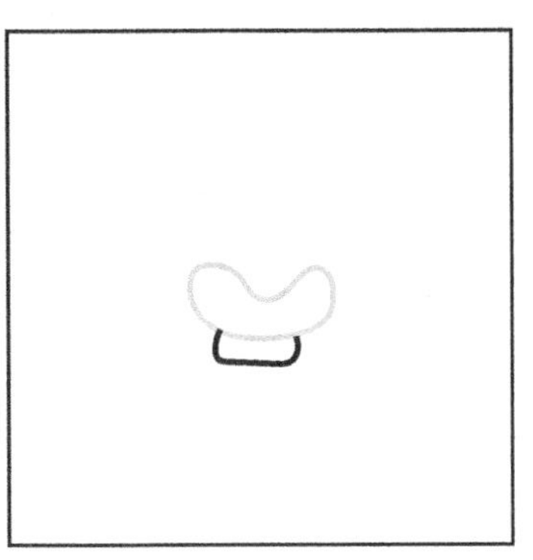

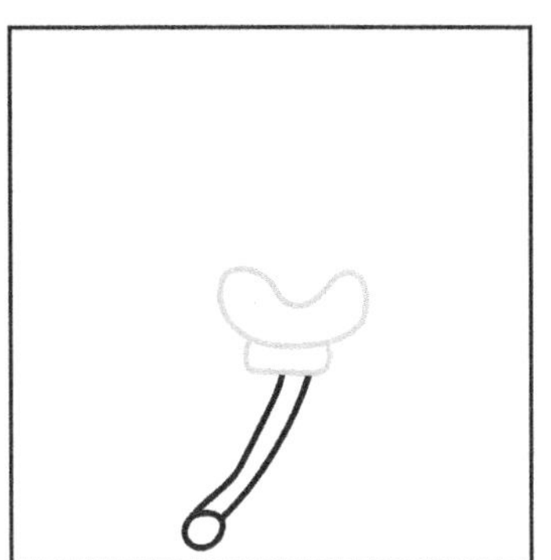

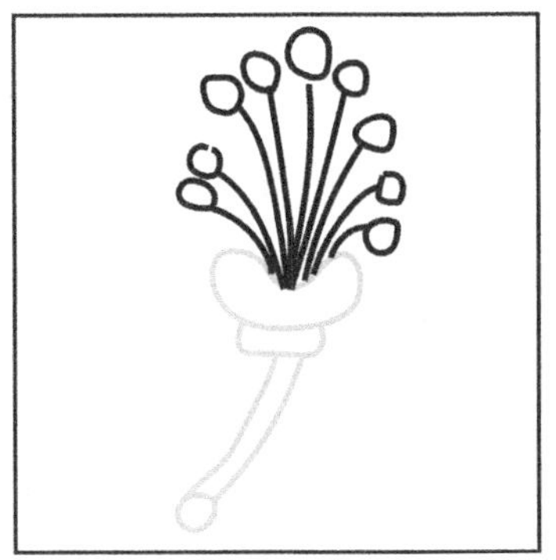

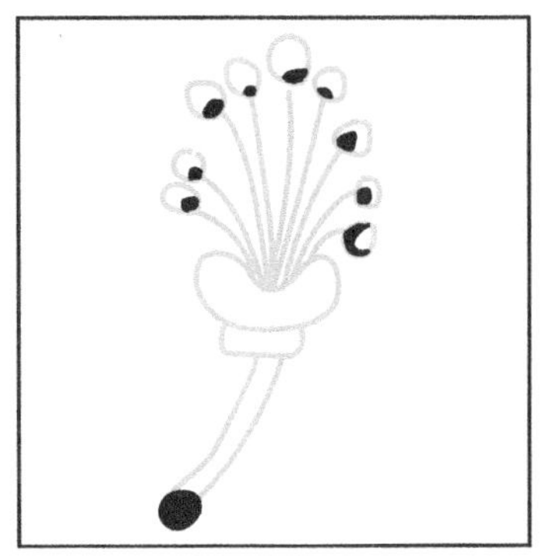

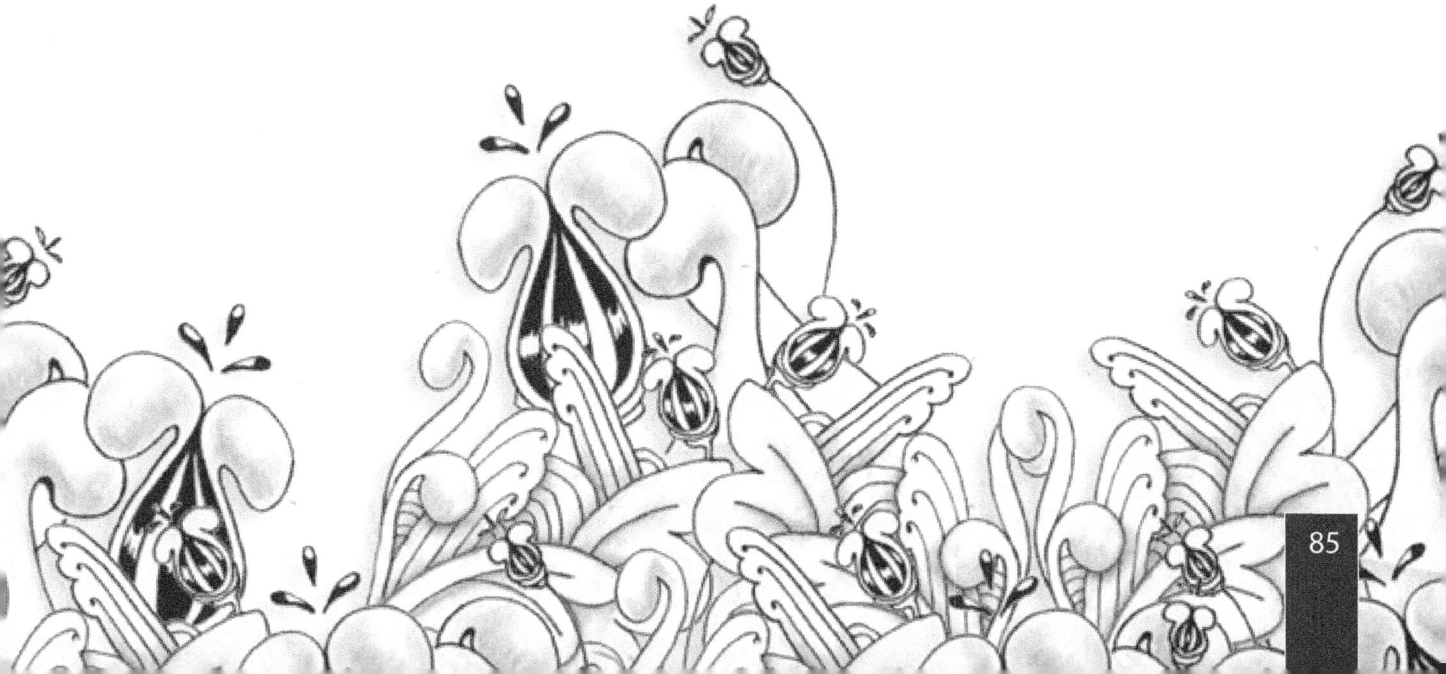

Veerap

Debbie Raaen CZT

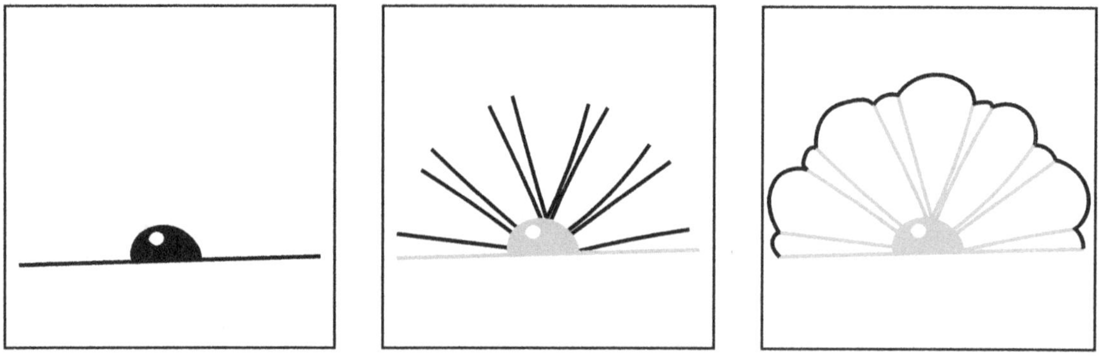

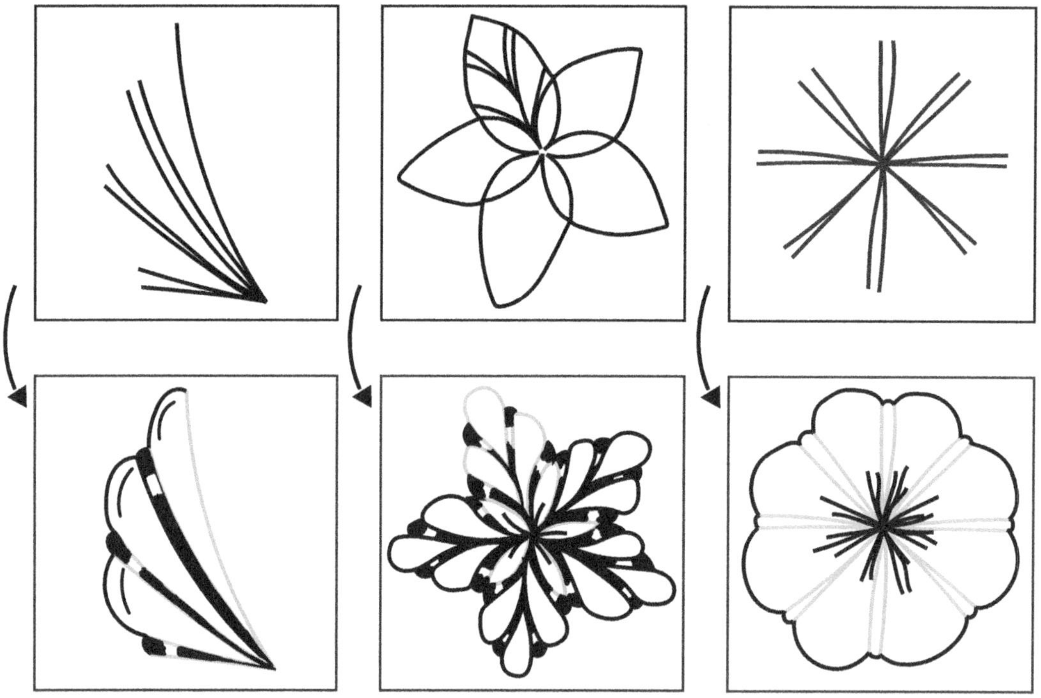

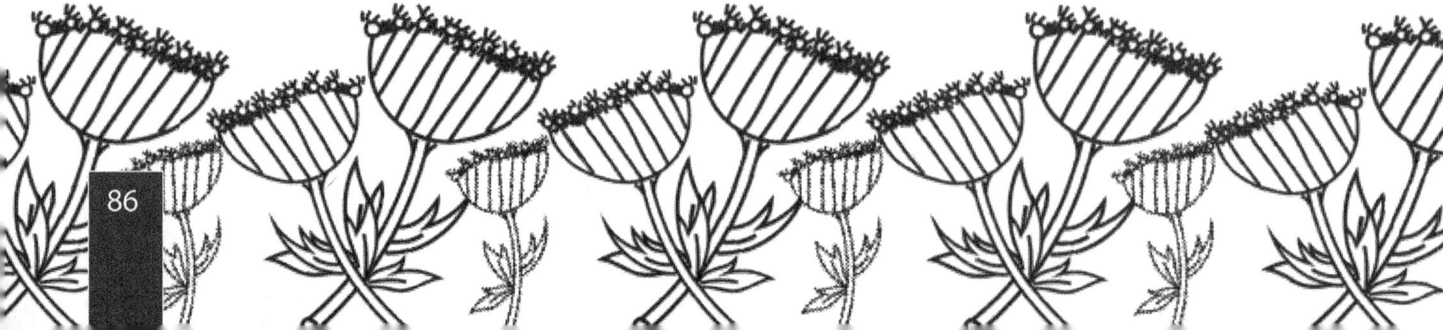

Yuliset

Annett Rumpler CZT

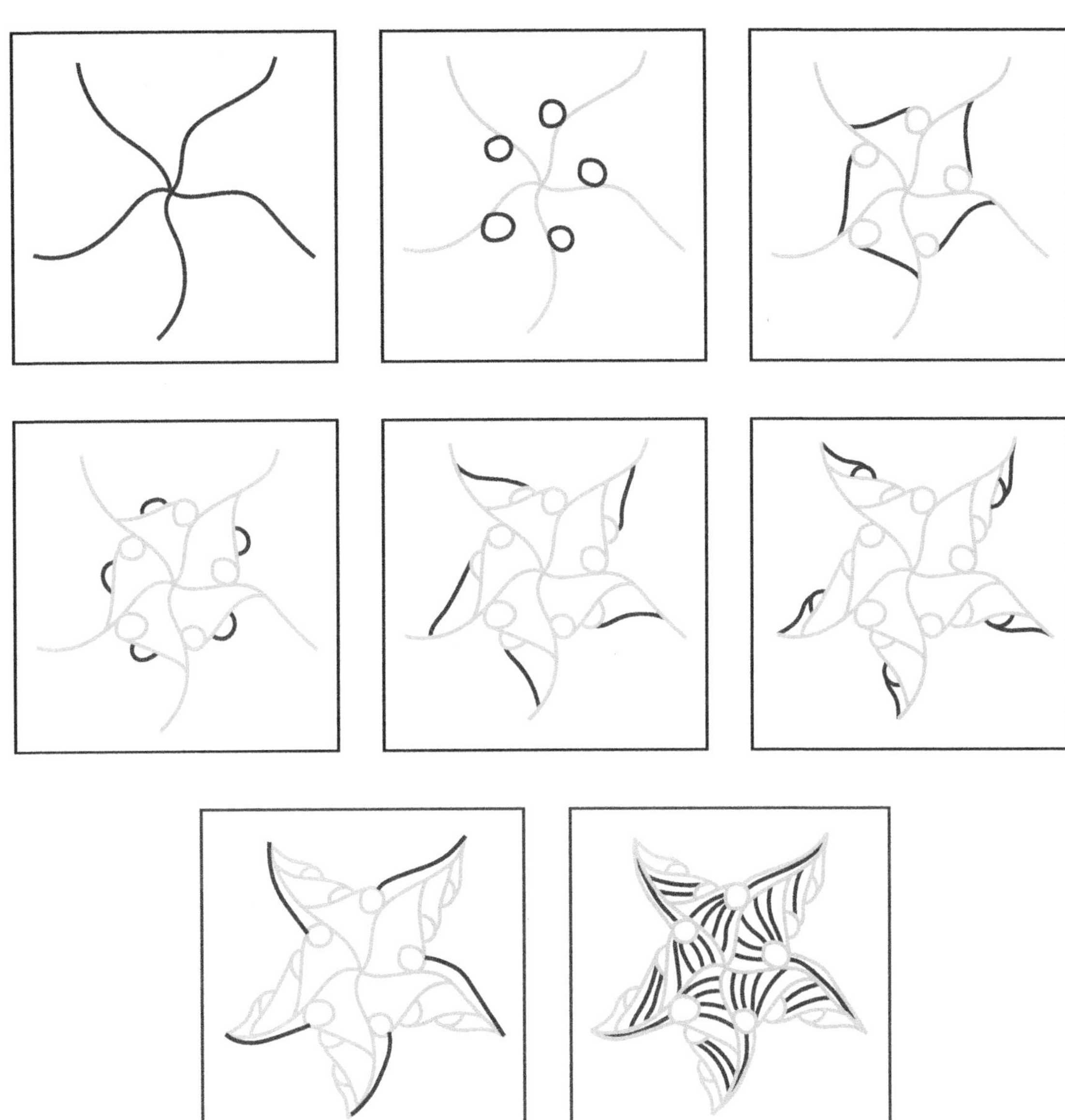

Tulipsi

Simone Menzel CZT

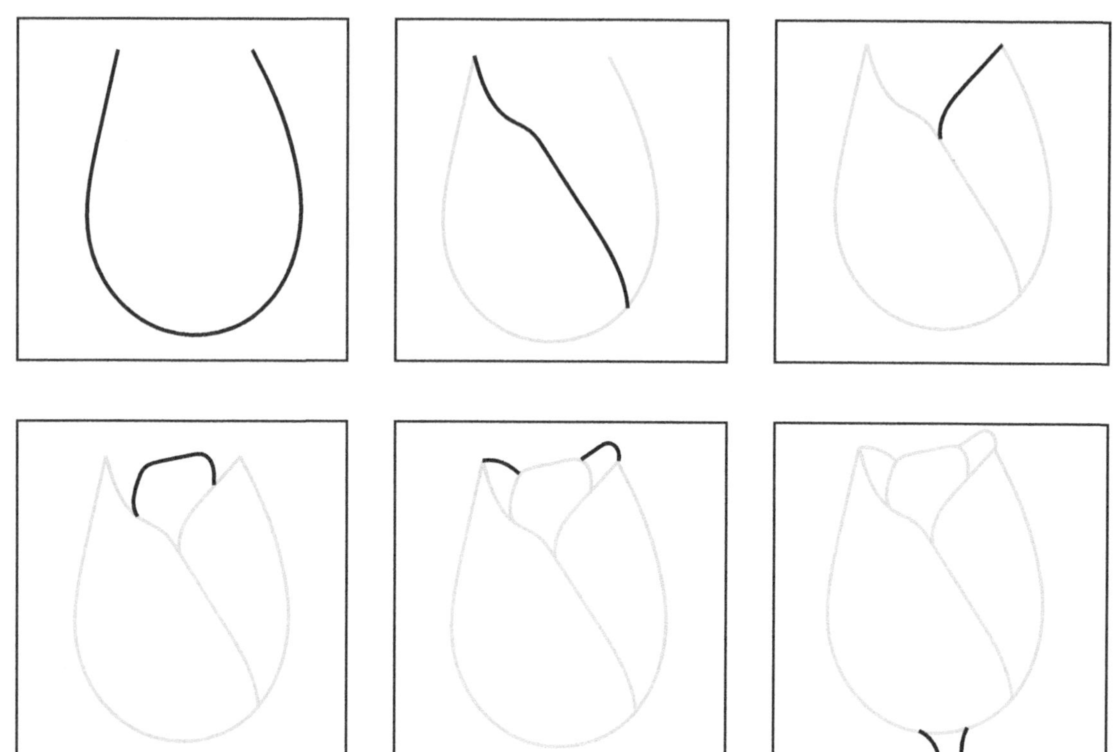

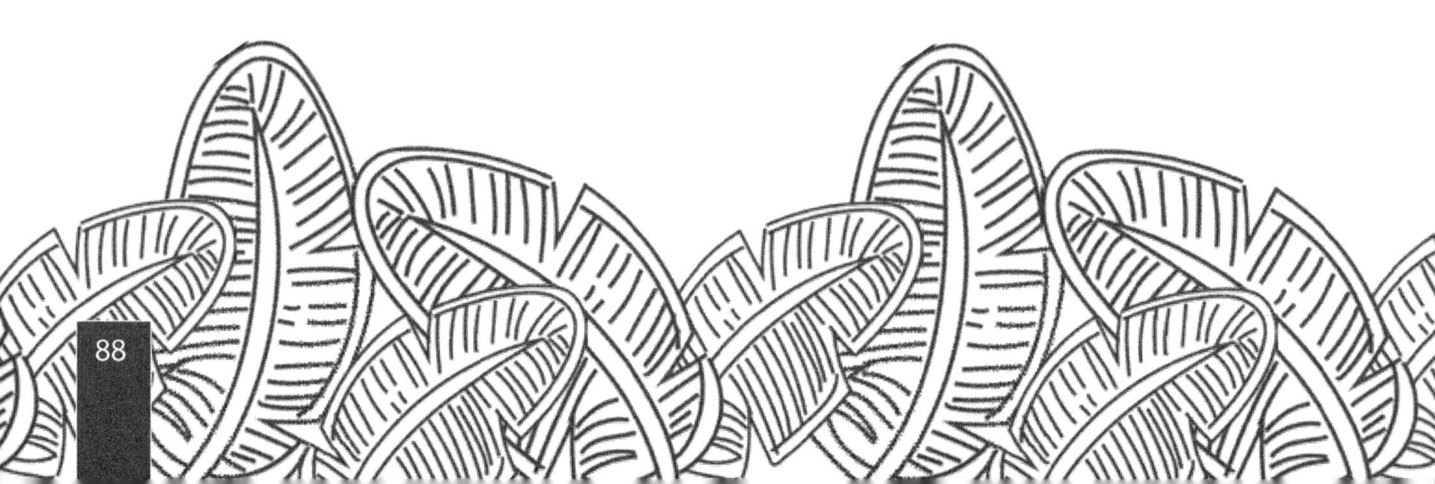

Spruce Cone Rose

Dolly Bolen CZT

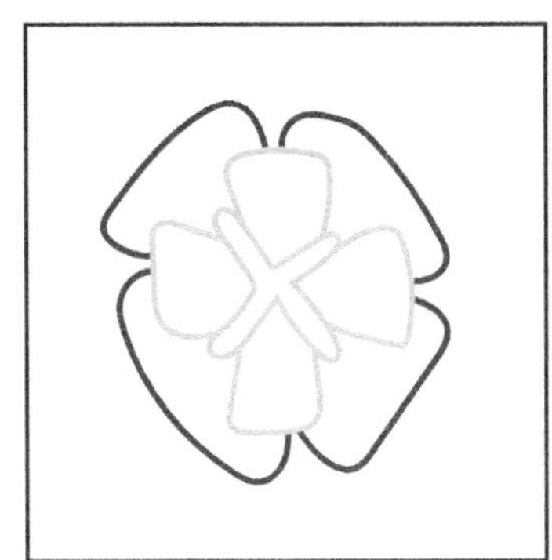
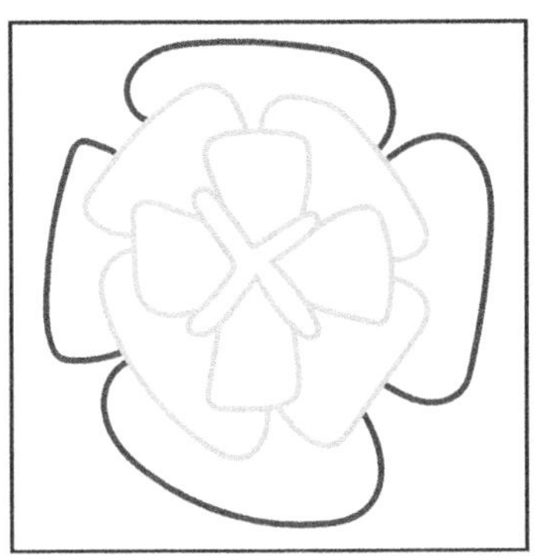
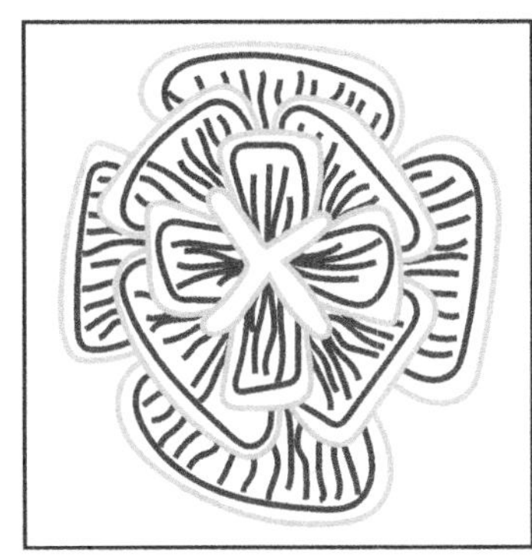

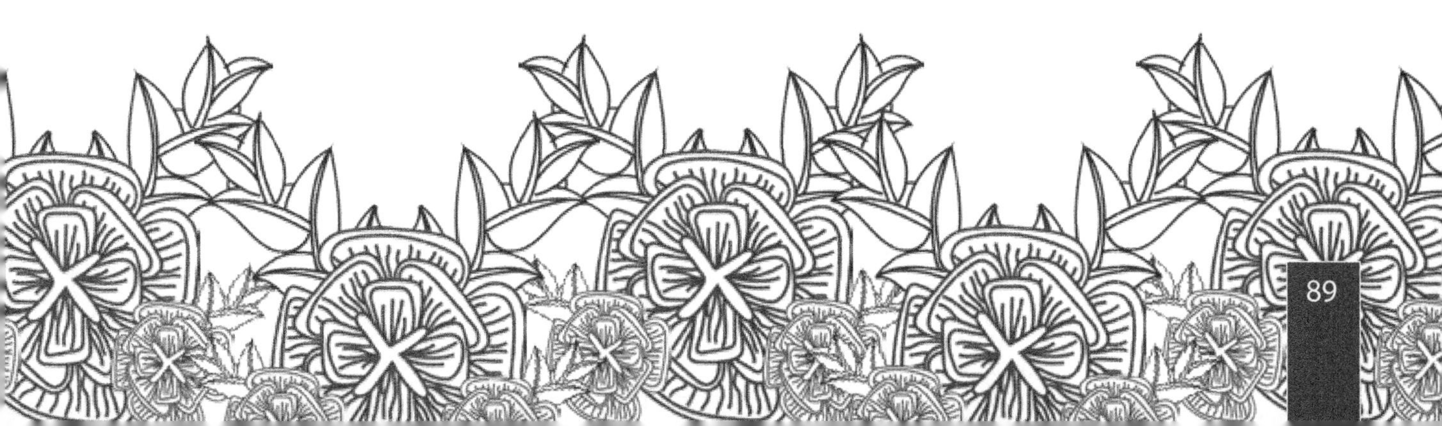

Stamen

Barbara Duel Johnson CZT

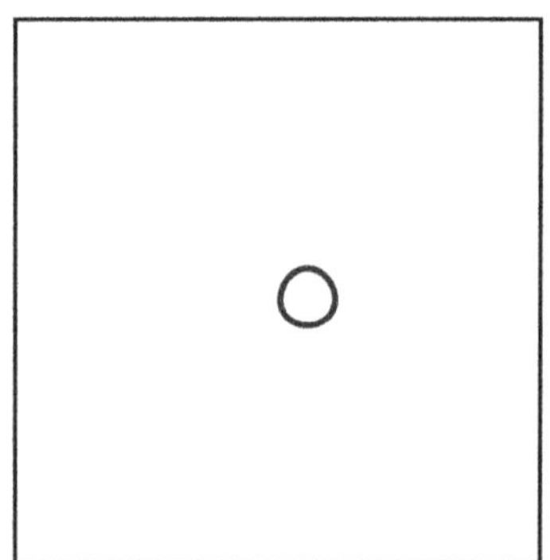
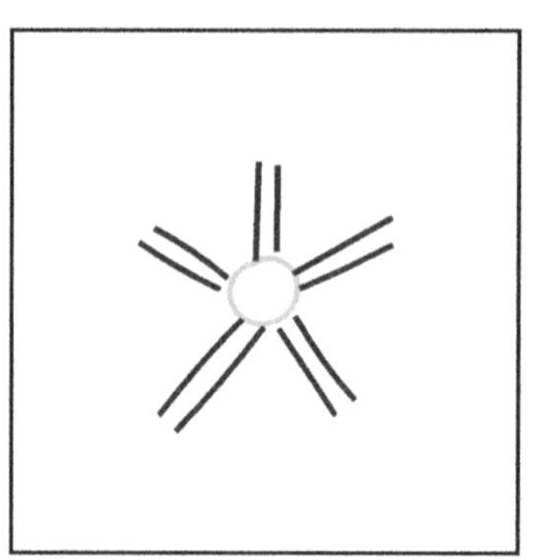
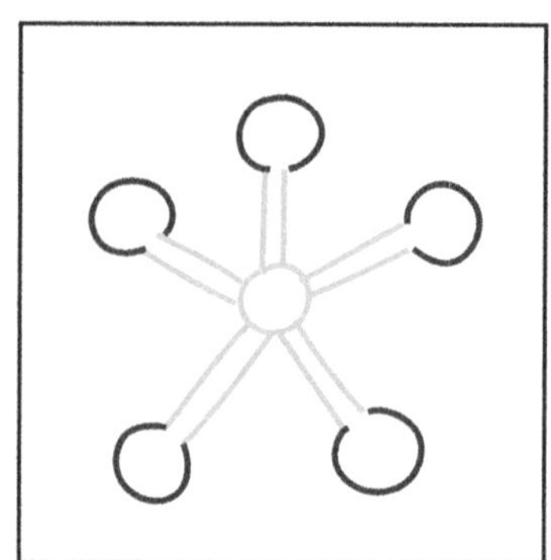
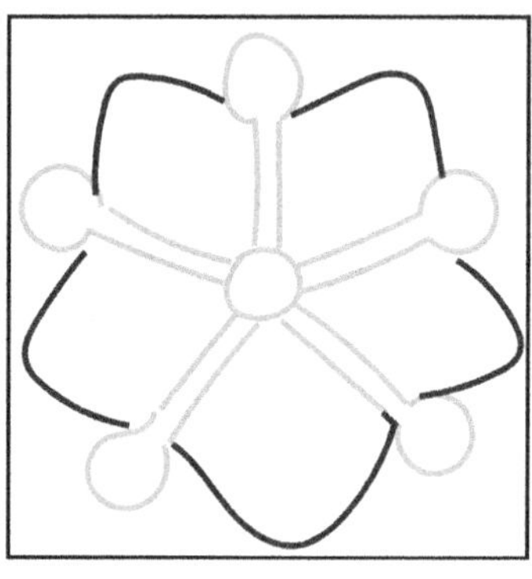
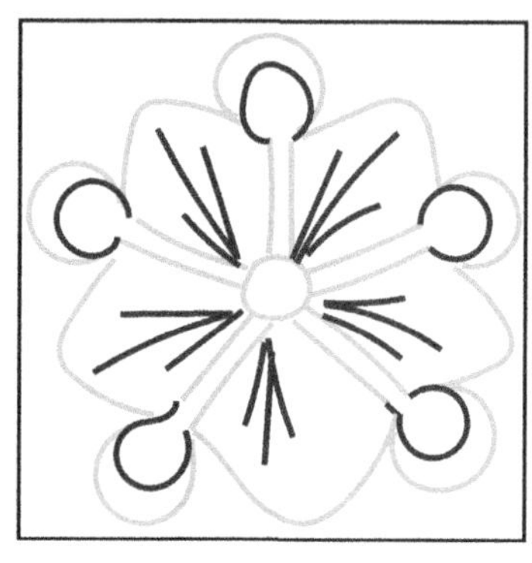

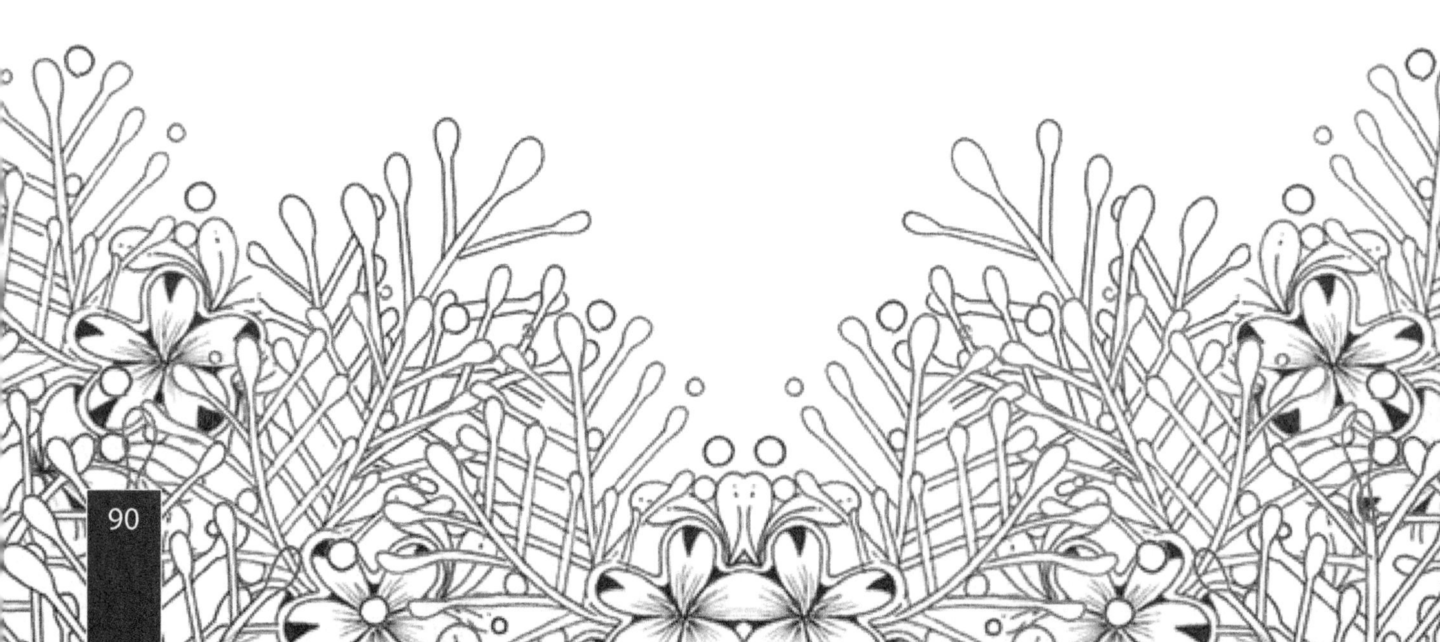

Wyfore

Official Zentangle Pattern

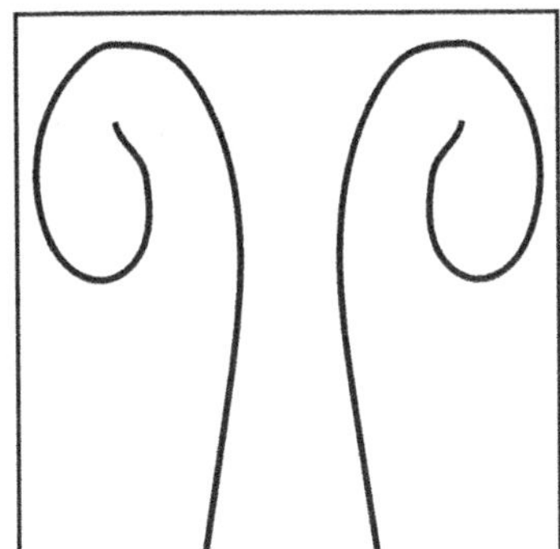
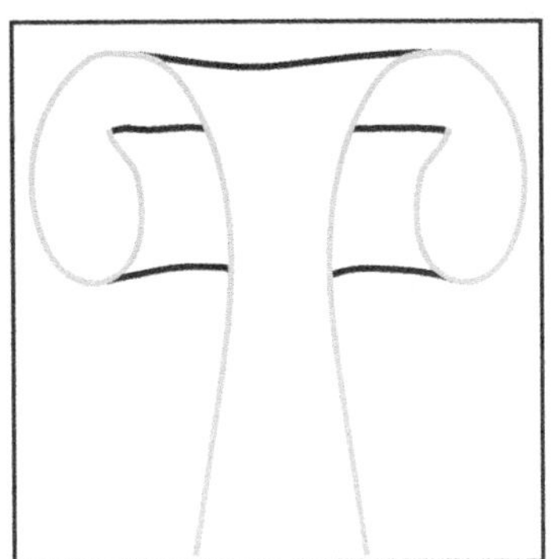
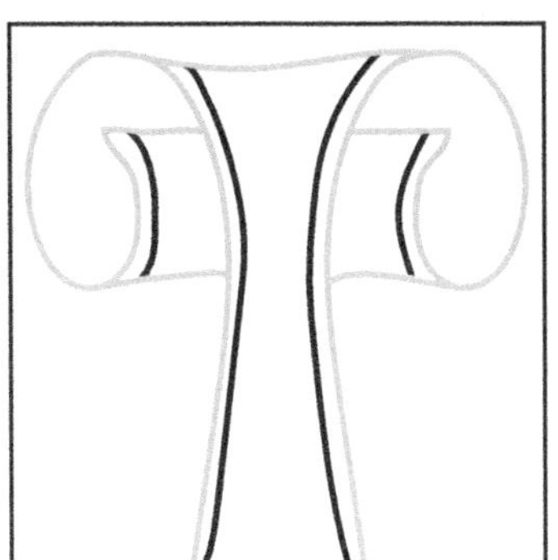
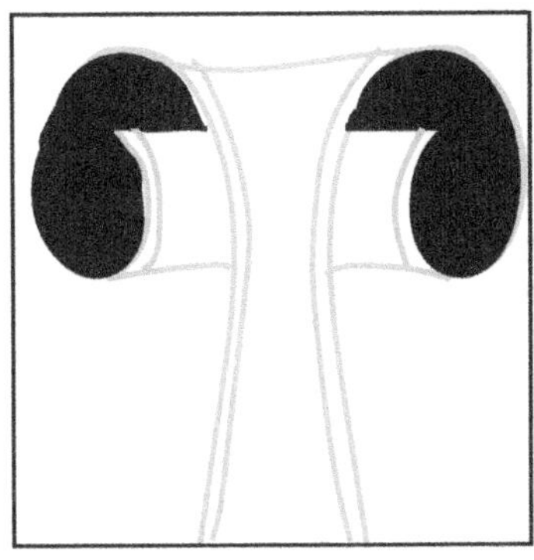
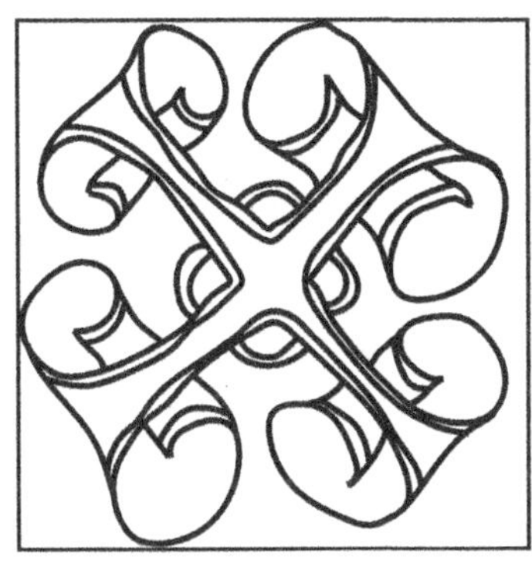

Tapijoka

Suzanne Crisafi CZT

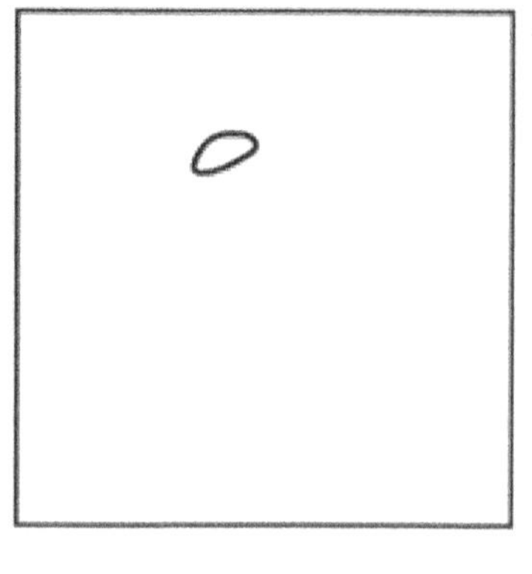
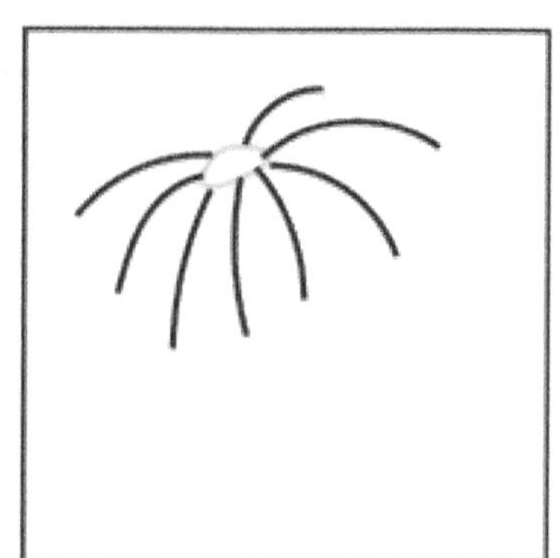
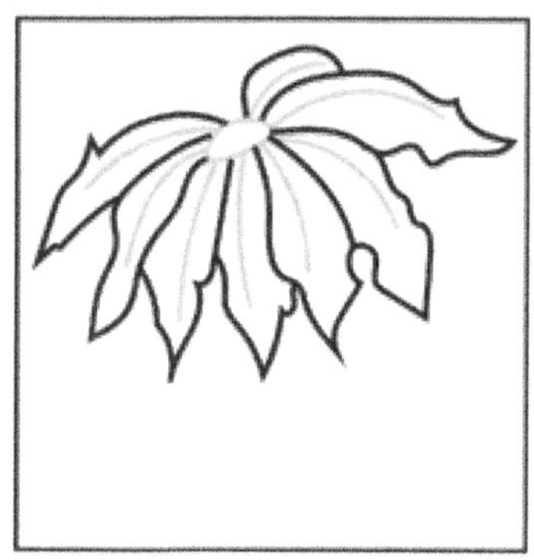
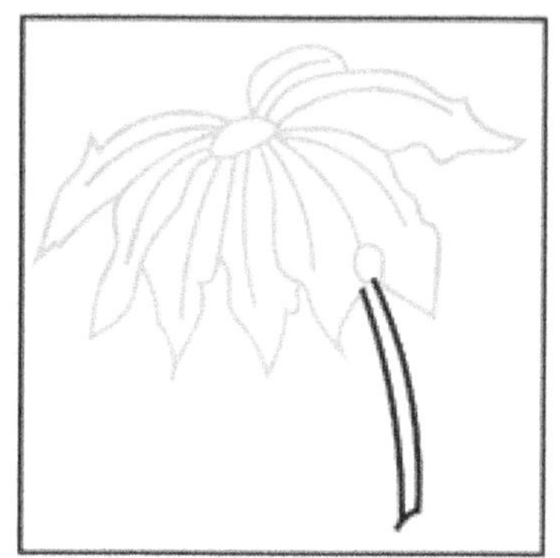

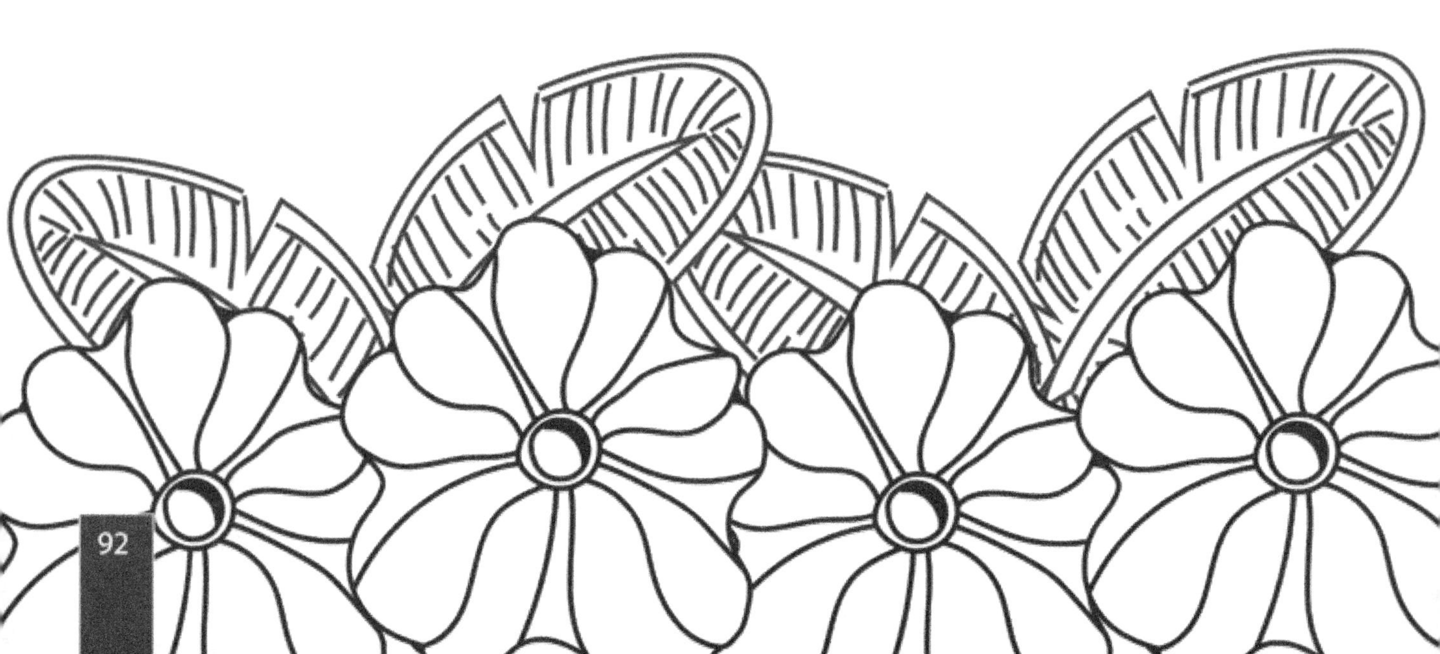

Ravel

Official Zentangle Pattern

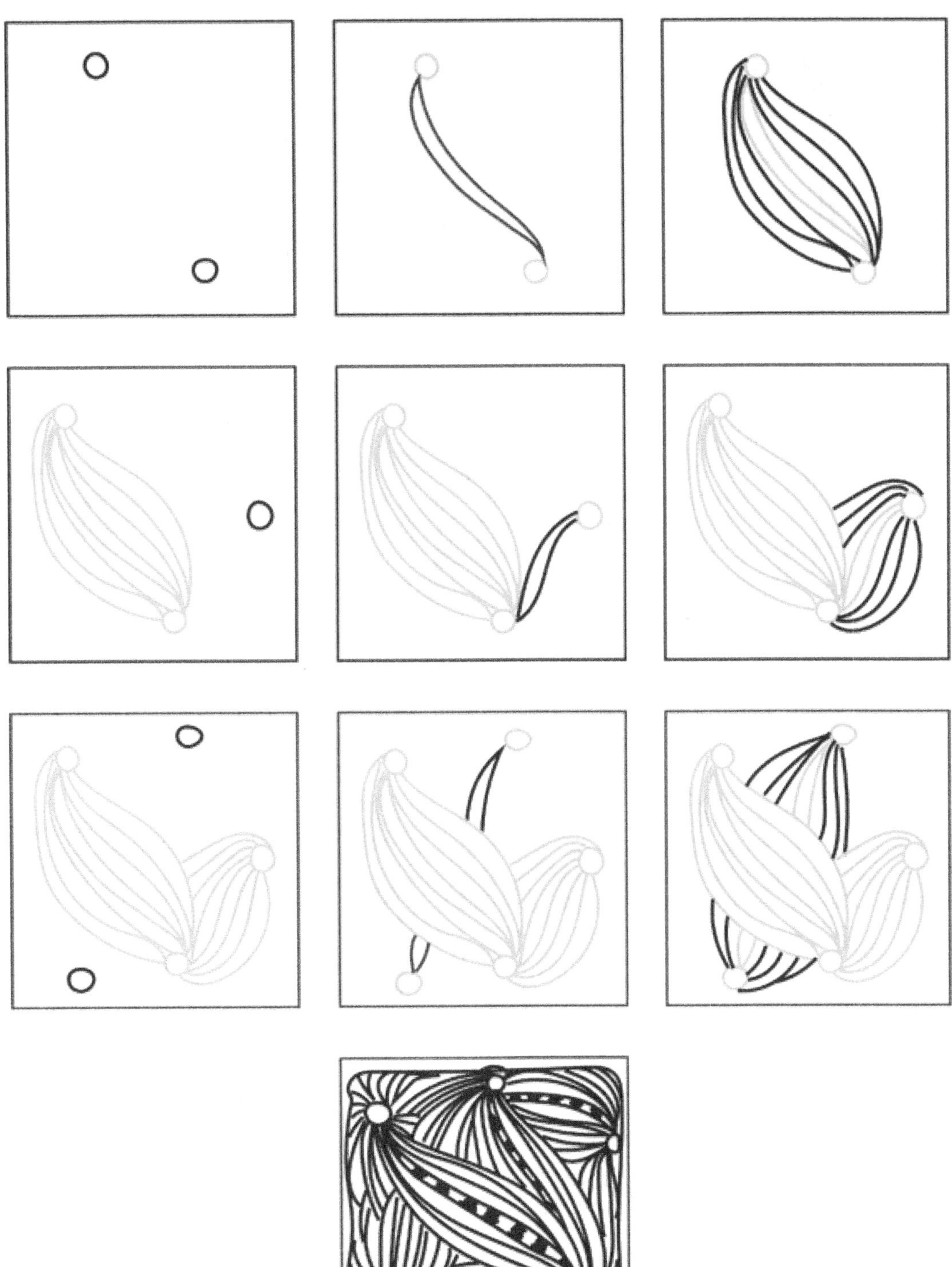

Schoggi

Annet Rumpler CZT

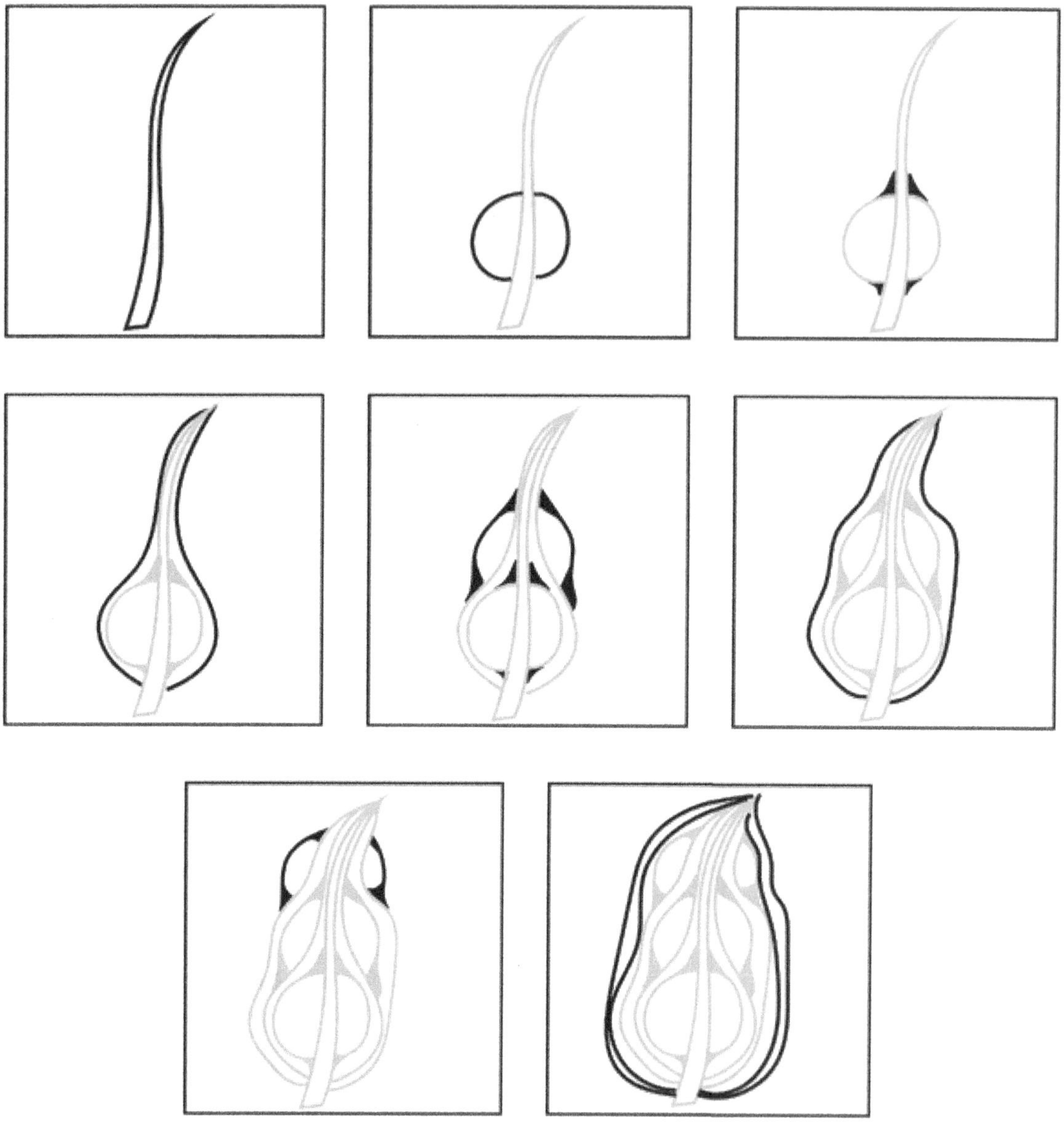

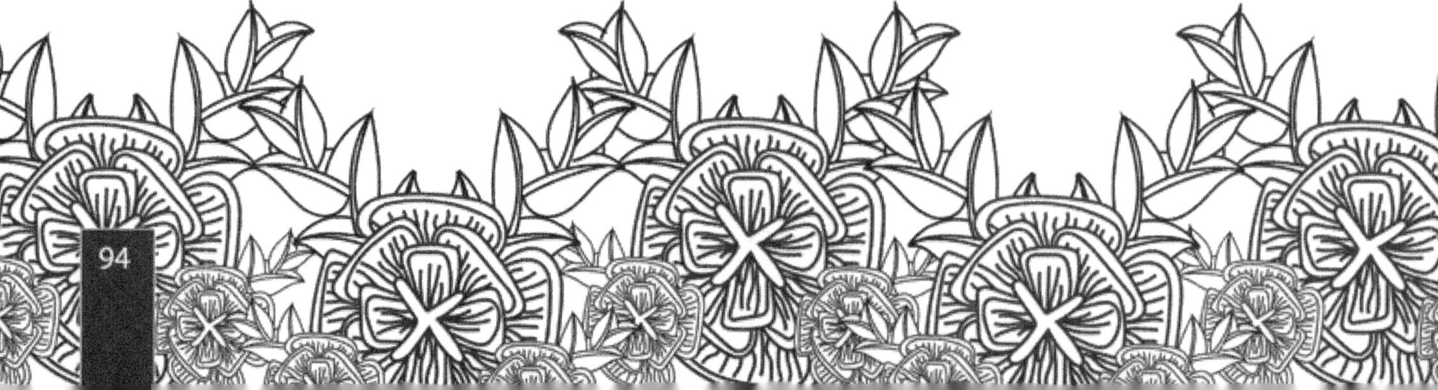

Tifnia

Carla Jooren CZT

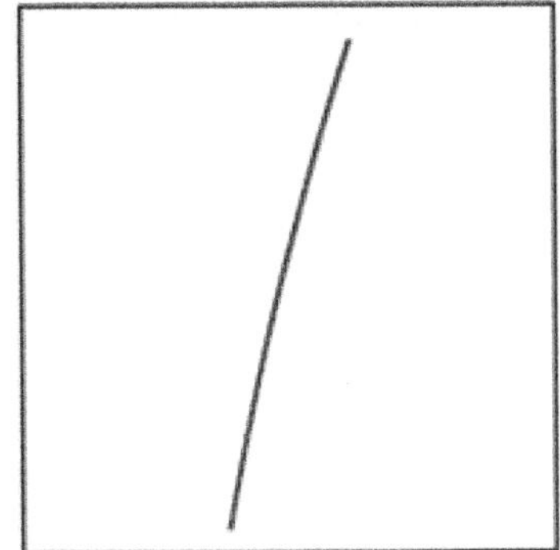
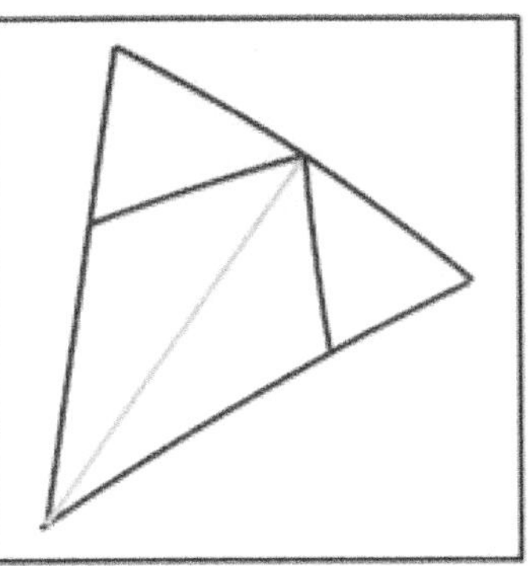
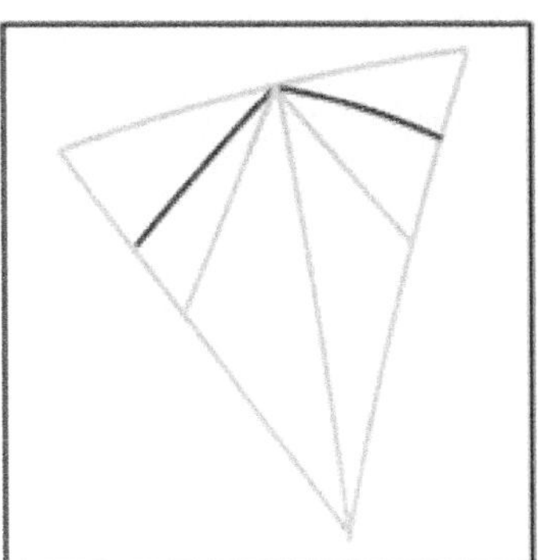
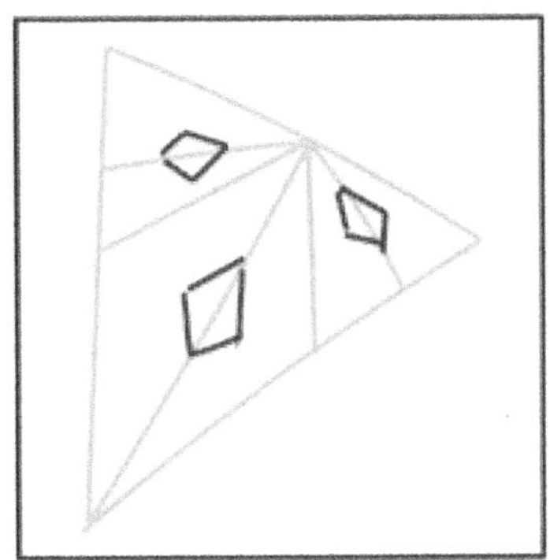
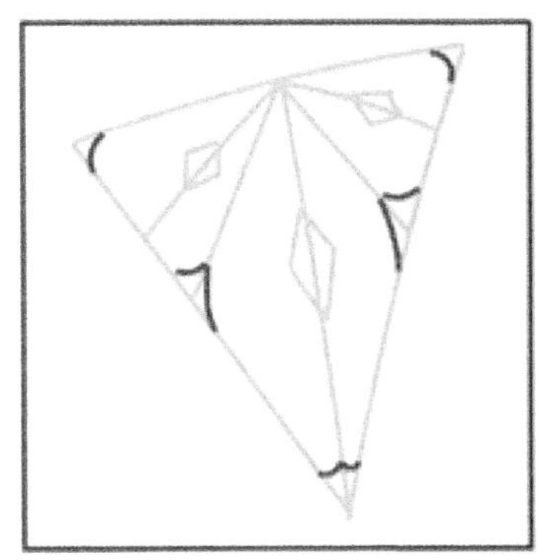

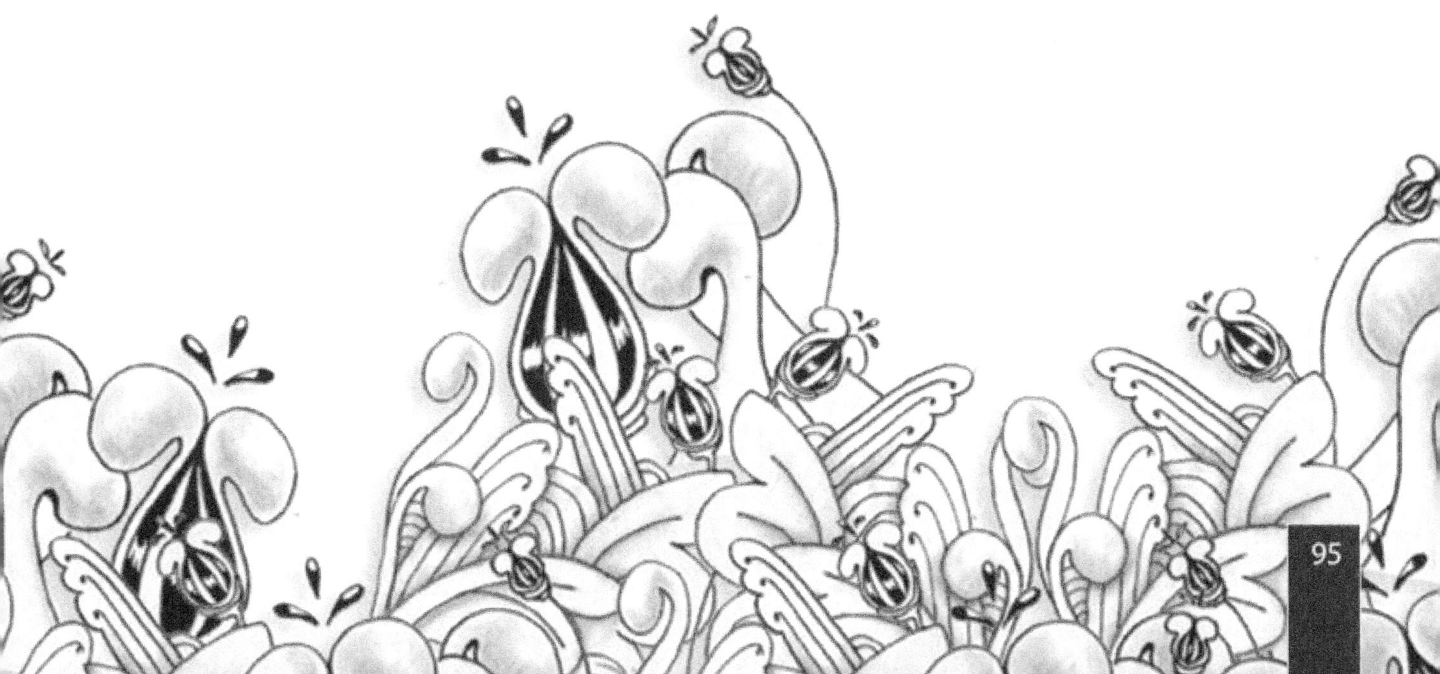

Sinko

Simone Menzel CZT

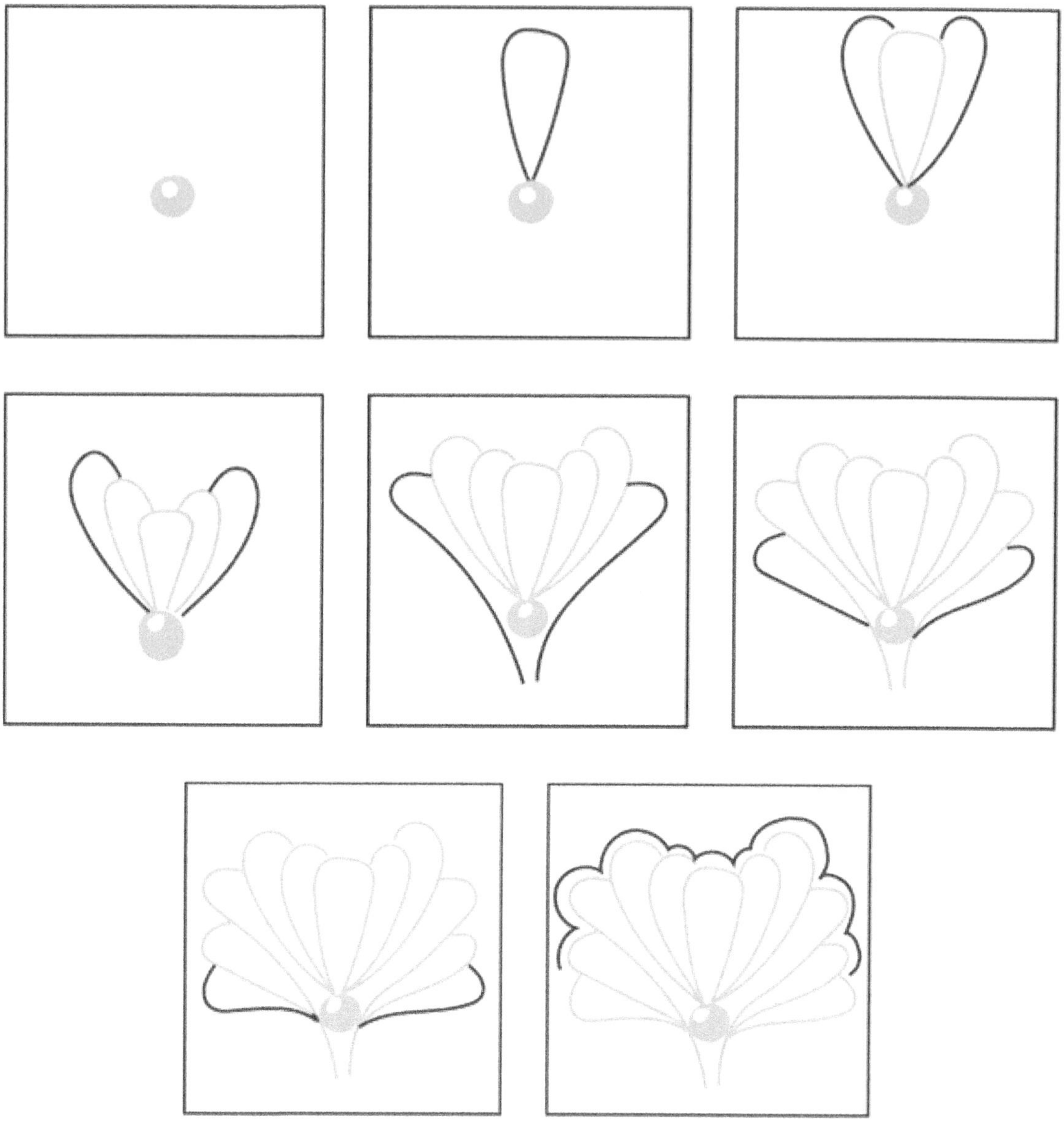

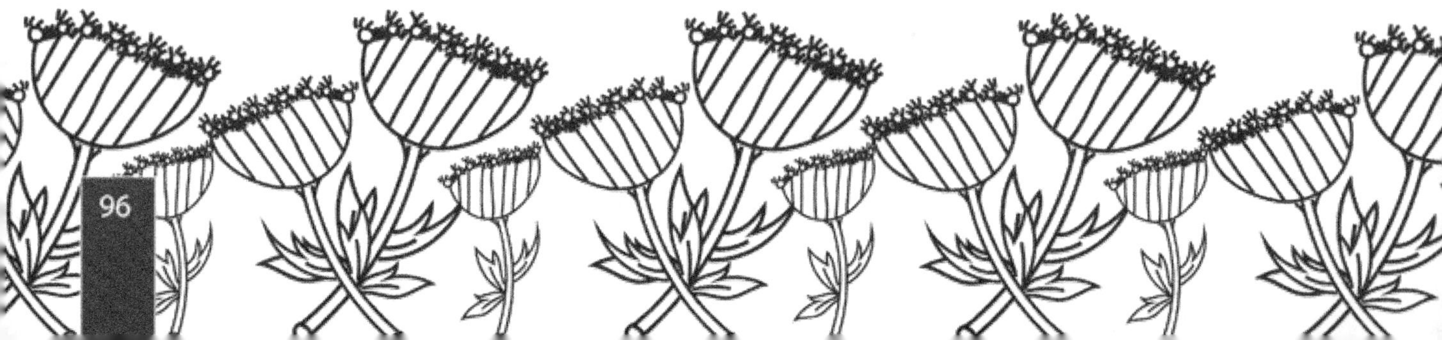

Sextant

Suzanne Crisafi CZT

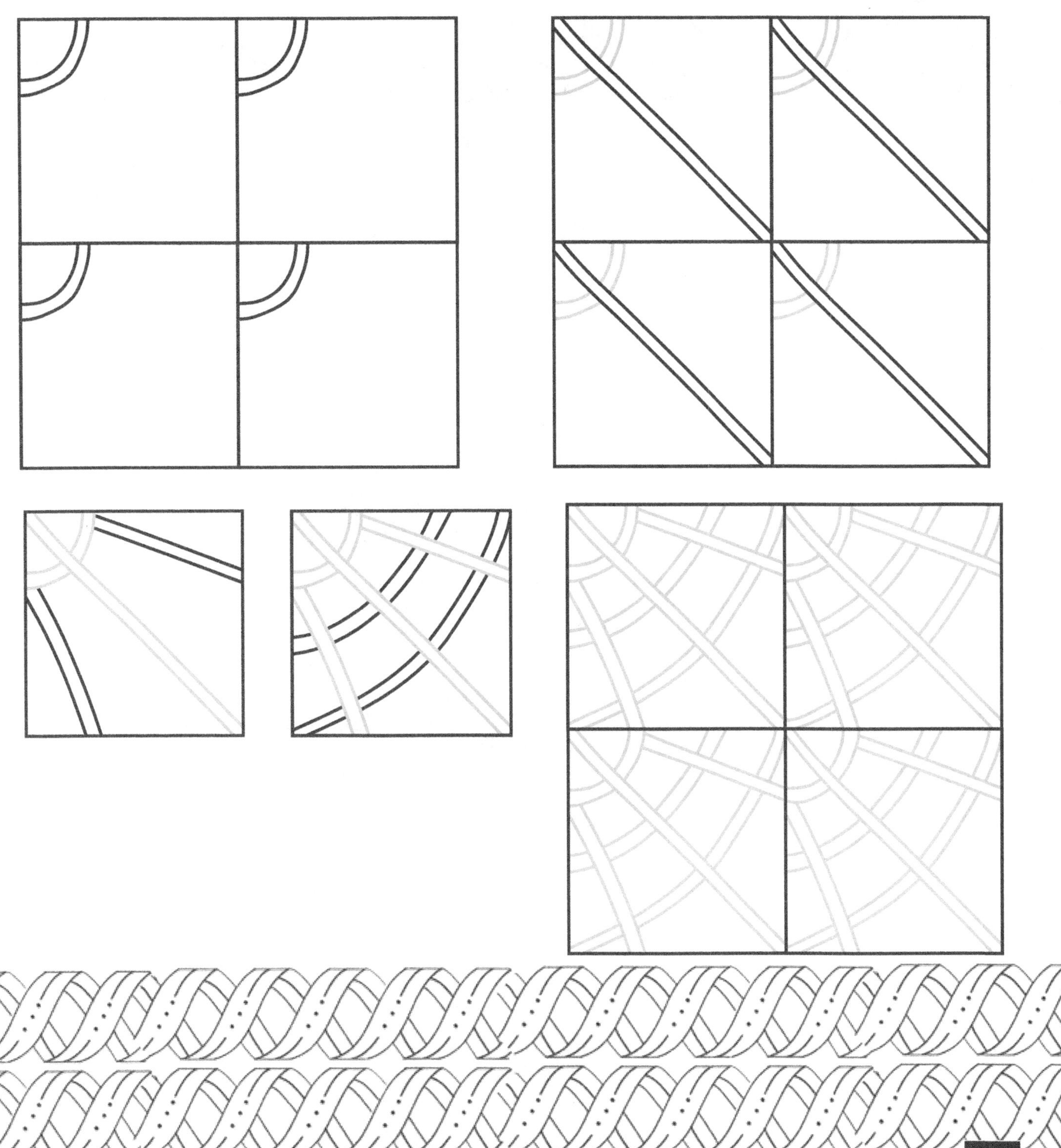

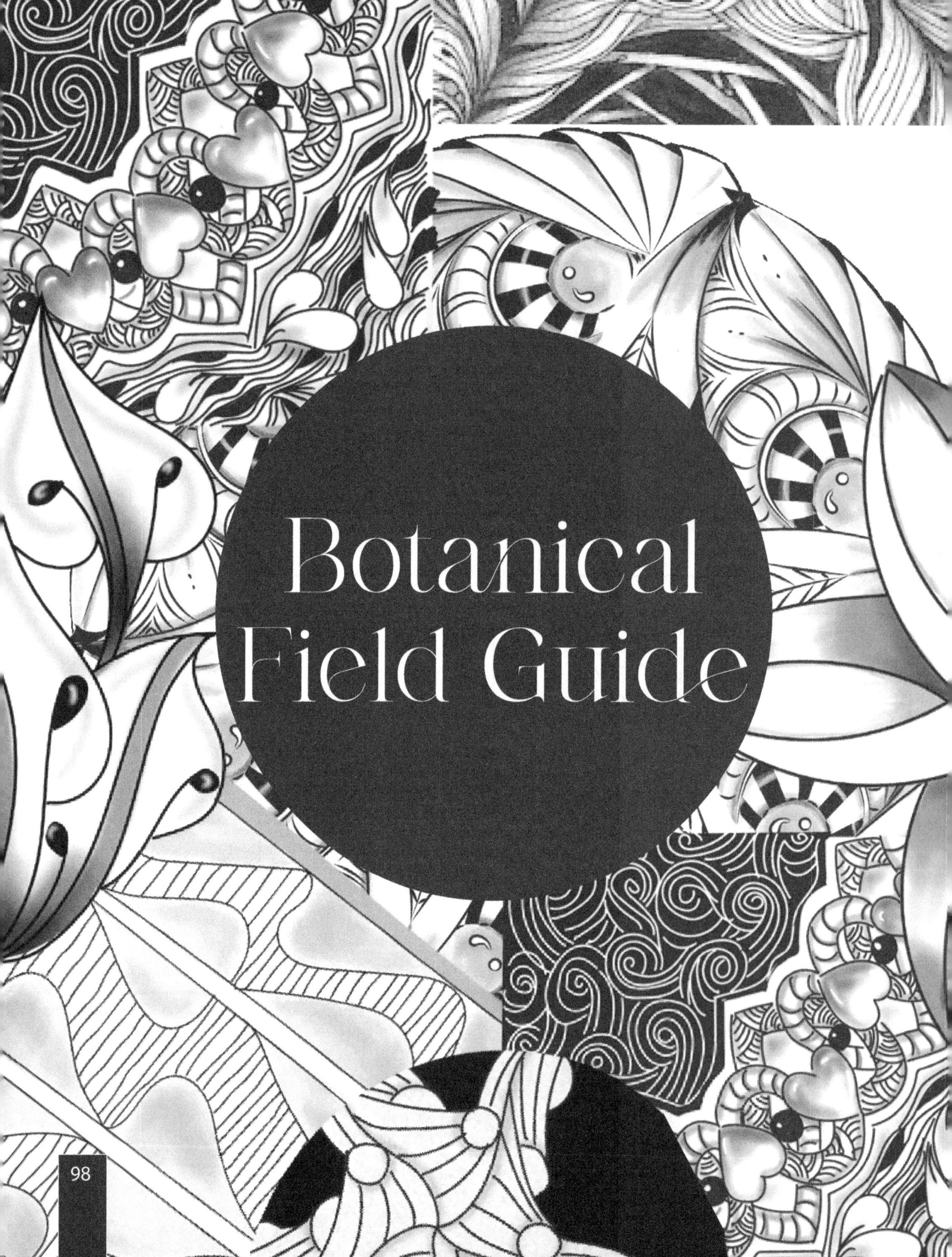

Botanical Field Guide

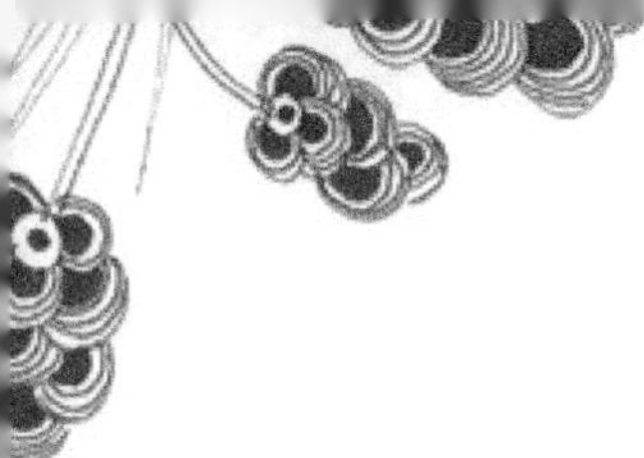

Botanical Tangles Field Guide

I wanted to do something a little different for the project section of this book and I was greatly inspired by the recently released ProjectPack 21 from Zentangle Inc.

I've created some field guide templates that you can fill with tangle inspired botanicals or botanical tangles. The difference between the two is as follows:

1. Tangle Inspired Botanicals are botanical drawings created from tangles that are not neccessarily organic. For example Crescent Moon or Darkbusters.

2. Botanical Tangles are already organic or flower themed and can be turned into nature studies easily.

I've created a free download for you that includes the cover for the guide and inside pages. In the coming pages I am also sharing some of the pages of my own field guide to inspire you.

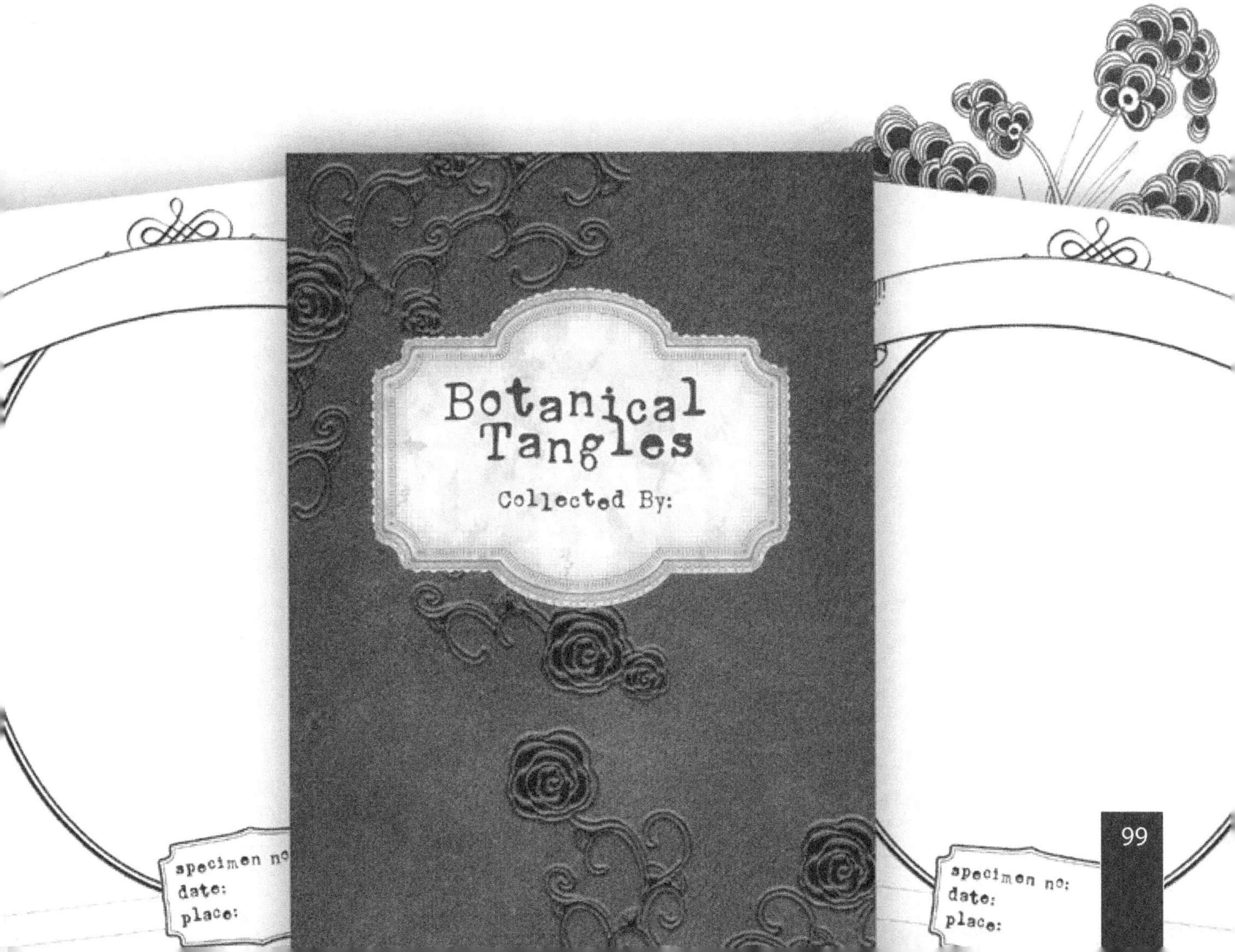

I've also created a video for you incase you want to bind your field guide the way I did.

All the information for the downloads and video can be found at: https://www.mzcreates.com/botanicalfieldguide.

I can't wait to see the pages of your field guide. Do tag me at @mzcreates to share your creations.

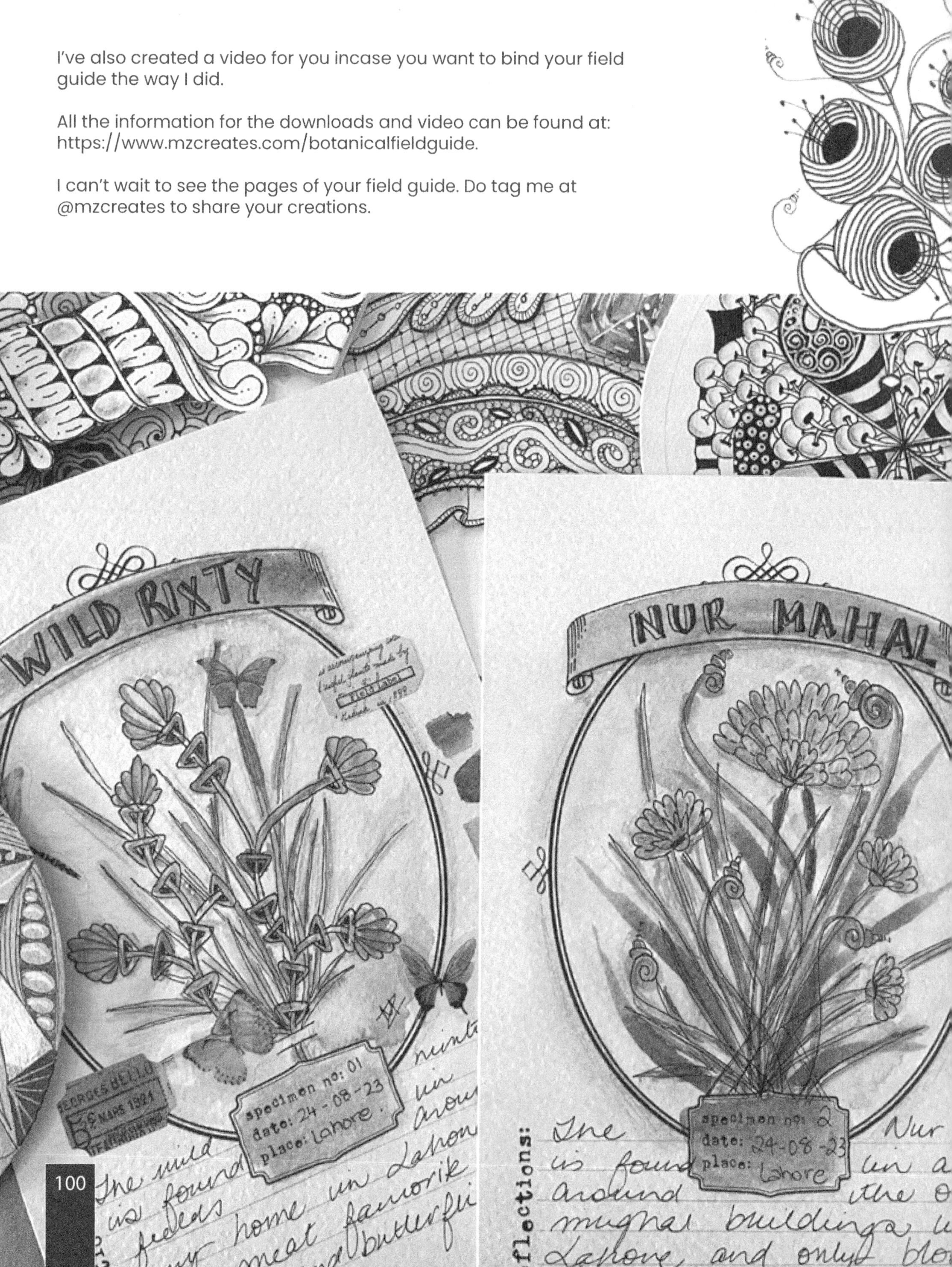

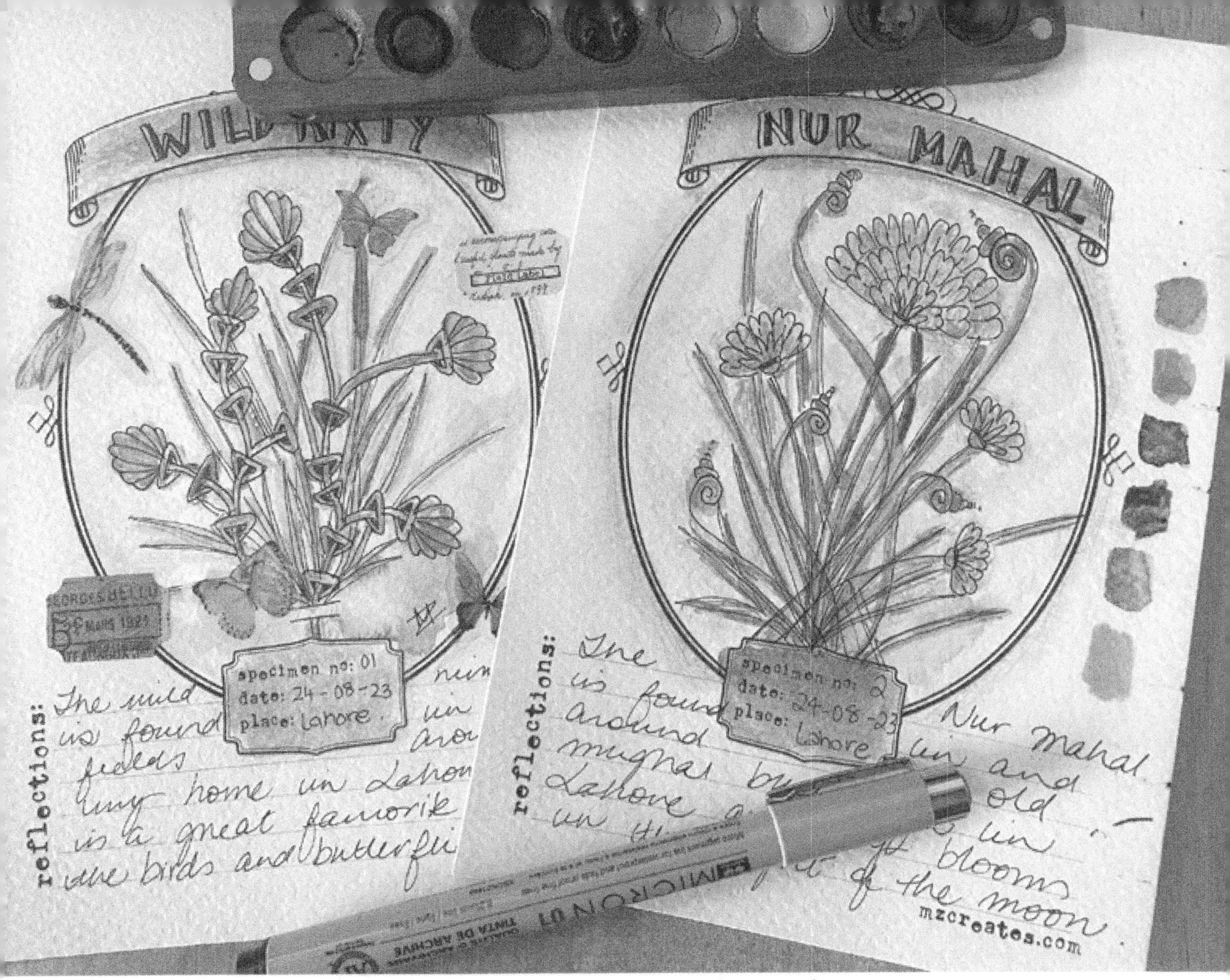

In the image above you can see that I used Rixty to create an image of an imaginary botanical called Wild Rixty. The page on the right features a new tangle I will release soon called Noor Mahal.

In this example I used watercolors to add some interest to my pages. I also added some stickers and journalling to give these fictional botanicals a history.

I have created videos for the process I followed to create the two pages above and you can find them on my YouTube channel as well.

When possible I do try to add some videos and downloads to my books so that they are more interactive and interesting for you.

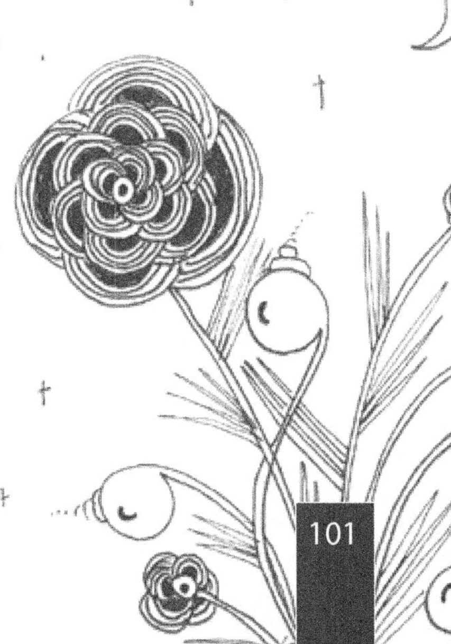

Crescent Rose and Pixie Bells have been created using Cresecent Moon as the base tangle and Dark Busters was created using the tangle of the same name.

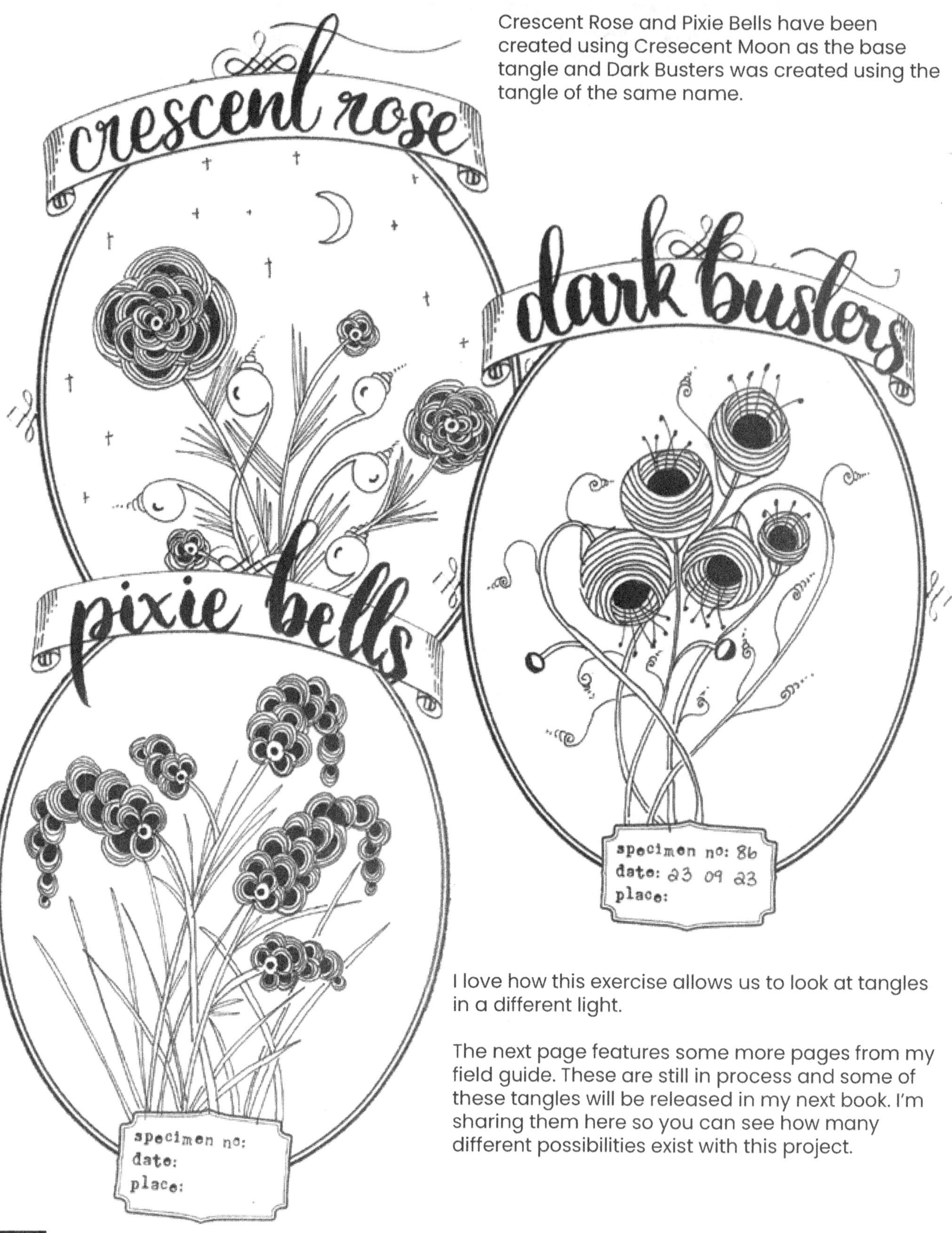

I love how this exercise allows us to look at tangles in a different light.

The next page features some more pages from my field guide. These are still in process and some of these tangles will be released in my next book. I'm sharing them here so you can see how many different possibilities exist with this project.

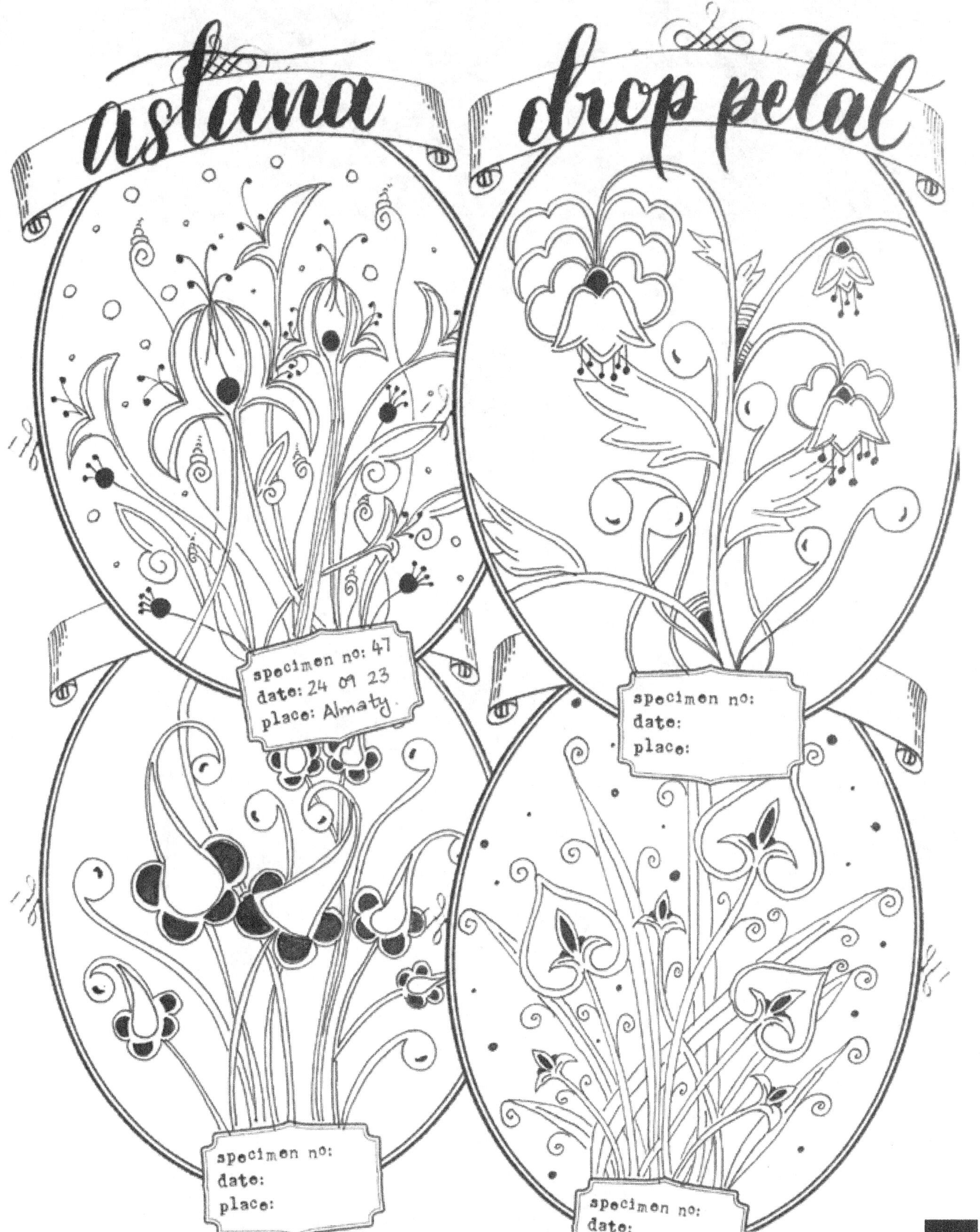
astana
drop petal
specimen no: 47
date: 24 09 23
place: Almaty.
specimen no:
date:
place:
specimen no:
date:
place:
specimen no:
date:

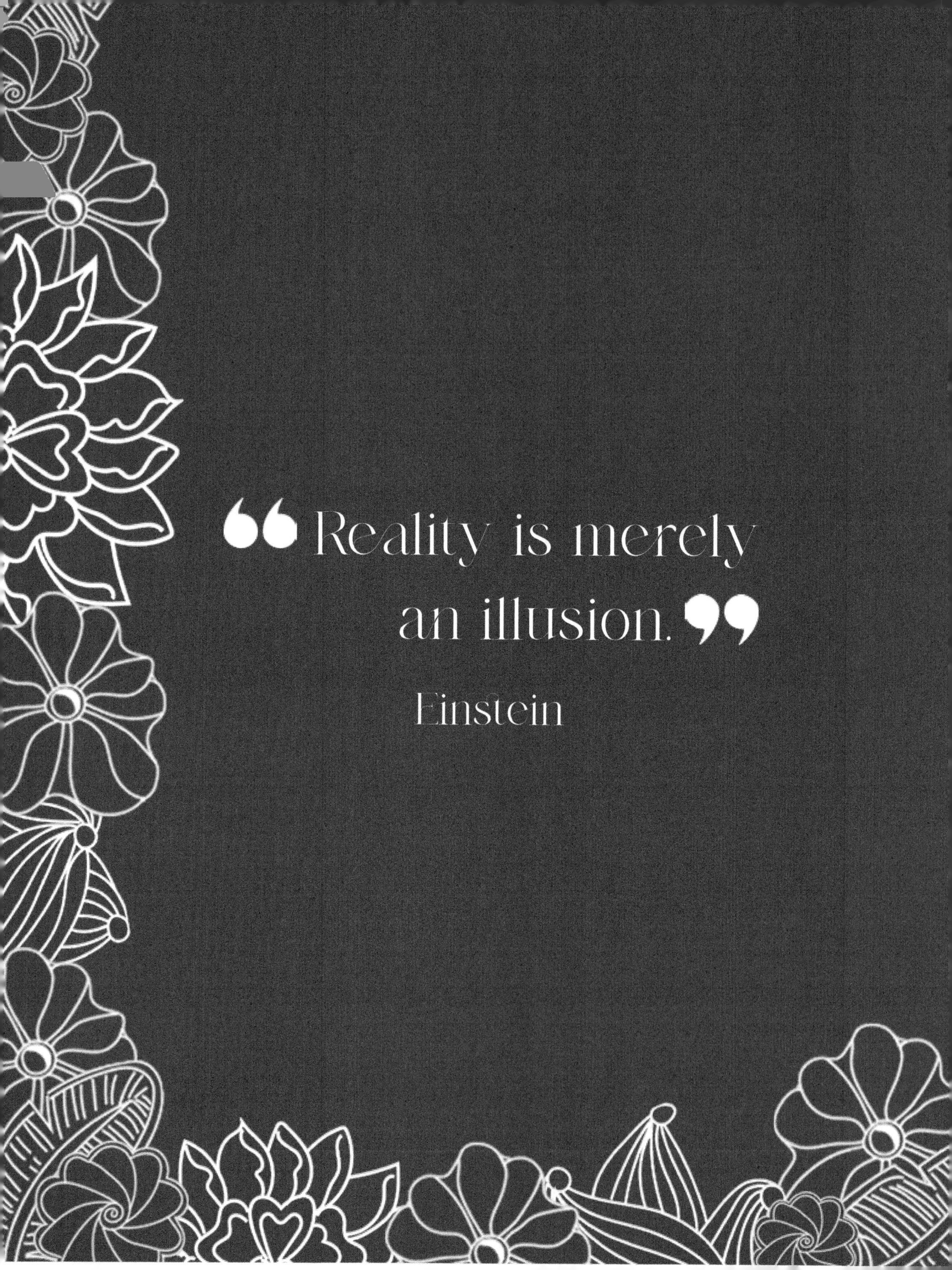
“Reality is merely an illusion.”
Einstein

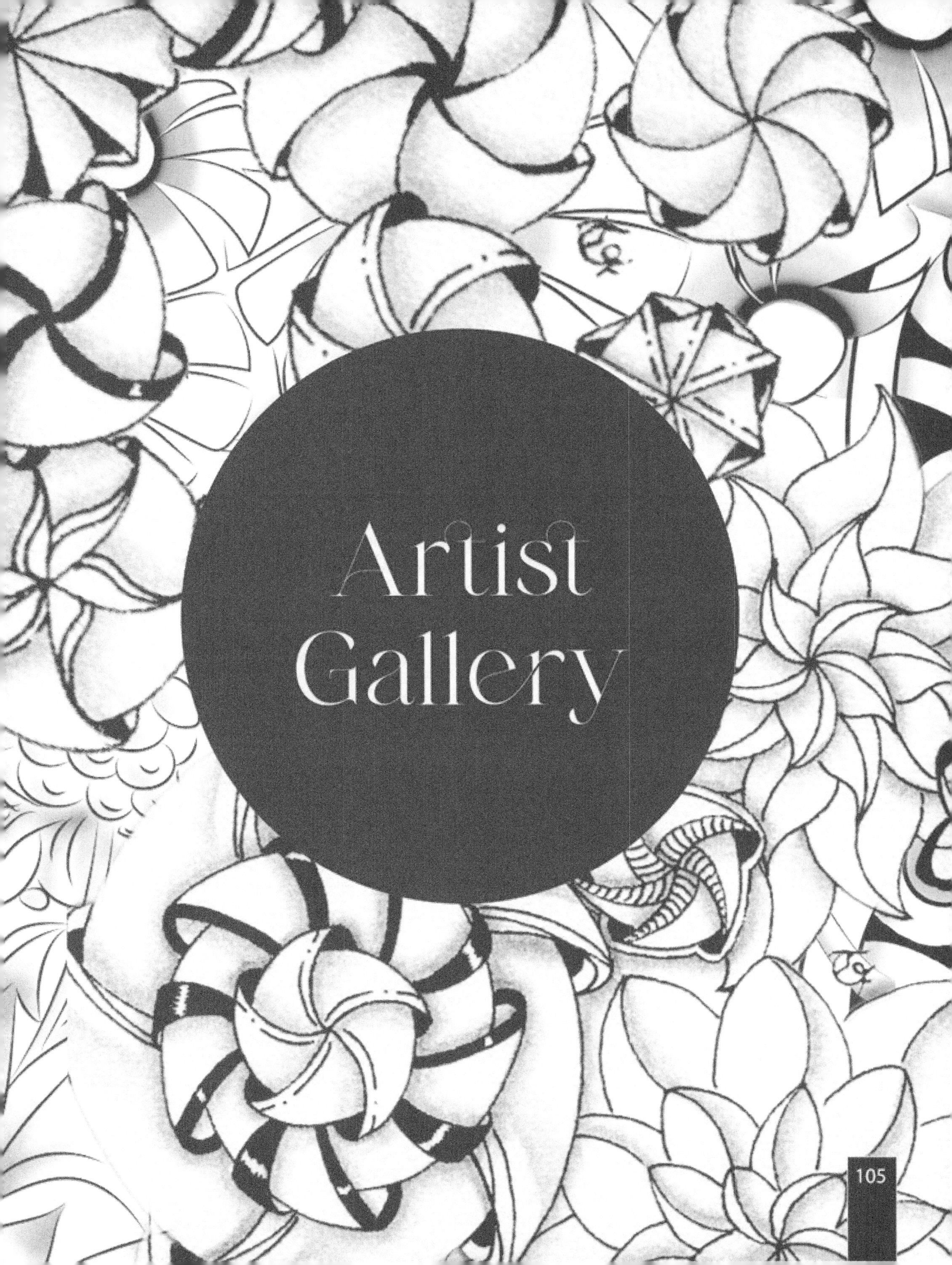

Artist Gallery

Theresa Fessler CZT

I have loved Theresa's work for quite some time now and was very excited when she gave permisssion to include her tangles in this book. I thought it would be fun to know what drew her to tangling.

1. What drew you to Zentangle in the beginning?

I have been drawing since I could hold a pen. Unfortunately I've never been happy with the results. I was so focused on everything that needed improvement that I wasn't able to notice the things that were already quite good. Although I enjoyed the drawing process I've always been disappointed by the finished drawing. Disappointed by myself.

But when I started following the Zentangle method I noticed that suddenly I liked these tiny pieces of art I created. This was an amazing experience for me.

It felt almost magical and I knew I had found something that brightens up my life.

2. Do you prefer the classic black and white or colored tangling?

I prefere the classic black and white, because color adds so much complexity. When I have time to tangle, I don't want to decide which colors to use, I just want to start tangling. But I also enjoy tangling (black and white) on a tile that has been previously dyed with watercolors.

You can find all of Theresa's tangles and her courses on her website:
https://streifenfuchs.de/tangle

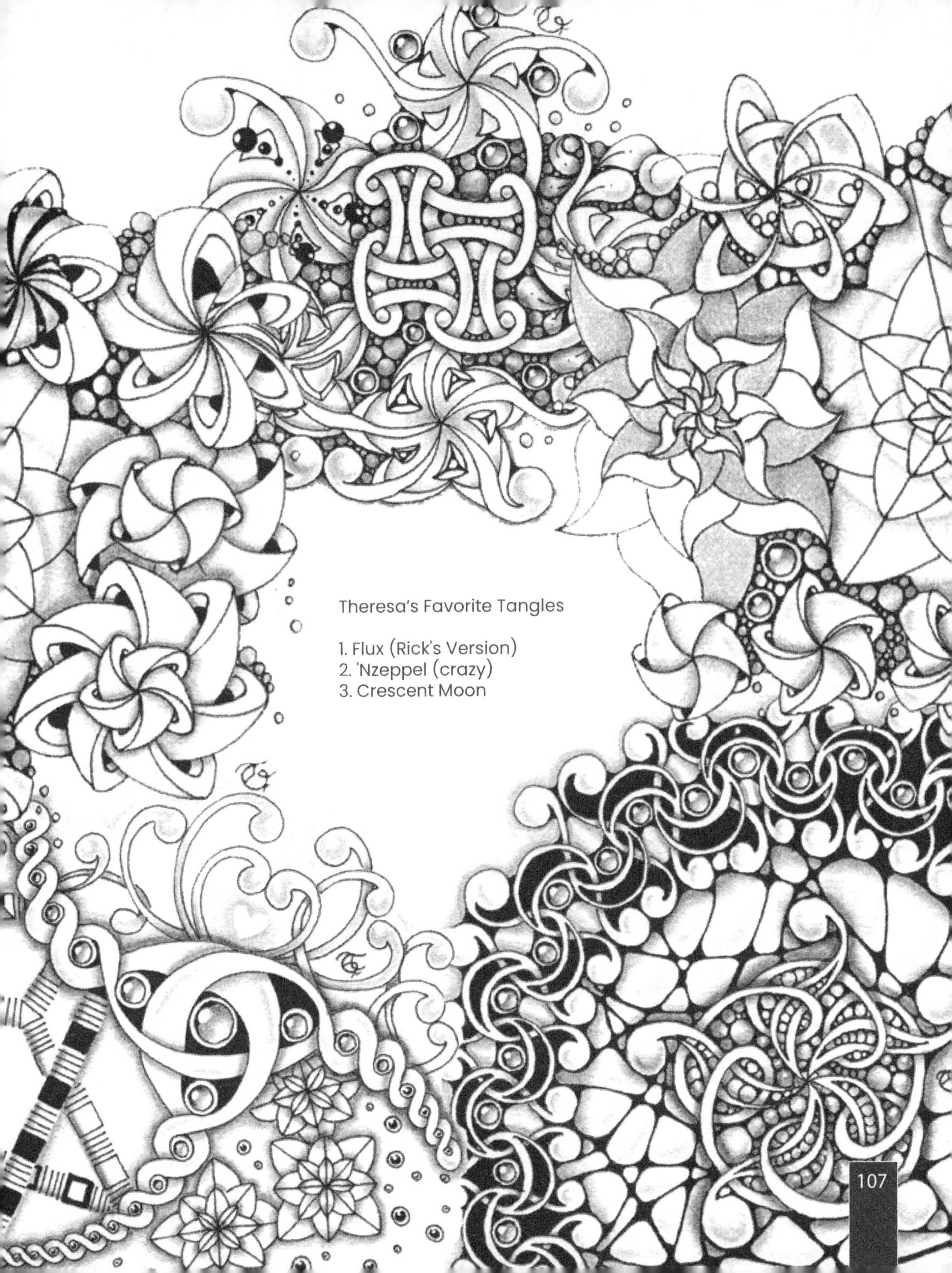

Theresa's Favorite Tangles

1. Flux (Rick's Version)
2. 'Nzeppel (crazy)
3. Crescent Moon

Miranda Gerber CZT

On these two pages you will see the art of Miranda Gerber. She is a CZT and does absoultely gorgeous work. Her organic tiles are especially beautiful! In this book you will find many tangles that Miranda has created and kindly shared with us. You can see more of Miranda's work and follow her on instagram @tanglewerk

Pick a tile from these pages and try and recreate the same composition with your own choice of tangles.

Pick a tile from these pages and try and recreate the same composition using tangles you've learnt in this book.

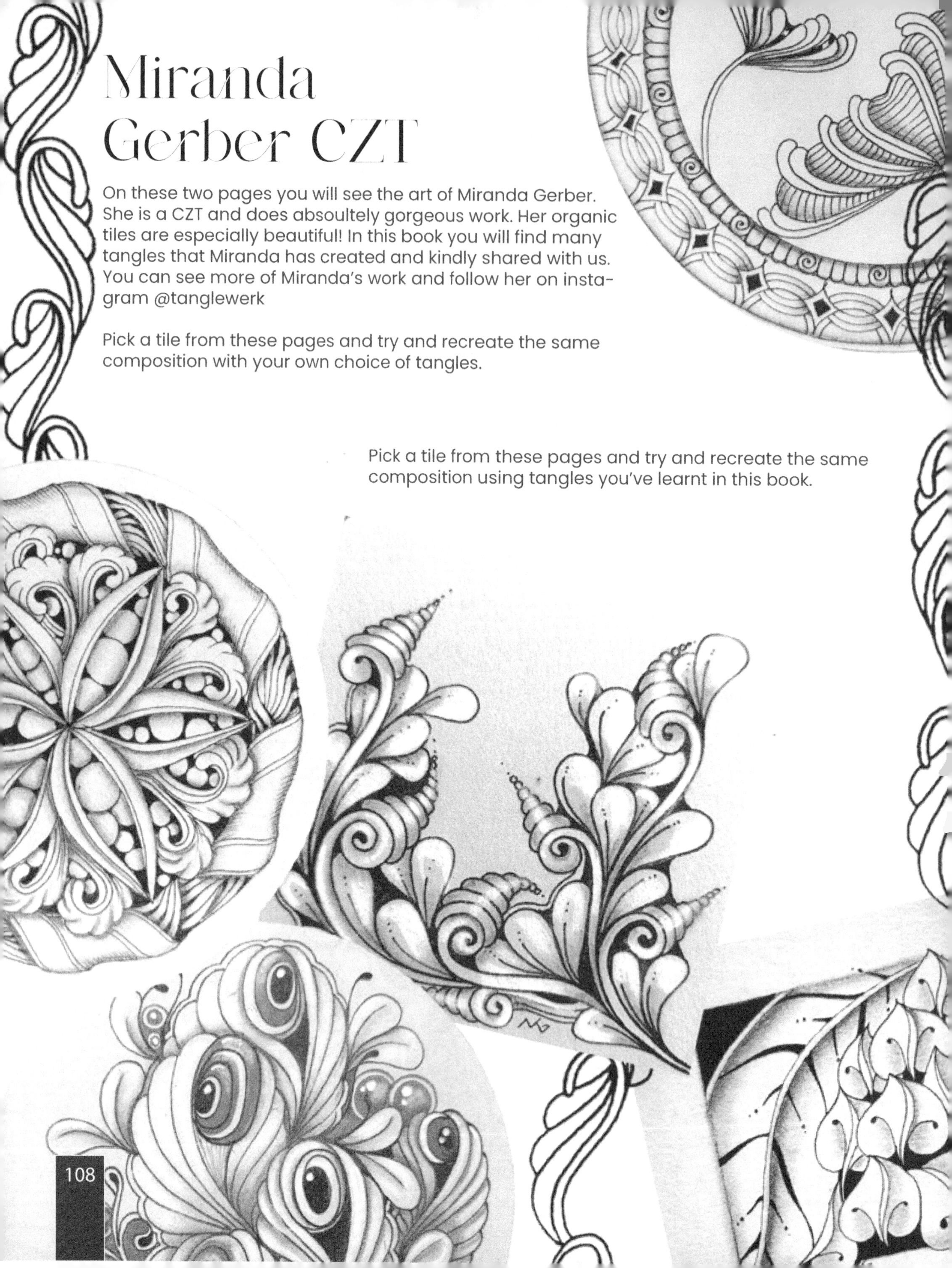

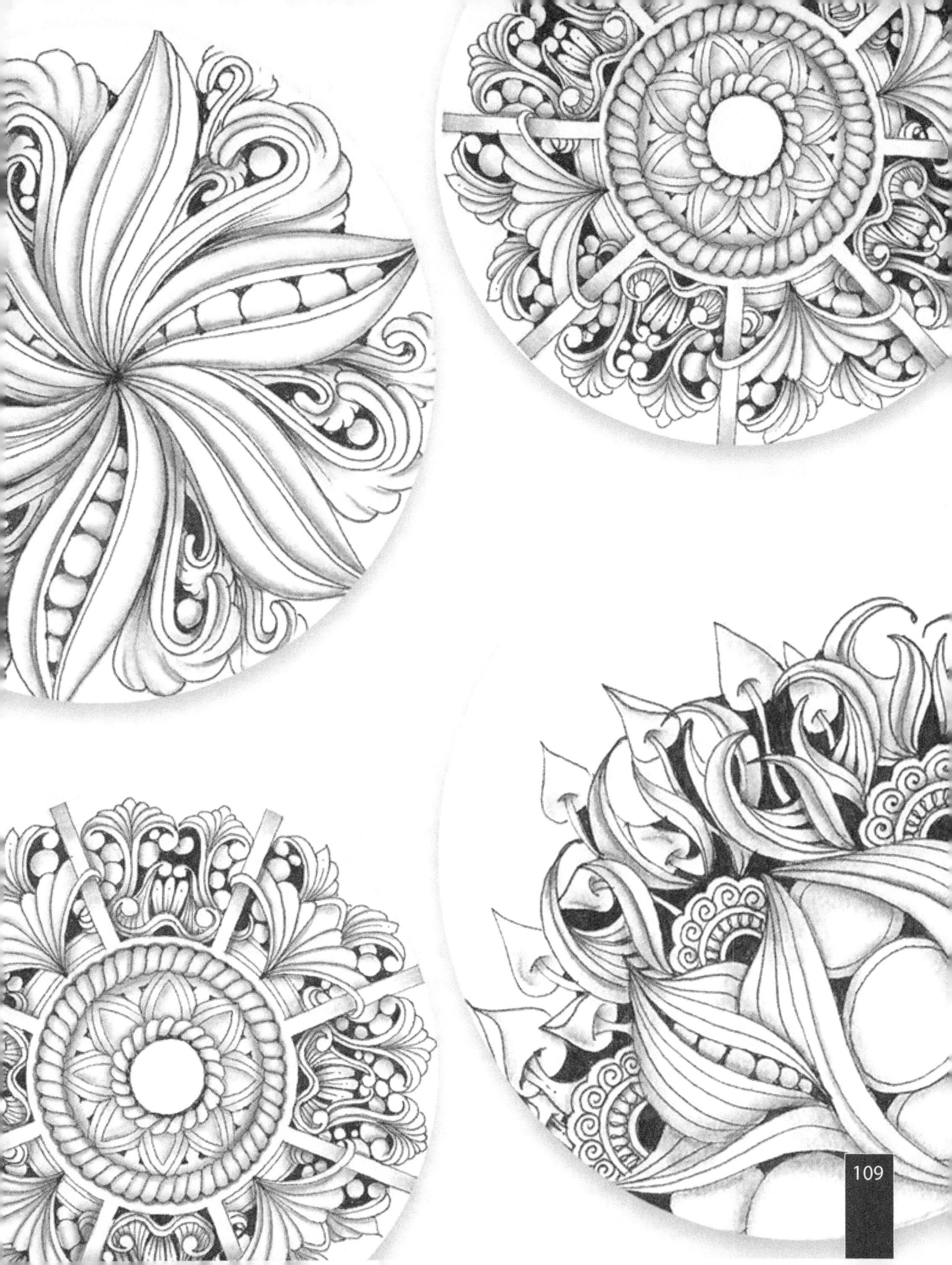

Aishwarya Darbha CZT

Aishwarya brings the mystique of the East to her art. You will see a lot of traditional Indian elements in her tiles and tangling. I love how intricate her work is and if you check out her instagram feed @tangleandinspire you will see that there is an explosion of color in her work which I love!

Aishwarya has a blog as well as classes you can take. Her tangle videos are really cool and so are her journal pages exploring other tangles and finding fun ways to create variations. You can fins some really cool images of her sketchbook on instagram.

Maybe you would like to try to expand on one of the tangles you've seen in this book? Create new versions or tangleations all your own?

tangleandinspire.com

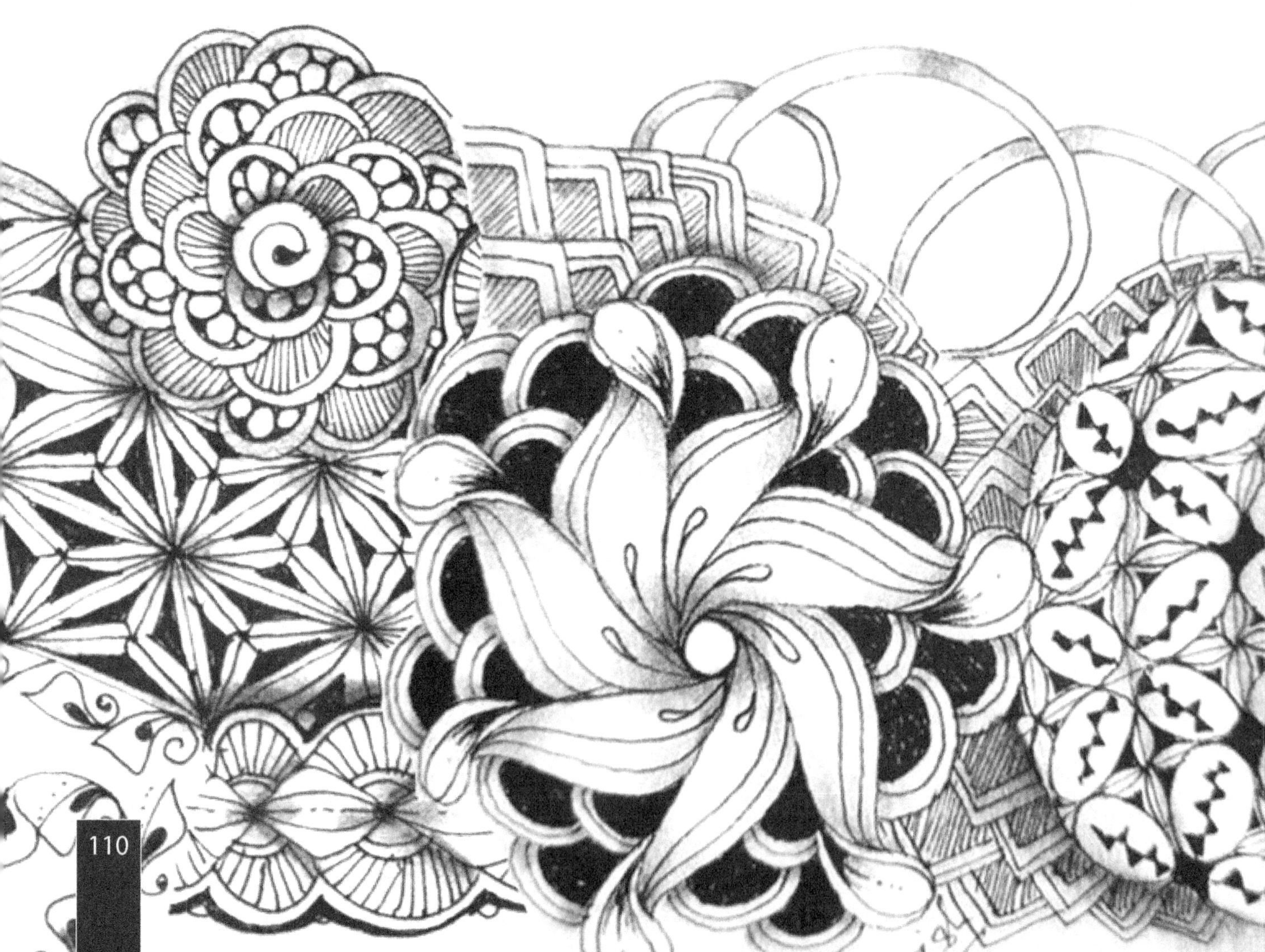

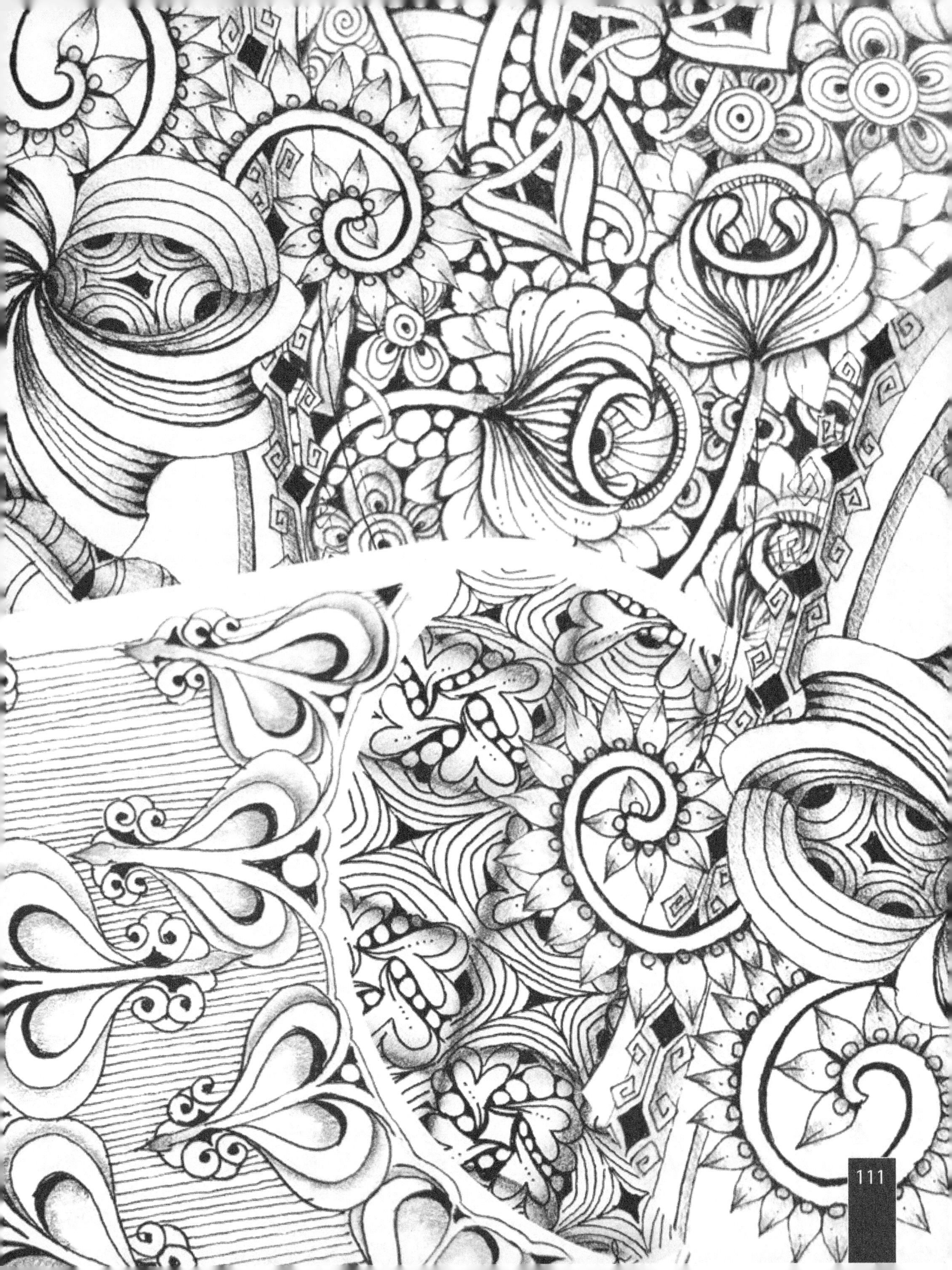

Henriette Robben CZT

Henriette's Instagram feed will blow you away. It truly will. She does such a variety of different things and has a treasure trove of ideas. Her attention to detail and her shading skills are both amazing.

By studying her finished tiles I learn a lot about how to incorporate different organic tangles in my art. I also see a lot of wonderful ways of composing a harmonious piece of art - something I struggle with at times.

I think looking at other artists' work and learning from it is one of the best things about the online art community.

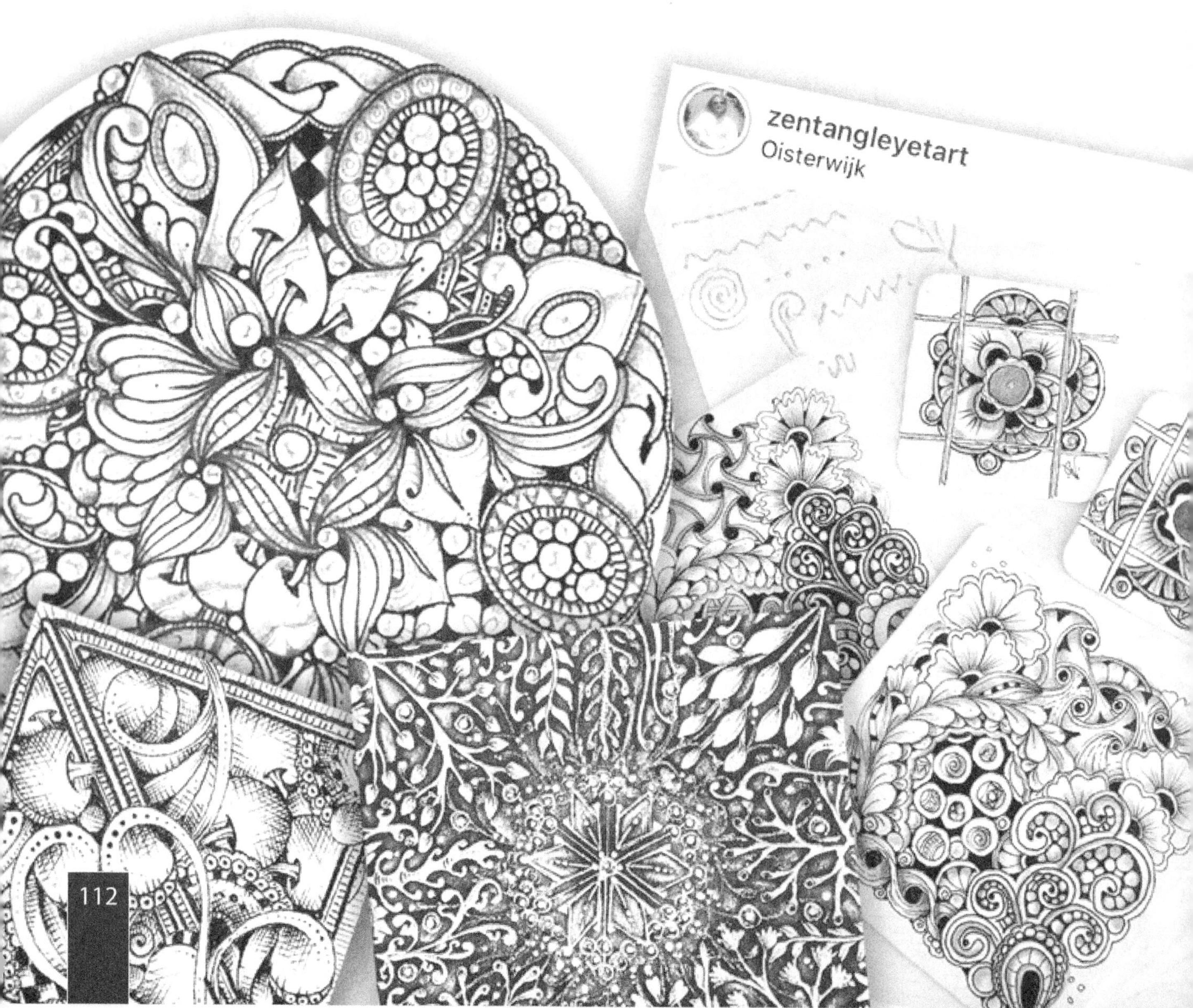

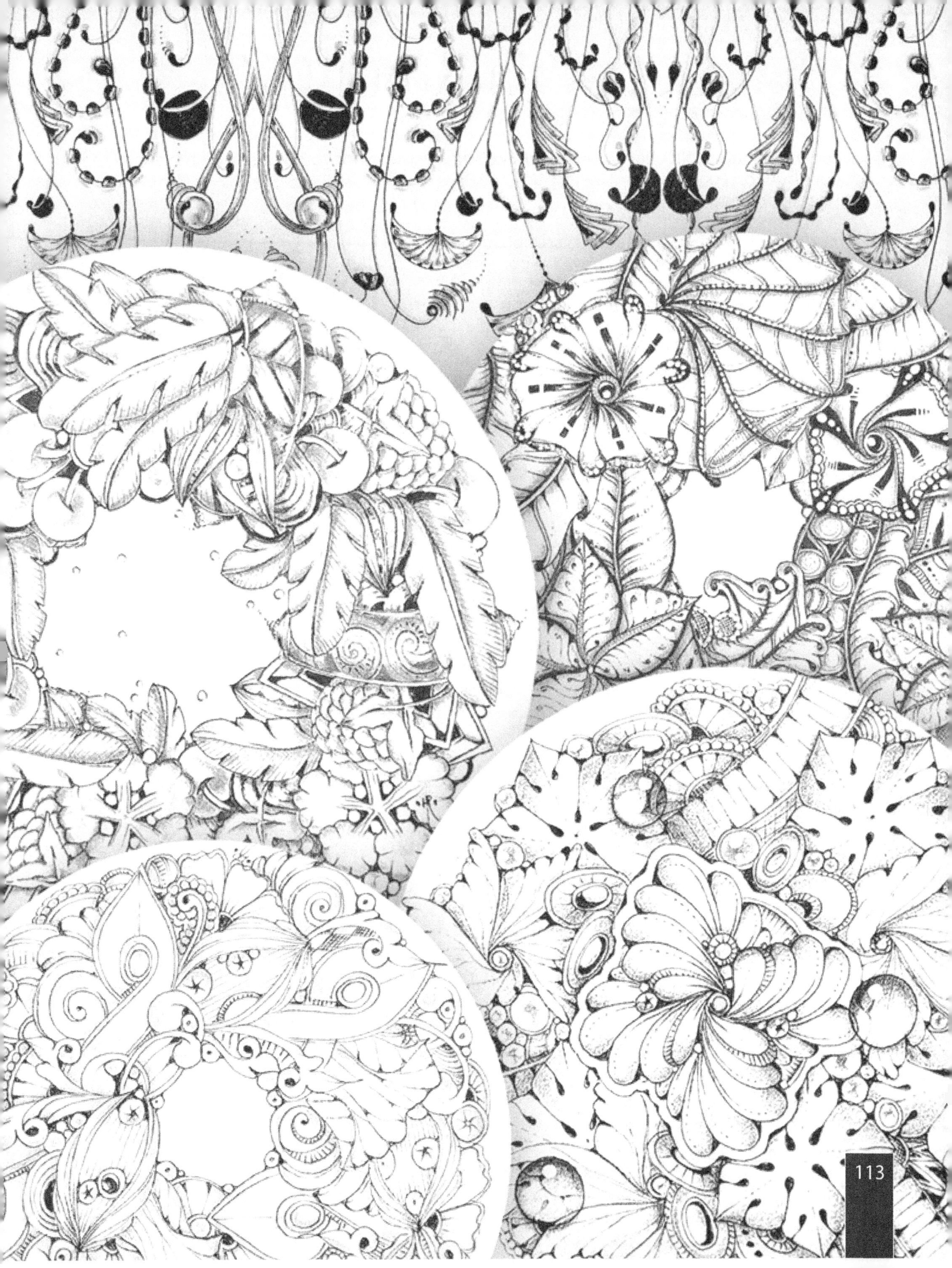

Rebecca Kuan CZT

Rebecca has a huge collection of absoulutely stunning work that you can see on her social media channels, both on Facebook and Instagram @rebeccasecretbox.

The images on these two pages are a sample of her work. Look at these tiles and note how the composition is so pleasing to the eye. Not every inch of the tiles are covered in tangles. Rebecca leaves some white space and also adds little bit of black for contrast and drama. I really love the finished look.

Which tile is your favorite?

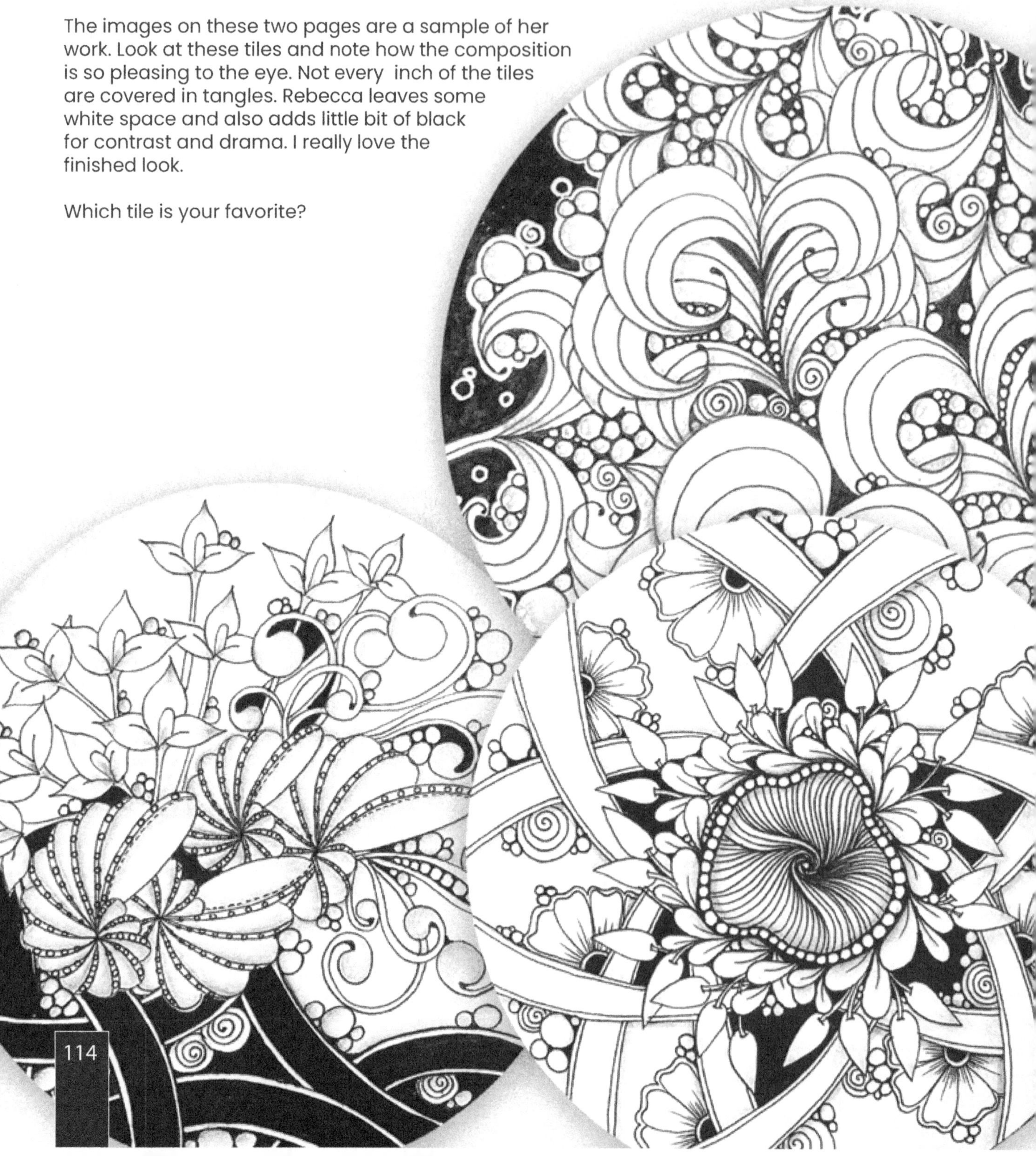

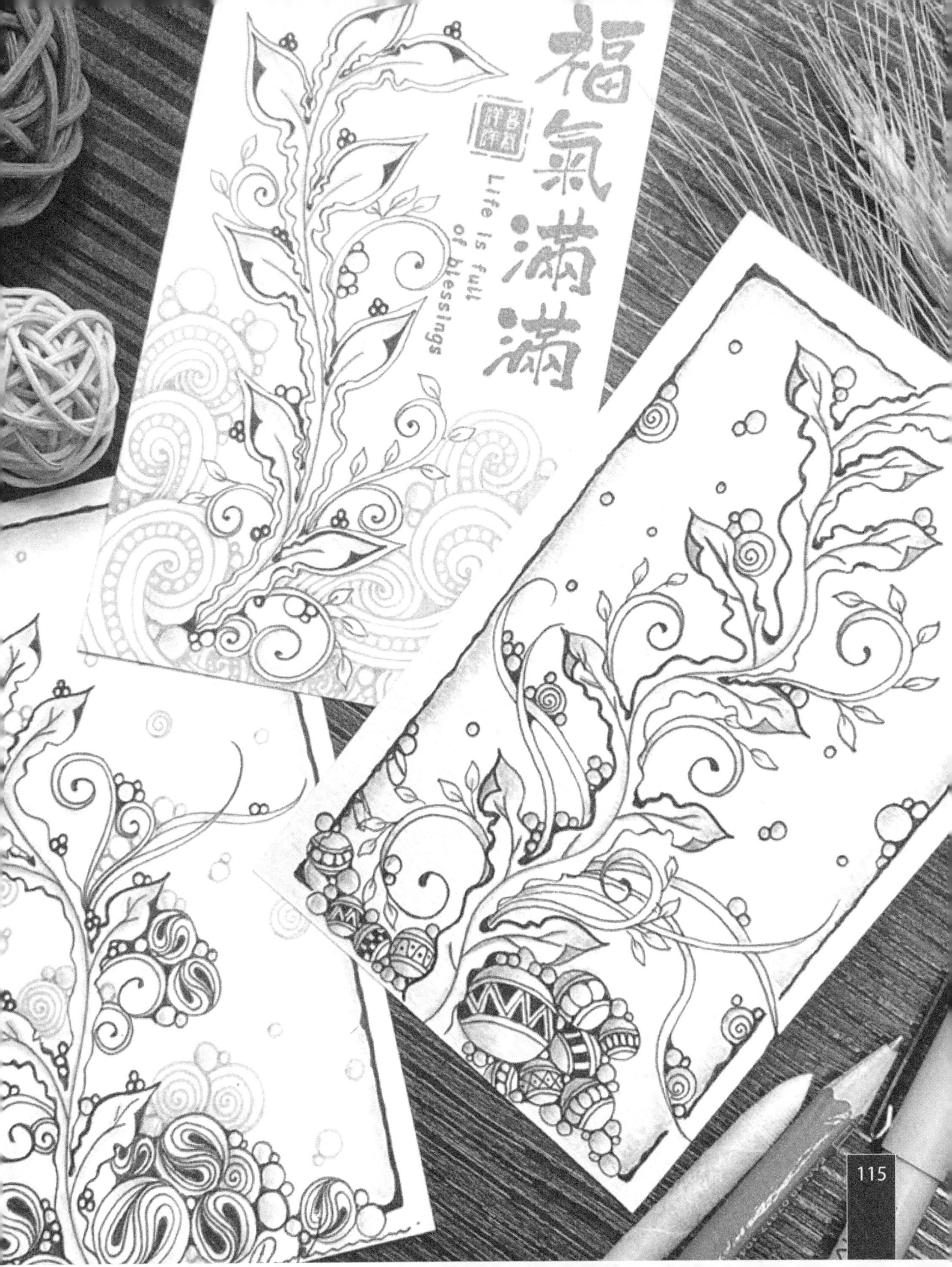
福氣滿滿
Life is full of blessings

Sunali Shah CZT

Sunali's work is so gorgeous and I am so glad she shared some of it with us as well as her tangles for this book. You can see more of her work and any classes she offers at:
https://www.facebook.com/sunali.shethshah

Sunali's favorite tangles:

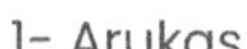

1- Arukas
2- Diva Dance
3- Waybop
4- Mooka
5- Flux

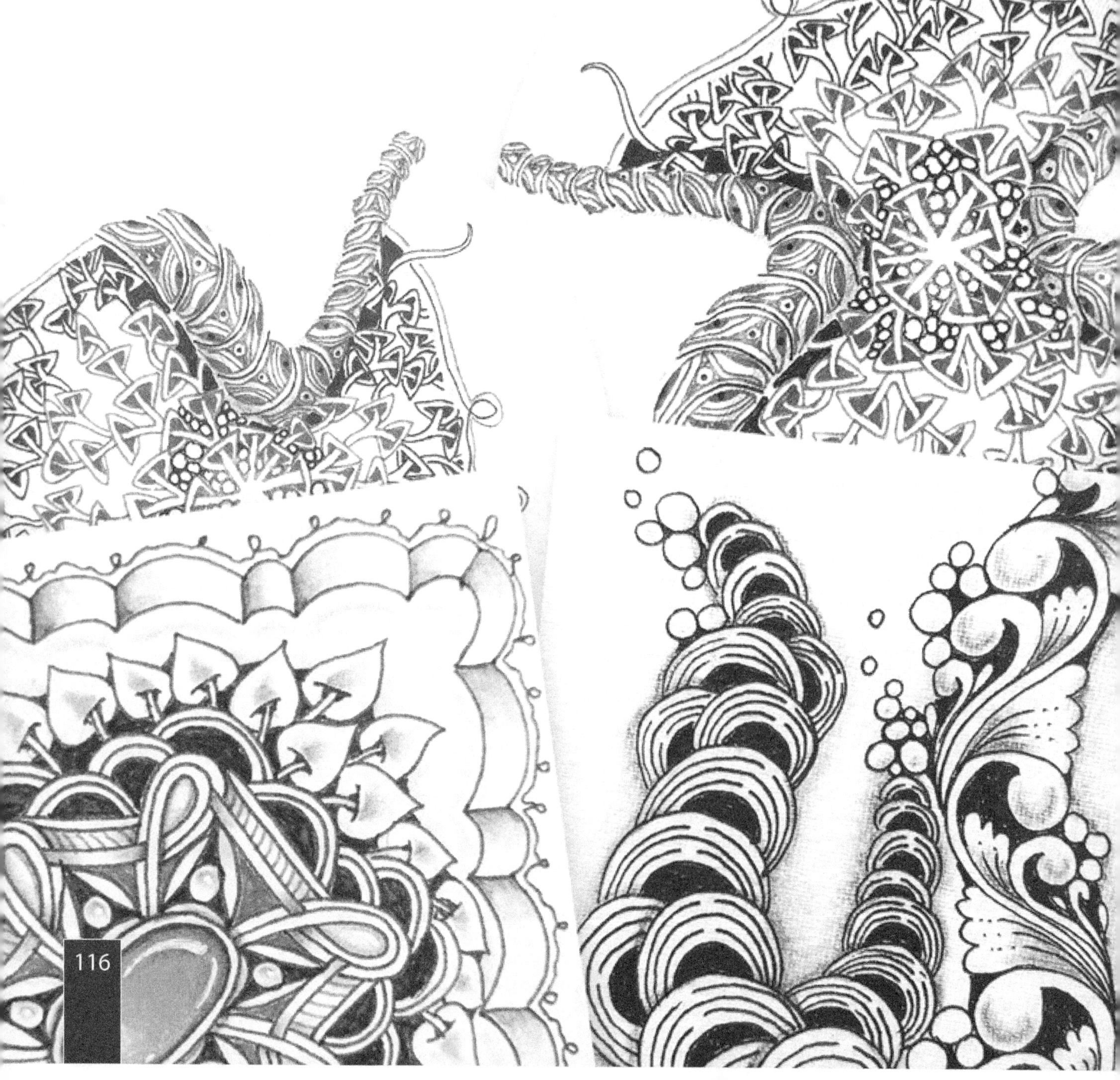

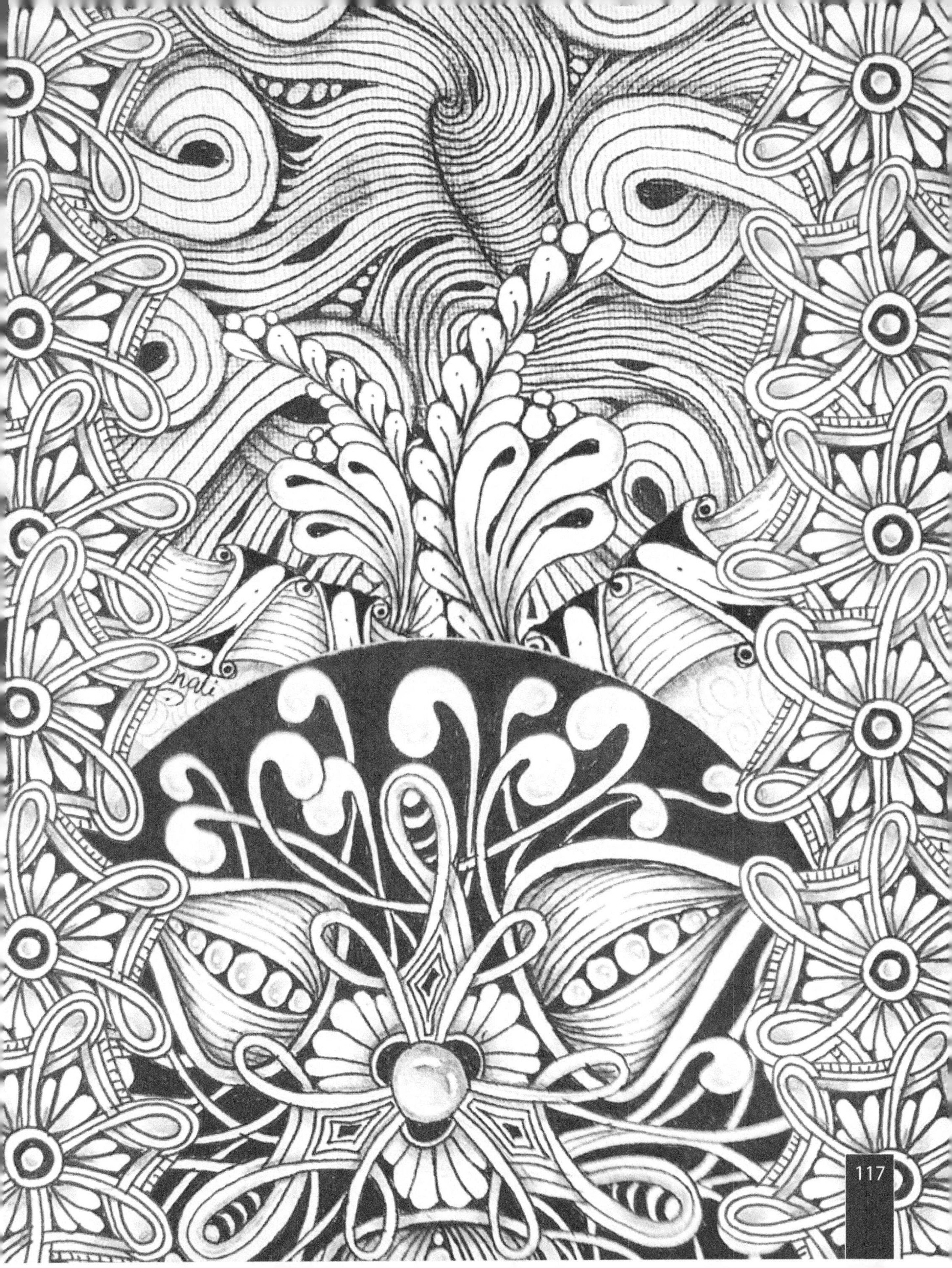

TILE SIZES

SQUARE TILE

BIJOU SQUARE TILE

ZENDALA TILE

3Z TILE

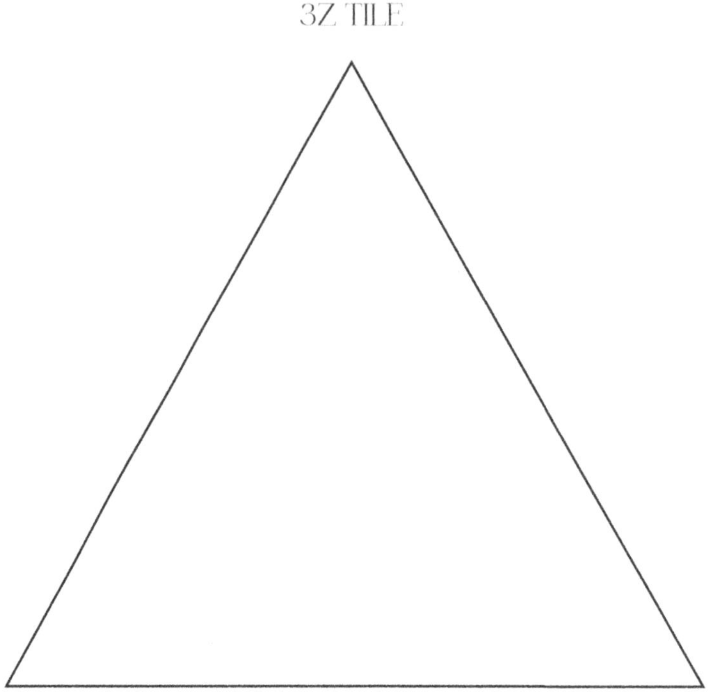

PHI TILE

About MZ Creates

Ever since I can remember I've been obsessed with numbers and creating. It could be any kind of project beading, stitching, papercrafts, painting, etc,. It really didn't matter. I would take to any new craft like a fish to water. The same was true for anything related to mathematics and numbers. I spent hours on end listening to music and making my way through numerous math problems.

This is the way I've always been. I know of no other way to be and I don't think I could change.

As time passed by, I got my graduate degrees in Mathematics and Operations Research but at the same time I started a creative blog and wrote several books for the Amazon Kindle. These books ranged from card making to mixed media and more.

Today when I would like to place myself in a neat little box and write a simple paragraph 'about me' I get stuck. I can't define myself, just an artist or just a mathematician, I've always been both and feel life without the other would be quite dull.

So now I run a software company and my creative blog. I'm a multi-faceted entrepreneur with an education in mathematics and a passion to create. I love pretty things, beautiful spaces, happy colors and elegant proofs. I hope you'll join me on my journey as I DIY my way through this precious and beautiful thing called life!

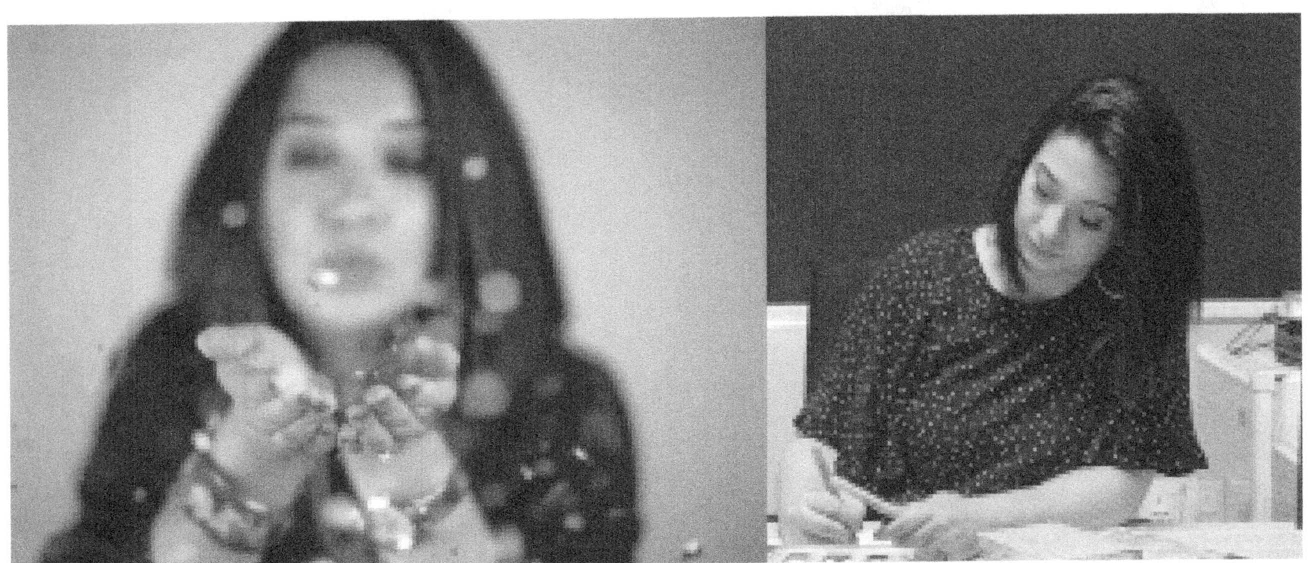

On my blog I stick to the workings of my right brain. All my creative DIYs, product reviews, book crushes and travel diaries are hosted there..

I love to create all sorts of things so you will find art journaling, mixed media, Zentangle® (I am a Certified Zentangle Teacher), drawing, watercolor tutorials and DIYs here. I love hosting fun parties with beautiful tablescapes, décor and fun and yummy cats. I also enjoy creating beautiful spaces. I feel if we are in a happy environment, we tend to be our best selves and so you will find some home décor tips and DIY's here as well.

Most of all though I just love sharing the joy of creating something beautiful on a budget yes I am super conscious of the budget aspect - and I hope you'll enjoy your visit with me!

If you're looking for a place to start maybe you would like to: Try my Free Zentangle® Art Class series on my blog Check out my YouTube videos - MZ Creates Follow me on Instagram @mzcreates

Love,

MZ

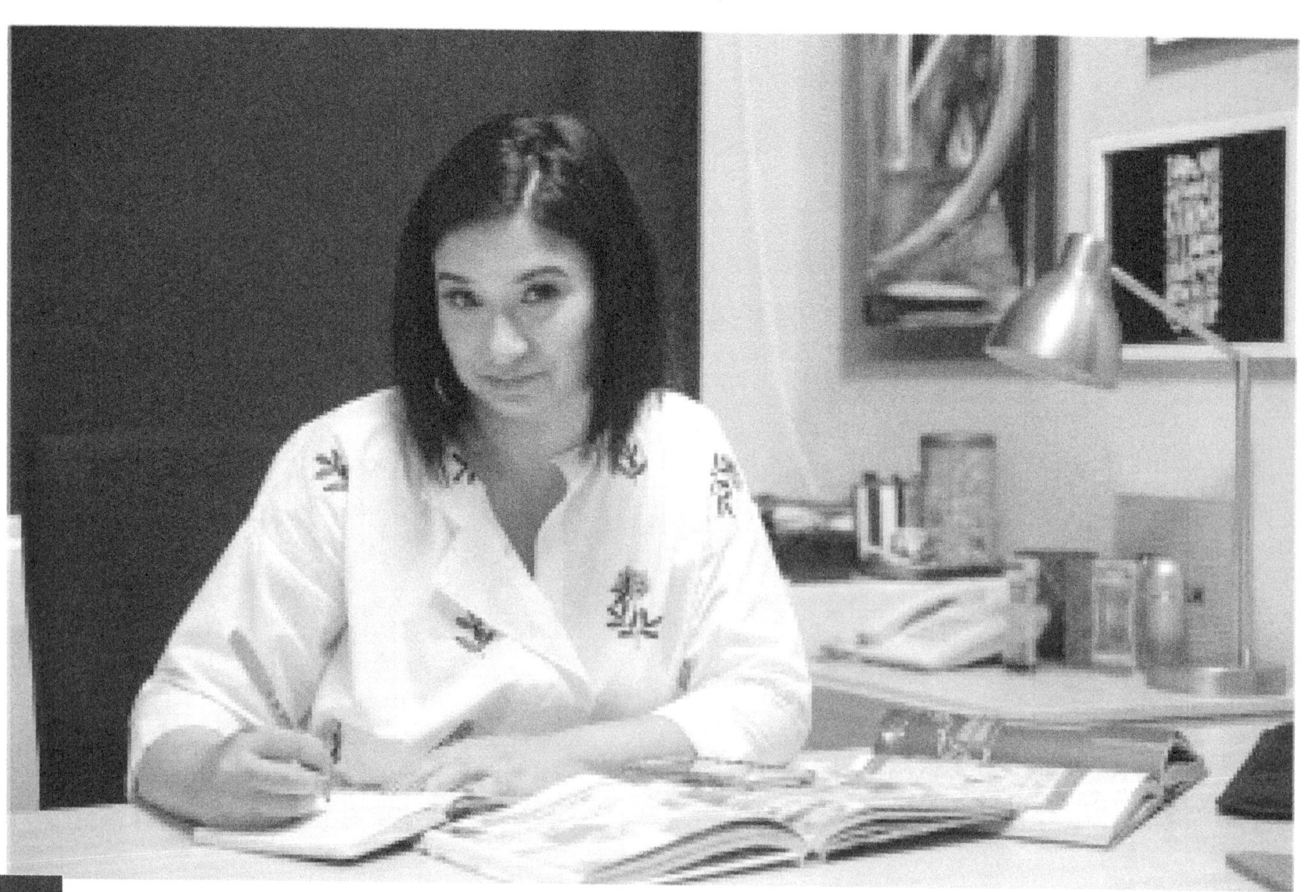

The first two books of
Botanical Tangles
by
Mahe Zehra Husain
are available on Amazon

Search for MZ creates on amazon for lots more fun creative books and activity books!

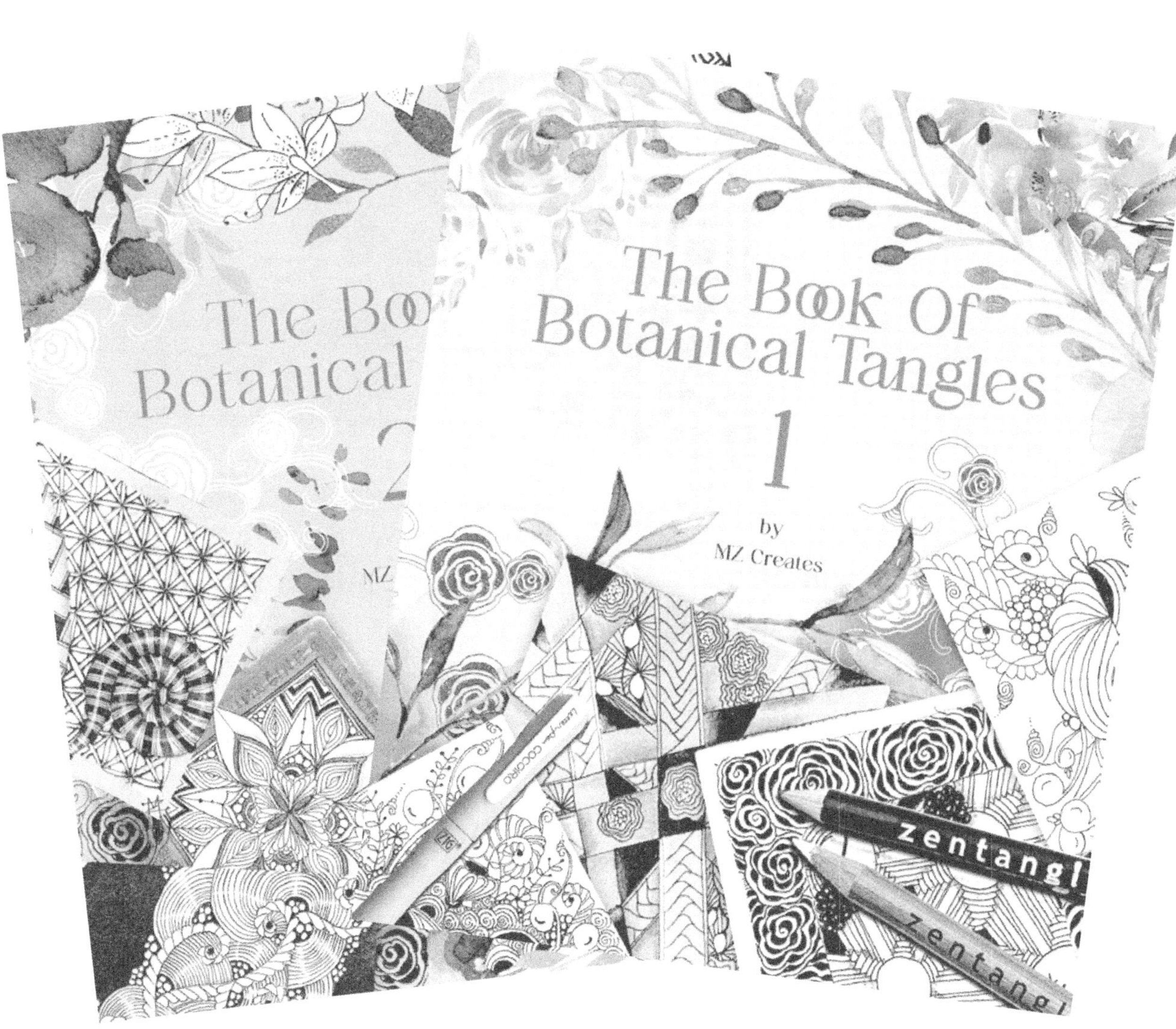

As you reach the final page of this book, I invite you to continue exploring your creativity with my exciting courses, which include Zentangle®, Art Journaling techniques, transforming old books into altered masterpieces, crafting customized vision planners, mastering lettering skills, and much more!

Continue your journey with MZCreates, just scan the QR code to access these exciting courses to keep the spark going.

As a token of appreciation, my readers will get a special discount!

Scan QR Code and enter **Promo Code** for exclusive **40% off**

Planner Bootcamp:	RAKSS7B
Vision Planner:	8RQMCYY
Lettering Class:	SA4TASE

So don't stop here.
Let's keep creating together!

Hugs,
MZ

Leave a Review

If you enjoyed this book please consider leaving a review on Amazon. That helps us to bring you budget drawing and art books.

If you have any questions, concerns or comments please reach out to us via www.mzcreates.com and we'll get back to you ASAP!

Search for MZ creates on Amazon for lots more fun creative books and activity books!

Browse MZ'S Books

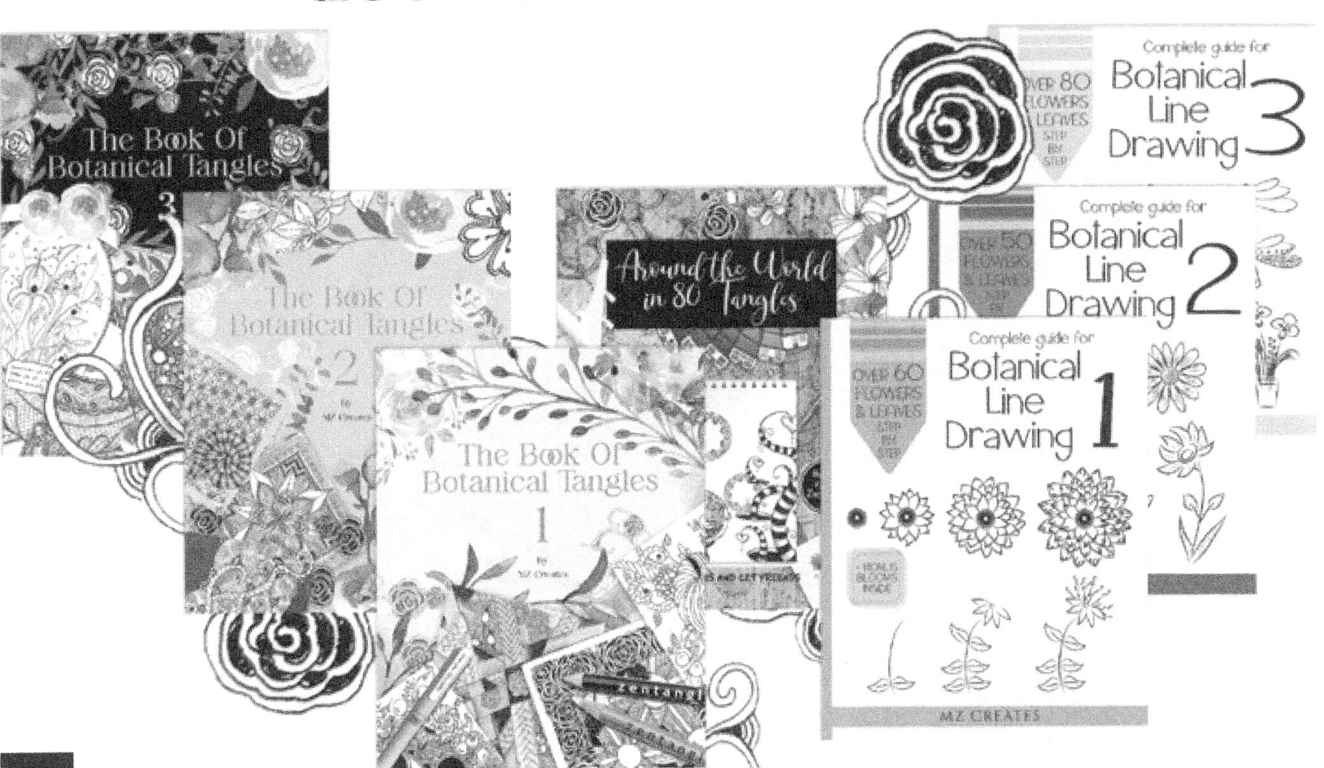

Discover a beautiful surprise!

Delve deeper into the enchanting world of
tangling with our exclusive bonus content.

Downloadable and printable pages include
sneakpeeks into other books and tangles !

To download follow this link:

https://www.mzcreates.com/bt3bonuspages

Enter your email and receive the download link !

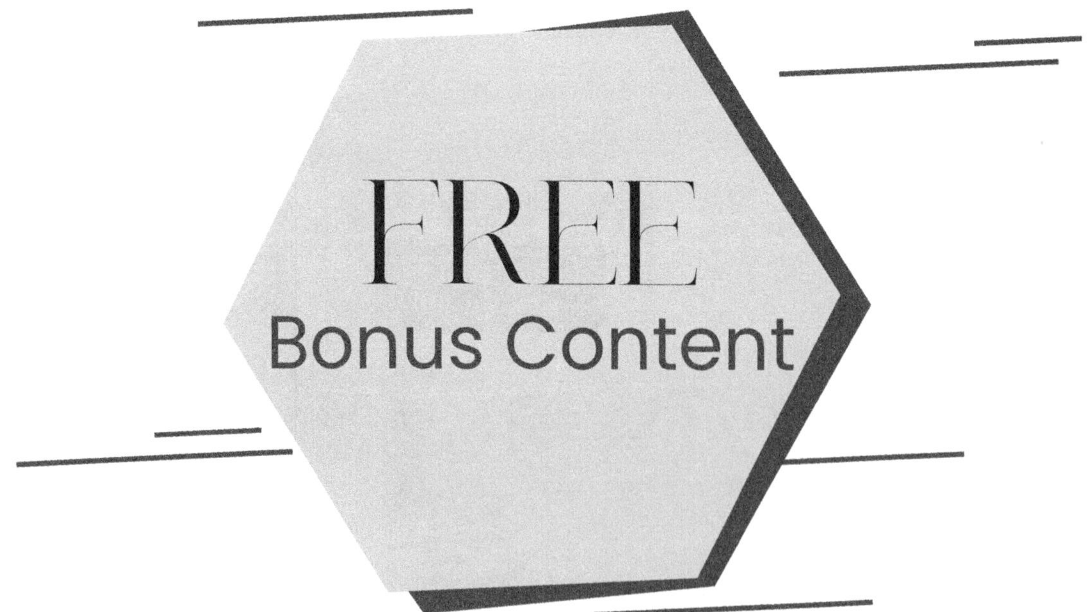

Made in United States
North Haven, CT
05 February 2025

65430925R00072